Memories of
Ira I. Boggs

In
Commemoration
of the
World War I
Centennial

Memories of
Ira I. Boggs

(1895 - 1983)

Coauthor
Dallas E. Boggs

TATE PUBLISHING
AND ENTERPRISES, LLC

Published by Tate Publishing & Enterprises, LLC
127 E. Trade Center Terrace | Mustang, Oklahoma 73064 USA
1.888.361.9473 | www.tatepublishing.com

Tate Publishing is committed to excellence in the publishing industry. The company reflects the philosophy established by the founders, based on Psalm 68:11,
"The Lord gave the word and great was the company of those who published it."

Published in the United States of America

ISBN: 978-1-68118-788-4
1. Biography & Autobiography / Military
2. Biography & Autobiography / General
15.03.24

To James Douglas Boggs
and other veterans
of our foreign wars

War memorial—on the grounds of state capital, Charleston, West Virginia

Pvt. Ira I. Boggs—Fort Oglethorpe, Georgia, 1917

Contents

1   My Childhood Years   13

2   My First Job   79

3   The War Years   123

4   Texas   175

5   California, Here I Come   209

6   Right Back Where I Started From   243

7   Marriage and the Family   267

1

My Childhood Years

I was born on a three-hundred-acre farm near Wallback, West Virginia, about fifty yards from the Clay County line. Dad and Mother both worked there, and that is where they met and married. My paternal grandparents, Henry Clay Boggs and Sarah Elizabeth (Geary) Boggs, owned the farm. My maternal grandparents, Cornelius Estep and Ona (Turner) Estep, lived in the same community, on some of the land owned by Grandfather Boggs. My grandfather Estep farmed and worked in the timber and lumber business. My maternal grandparents were active church members, and Granddad helped another neighbor, Frederick McGlothrin, hold revivals.

My older brothers Alvah, Guy, and Ray, were born in a hued log house with a puncheon floor just across the creek from the Wallback Post Office. A puncheon floor was made of split logs with the split side up. It was hued level with a foot ax (an ax shaped like a mattock). Right before I was born, the family moved into an unpainted plain lumber Jenny Lind house on the same farm and about a half a mile down Sandy Creek. I was the baby when we left there and moved to Looneyville in the same county (Roane).

Sandy Creek is about thirty miles long. It heads near Clay and Ivydale and empties into Elk River at Clendenin. Elk River is noted as one of the most meandering rivers in the world. It is so crooked that the distance by river from Clendenin to Ivydale is about sixty miles or more. At Jacks Bend (near Procious), you can ride a five-coach train and see most of the front end of the train from the passenger car. There are many such curves on Elk River. Two other examples are Horseshoe Curve (a bend on the railroad above Clay, across the river from where the river meets Route 4) and the World's End (a large form of cliff a few miles north of Clay).

In those days, children, women, and everybody worked with a hoe, an ax, or other tools—a horse and plow or an ox and plow. I've heard Granddad Estep say he would rather have Mother drop corn than any man who ever worked for him. There were mechanical hand planters in those days, but they were expensive, and some people didn't have them. Few families grew more than fifteen or twenty acres of corn, ten acres of hay, twelve acres of pasture land, and a few acres of wheat or oats—just enough to produce food for the family and a cow or two and a team of horses or oxen. We had our wheat and some of our corn pressed and ground into flour or meal. The nearest mill was in Newton, a small village about four miles from our home, at the three forks of Big Sandy Creek.

Most people used wood to cook and to heat their homes. Some people burned coal, but nobody in our area had gas. (There were very few gas wells in the state at that time.) Our wood-burning fireplace was about five feet long by four feet deep. Dad would carry in a chunk of wood—about as big as he could get on his shoulder—and bed it on the floor at the back of the fireplace. We had an iron rack on each side of the fireplace to hold the wood up so air could get to it. Dad would bring in another large stick of wood—we called it the fore stick—and put it in front next to a big flat rock (the hearth). To boost the flames, he usually put some smaller sticks of split wood between the fore stick and the backlog. It made a whooping big fire that warmed the whole house.

We had one big bedroom next to the sitting room and another bedroom next to the dining room. In those days, the parents usually had a bed in the corner of the sitting room. For the baby, there was a cradle that was usually homemade (from boards or small timbers), and it rested on runner boards (rockers) that were beveled on each end. Mother sat and breast-fed us while knitting stockings, sweaters, and other clothing. She knitted our mittens from yarn that she spun from wool. Sometimes, while knitting with her hands, she rocked the cradle with her foot and sang to us until we fell asleep.

I watched attentively as Mother and Grandmother made yarn by pulling big fleeces of nice white wool that they got from Dad's and Granddad's sheep. They sat for hours while making yarn and knitting clothes with it. They dyed it different colors and left some of it natural, with contrasting shades for the toe and heel of socks or the tops and bottoms of mittens. Those homemade items were very warm and comfortable, and they would wear for a year or more. To make diapers, sheets, and pillowcases, Mother bought goods, such as white linen, from the local store. (Children usually wore diapers until they were at least three years old.) Sometimes she splurged to buy calico for her clothes and for the children's dresses.

Boys wore dresses until they were about old enough to start their schooling. I remember when Alvah and Guy wore dresses and when they got their first pants. Mother made their jeans out of denim. (Jeans were warm enough for winter, and they lasted a long time.) She made their top shirts with cotton and their underclothing from gingham and other lighter material. She lined their denim jackets with linen or calico. At that time, there weren't so many different kinds of cloths to choose from. Poor people used calico, gingham, or chambray. Wool and silk were too expensive for most uses. Children didn't wear belts. Mother put buttons on the waists of our snug-fitting shirts and cut matching buttonholes in the pants to hold them up.

We were very proud of the new clothes that Mother made for us, and we took great care to keep them clean so we could wear them longer. Mother usually made our hats and caps too, and she knitted toboggans (with a long top and a tail that hung over our backs) for children and women. Everybody wore hats in those days. It wasn't natural for anyone to go to church without a hat.

Men wore galoshes (suspenders) to hold their pants up. I remember when the first belts came into style. Uncle Milton had been away working on a timber job, and he came back with a belt. He wore his shirt bloused down over his belt so you couldn't see it. This was in style for some time before they started wearing shirts neatly slipped down in their pants, then you could see the belt, which was made of leather, platted cord, or other heavy material.

Children wore shoes only during the winter, and young men often went barefooted to church or other gatherings. Dad usually bought our shoes from the nearest store, but he sometimes had them made from cowhide at our local shoe shop. We usually wore broad-toed shoes that we called brogans. They were strong, and some would wear all winter. To get them to wear that long, we usually had to half-sole them. Shoes were too expensive for poor people, and most children did without them. In winter, we stayed indoors most of the time until we were old enough to go to school.

Granddad Estep was one-eighth Cherokee Indian. He owned the blacksmith shop where he built wagons and sleds. He cut blocks from specially cured logs that he kept on hand. For the axles and frames, he chose gum trees because they wouldn't split. He made shafts from tougher wood such as hickory. For large wagons pulled by two horses, he made a single shaft (or tongue). On smaller wagons (for one horse), he fastened a tough piece of wood on the inside of each wheel. Each block held a wooden shaft that he left long enough to reach the hames (a part of the harness that is cushioned by a soft collar to protect the horse's shoulder from bruises and frictional injury) on each side of the horse. The shafts, when attached to the hames by iron rings, served as handles to guide the wagon, and they were fashioned so that the horse could hold back on the wagon when going downgrade. Most wagons had wooden wheels with a strong iron rim around the outside of each wheel. The wheel was coupled to an inner rim that fitted the axle. Spokes of wood coupled the outer rim to the inner rim.

Each end of the spoke was cut to a small round shape that fitted slots in the rims. The outer rim was very thick and strong, and it would roll along for years. The spokes would finally decay.

Granddad Estep was a first-rate blacksmith. I've seen him repair wagon wheels by making spokes and fitting them into the wheels. He could also repair worn-out iron rims. I often pumped the bellows to push air through the coal fire to make it bright for heating the metal. I watched Granddad pound the metal out thin and weld it. He pounded it fairly thin until it was about ready to weld. Then he put it back to reheat it until it was white-hot, with sparks flying from it. Before he pounded the metal again, Granddad put a small amount of some kind of chemical on it (I think it was saltpeter, but maybe it was borax) to keep it from flaking. He would round it off and then put it together and pound it so smooth that you couldn't see a seam in it. Then he would reheat it to a red-hot appearance. He held it over a rain barrel until it cooled to just the right temperature, which he could determine by the color changes. Then he dipped it into the water to temper the metal to the right hardness. He wanted it to be a bit flexible, with some spring in it, and not so hard that it would be brittle. Those wheels and axles were strong enough to carry several thousand pounds.

Granddad used his wagon and his team of horses to haul corn from the fields. He'd put a high body on the wagon, one that would hold twenty to fifty bushels of corn ears. He had to drive the team over rocks, stumps, and steep places to pick up his corn. He went over such rough places that his wagon could easily turn over and spill the corn.

We didn't have car wrecks, but we did have dangerous trials and tribulations in those days. Sometimes a wagon would push a horse so hard that the horse would run away. Some horses were naturally wild and stubborn. They could tear a wagon to pieces while crippling themselves or the driver. They sometimes caused the load to turn over on the driver and kill him. Sometimes a horse would run away and cripple or kill a neighbor (or a member of the family). The mowing machine was also dangerous. A team could run into an insect nest and get stung, and a spooked horse might run away with the mowing machine, hay rake, wagon, or buggy.

Even riding a horse could be dangerous. A rider could get raked off by a branch on a tree (or thrown off otherwise).

When the ground was wet and soft, Granddad used a sturdy sled to haul his corn. It held as much as the wagon, and he could take it over rougher ground. He made his sled of tough white oak. He put four-by-four blocks between the upper and lower runner sills. Then he bore a hole endwise through each of the blocks, put a strong bolt through each of them, and fastened them tight to keep the sled compact and strong. The tongue on his sled was as tough as the one on the wagon. He'd put a horse on each side of the tongue and raise it up to the horse's shoulders while he hooked the breast chain to the harness. On a steep grade, the horses could hold back on the chains and support a very heavy load. When a sled was nearly worn out, Granddad made new runners for it. He would cut a small white oak or hickory tree and split it in half. He bent and shaped the wood by fastening one end to a tree or a building and putting weights on the other end. He burned and seasoned the wood to make tough and long-lasting runners.

My grandmother Boggs was almost blind. When I was just a young child, she would take me to the garden with her and have me pick ripe tomatoes for her. She said, "I can't see if they are red." She talked to me all day long while she went about her work. One day, Ray and I were at her home while Mother had to be away. Grandmother was washing clothes, and Ray and I were playing in a tub of water. Grandmother told us not to play in the water, that we would get our clothes wet. We were small and forgot that we shouldn't play in the water. When we started playing in it again, Grandmother picked up a stick and whipped us with it. We cried. It didn't pain us any, but we were embarrassed. It hurt us very much that Grandmother had to whip us. I loved my grandparents, and I thought they didn't love me anymore. Our older brothers and our uncles teased us and said we didn't have any nerve, crying over being whipped with a straw.

Granddad Boggs was a small man while Granddad Estep was a large man. Granddad Boggs was jolly, even though he had asthma and was feeble before he was old. He walked with a cane when he was fifty. My granddad Estep was jolly too. He would take me on his lap and tell me stories and have me saying words like *rhinoceros* and *hippopotamus*. Then he would laugh.

Grandmother Estep was very kind, and she would hunt pretties for us to play with. Children didn't have as many toys to choose from as they do these days. We made our own—when we could find proper material. We used Mother's thread spools to build toy carts and wagons, and we made roads over a clay bank on the edge of our yard to run them on. We also molded dishes and other trinkets out of tough red clay.

What mischievous things children will do for amusement! Granddad Boggs kept sheep in a field near our house, and they were a menace for us. One big buck butted us when we came near him. We hated him so much that we stacked a pile of rocks on the opposite side of the fence to throw at him. We'd get rocks as big as we could lift to the top of the six- or eight-rail fence, which was about six foot high. The sheep would back away from the fence, and when we dropped a big rock, he would run against the stone and butt it. We finally got into trouble for bloodying his head. Granddad noticed it, and Dad stopped us from having our revenge on the mean old buck sheep.

We had to go daily into the field to hunt for the cows and bring them in for milking. When the cows were near the sheep, Dad would go get them. One day, Dad wasn't at home when it came time to bring in the cows. When we went to get them, the big buck ran after us. All of us except Guy escaped over the fence. Guy lay down flat on his belly. The buck came up to him, but it didn't hurt him. (Dad had taught us to lie down so he couldn't butt us.) One of us climbed back over the fence and called the buck. When the animal was distracted, Guy nearly flew for the fence.

As spring approached, we noticed the birds coming from the south and building their homes. We got to know nearly every species by the shape and color of their eggs and their nests. A pair of bluebirds drilled into an old snag near the house to clear a hole in it big enough for their nest. Bluebirds have bright blue feathers and rust-colored breasts and throats, and they are easy to recognize for their cheerful songs. (There were lots of bluebirds in those days. Now you will hardly ever see one of them.) They built their nest a few inches down the heart of the stump so their little birds wouldn't fall out. They laid big blue eggs. Sometimes, we climbed trees to see into nests. Some birds would fly at us and flap their wings to scare us away. We were careful not to molest the little creatures or their nests in any way. Dad and Mother always told us not to touch the beautiful blue eggs or the babies. That might cause the parents to leave, and the eggs wouldn't hatch or the little birds would die. They also told us not to blow our breath on the eggs because that would cause the ants to eat them.

We often found a partridge nest hidden on the ground in clumps of grass or weeds. The little ones would crawl under leaves and hide where we could never find them. The mother bird would start running or fluttering along just fast enough to keep us from catching it. That would distract us from the baby birds. Then when she got her babies out of danger, she would rise and fly back to the nest.

It was another sign of spring when the frogs and toads began to squawk and holler. We followed their sounds to find them and bring some of them to the small pond in a little creek that ran near our house. We had quite a batch of toads and frogs. Sometimes we noticed a little toad climbing on the big mother toad's back. Another toad would try to take a ride. It would grip the mother toad's back with its hands and kick the other frog end over end, as if to say, "This is my ride." We had names for some of the champion fighters.

When we heard a toad holler at a distance, we went on a hunt for him. We made croaking noises to imitate him, and he would answer us until we could find him. Sometimes he would be hiding under a log or rock, and we would gravel him out. One day one of us was graveling after one and got hold of a snake. That spooked us for a while. We went home and told Mother of our adventures. Mother didn't want us to play with the dirty things. She told us that the toads would make warts come on our hands. Once I caught a pretty green tree frog and took it to the house to show Mother. It wet on my hands, and I rubbed my face and got the water into my eyes. It smarted so badly that I thought I had gone blind. Mother fixed some thick cream and washed my eyes, and they finally quit hurting.

One day, Mother sent me to bring in the cows. (She wouldn't send me so far that she could not see them or hear the bells. They were usually in a pasture field of fifteen or twenty acres, and one or two cows wore a bell so we could find them by following their sounds.) Walking along a cow path, I came upon a big black snake. I got a rock and mauled it. A little further along the cow path, I found another one and mauled it. As I came back with the cows, I picked up the snakes by their tails and dragged them back with me. I wanted to show my kill, but they were not dead, just wounded. When Mother saw me with the snakes, it scared her silly. I was only about five or six years old, and they might have wrapped around me and killed me.

Another time, when I was about the same age, Mother and I were picking greens in the cow pasture. Mother said, "I hear a locust." (It was probably a seventeen-year locust, a cicada. They are large, shaped like a horsefly, and make a lot of noise.) I didn't know what a locust was, and I don't suppose I asked Mother. I formed an opinion that it was an animal, like a little colt.

I remember a lot of talk about the Spanish-American War. We lost almost three thousand soldiers in that war. I was only three years old. Dad wanted to go, but he had five children at that time. The war was in the South, and the soldiers from the north were not used to the Southern climate. Many of them came down with yellow fever, and it seemed that almost everyone that had it died. (Yellow fever is somewhat like malaria fever. Our boys in the Pacific had that in World War II.) If the doctors had known as much about the disease as they do now, we wouldn't have lost many soldiers. I remember the talk of Theodore Roosevelt's charge up San Juan Hill in Cuba. He became quite a hero to the American people.

In 1899, while we lived at Looneyville, there was a terrible cyclone (what we would now call a tornado). I was only four years old, but I realized that my life was in very great danger. It's the first real scare that I remember, and I've never had another reason to be as scared as I was in that storm. I remember it as if it were yesterday. The clouds were so black and heavy that it was almost dark at about 4:00 p.m., and the air was full of leaves and brush. We heard the roar for several minutes before it came, and we realized it was going to be a bad storm. Dad, Uncle Cleave, Uncle Claire, Uncle Owen, and Uncle Martin were putting up a stack of hay. They hurried to finish the job and then ran for the dwelling. The haystack was torn to pieces, and the hay almost blew away. We lived in a big hewed log house. Some logs were twenty or twenty-four inches in diameter, hued to about eight or ten inches thick. The building rocked until we thought it would go to pieces any minute. If it had been built of lighter material, the house would have been blown apart. Afterward, I was always scared when the elements looked dark before a storm.

I don't know how many times it touched ground, but the main part of the storm swept through a strip about twenty-five miles long. It also passed through King Shoals Creek, where Granddad Estep lived. Uncle Bob, Uncle Elmer Estep, Benny Belcher, and others were in the woods cutting timber and hauling logs. They tied their horses to some trees and ran under a rock cliff. They anticipated that their horses would be dead when they emerged, but they just found them covered with brush and not hurt enough to mention. At the head of King Shoals Creek, the cyclone twisted and wrung off three- to five-foot-thick hickory trees as you would a switch. Acres of the timber were stripped clean. Huge hickory and white oak trees four or five feet through were wrung off of the stump as if they were six inches through.

A day or two after the storm, I walked with Mother to the post office. The timbermen were cutting logs from big trees three to five feet thick that had fallen across the highways. Some of them were twice as tall as I was, and I couldn't see over them. They cut the logs thirty feet long and hued them square with chopping axes. Then they dressed them with big, wide axes that they called broadaxes to make square timbers for shipbuilders. They had to use a yoke of big oxen to haul one log. They hauled the logs about three miles down Poca River. This was so near the head of Poca River that it was too small to float them. They left the logs there until a flood came and floated them into the Kanawha River and below to Nitro. They later took them to a shipbuilding dock.

A man at Newton was carried away by the strong wind. He grabbed a small bush and held onto it. He was whipped around on the ground until he was worn out. A baby was blown away, and they found it clear over a mountain almost unharmed and still in its cradle. In the spring of 1903, when we moved to Upper King Shoals, there were acres of devastated forest land without a whole tree.

When we went to church, visited someone, or just went on an outing for a merry time, we would take a large sleigh or sled bedded with hay or straw and some blankets. Traveling in a sleigh or buggy with a good strong galloping horse, we could make twenty to forty miles in a good day's drive. Our family was very devoted to the church. I must have been about four years old when I remember going to the Flatfork Missionary Baptist Church with Mother. I can still see the minister, Preacher Cal Burns. He was a medium-sized man, but slender. He preached for an hour or longer, and I got so restless that I was glad when we started home. I remember the neighbors—Bowens, Looneys, Hutchinsons, Drawdies, Smiths, Vineyards, and others. The preacher came home with us one day, and I can still see him talking and reading his Bible.

We children were very fond of our pets. One was a big cur dog named Ponto. He was about the size of a collie, but black, with a white ring around his neck. Dad and some neighbors were building a private road up to our dwelling and the farm. They put off some blasts of powder. (Dynamite wasn't used so much those days.) They set off the blast before they noticed that our dog had run into the area. Ponto didn't get hurt badly, but he was always gun-shy after that. When it thundered, he would come in the house and crawl under the bed.

Ponto was a good watchdog. When a hawk came near the chickens, he would run and bark at its shadow. That scared the hawk away. Ponto wasn't a mean dog, but he did bark at strangers. One time a neighbor came by, and the man ran from him when he barked. That is the only person I ever knew him to bite. Dad told the man that the dog would not have bitten him if he had not run, but Ponto became disobedient, and Dad gave him to Uncle Owen. We didn't have another dog for several years.

We had a big red Hereford cow that we kept for a long time. We called her Molly after Molly Bryan (William Jennings Bryan's wife). Dad sold her after she got old, and we cried when they took her away. We didn't think Dad should sell her to be killed for beef.

One cold February morning, Dad brought a little lamb in from the herd. Either the lamb's mother had died or she gave birth to three lambs and couldn't take care of them all. We fixed a bottle and raised it on cows' milk until it was old enough to live on pasture with the flock. We didn't want to see it go. A lamb makes a nice pet.

We had a sorrel colt named Maude, with a white tail and white mane. Near our dwelling, there was an old well that was covered over with rails and timber. Maude was picking around the well and fell into it. Dad got her by the leg and coaxed her to be quiet. Mother ran several hundred yards and got a neighbor, Jack Hutchinson, to help get Maude out of the well. They got her out, and she wasn't hurt. Maude ran off the hill, and for ages, she never got near that well again. She was a draft horse (Percheron stock), and she grew to weigh about twelve hundred pounds.

Maude was a fast horse, especially with a plow. She was mean and hard to control at times, but we could plow more ground in a day with her than with mostly any other horse. Maude was always afraid of a hole, or even the appearance of one. Sometimes she would have to cross a hollow in plowing and would break through into a waterspout. She got so scared that she would shy around the hole and break down the corn. At times, she jumped clear across the drain. We had to completely loosen our grip on the plow and just hold the lines to keep her from running away. I've been jerked and dragged while holding onto the lines, but I never got seriously hurt that way.

Ole Maude had a pretty sorrel colt with a white mane and white tail. When it was born, we just couldn't stay away from that pretty long-legged colt. Dad kept telling us that Ole Maude liked her colt more than we did and that we had better not go too close to her, or she might think we would hurt it or take it away from her. but my brother Ray, ventured to the colt and put his hands on it. Maude was eating her dinner, but she saw Ray and jumped at him and left her teeth marks on his chest. After that, Dad didn't have to tell us to keep away from Ole Maude and the colt. We ventured back when the colt was a month or so old, but Maude was gentle by that time, and so was the colt. It made a strong horse. We named him Fox, and we kept him for about four or five years before we sold him to a neighbor whom we trusted to take good care of him. Ole Maude had another mare colt that we called Dinkey. It was a pretty black horse not quite as large as Fox. We sold it at about three years old. We children didn't like to see the colts go, but Dad would tell us he would get us some pretty new clothes. We kept Maude until she died, when she was seventeen years old.

In the fall of 1901, the year I became six years old, I started to school at the Red Knob School, a one-room schoolhouse. I walked about a mile through a farm where there was usually a herd of two to three hundred beef cattle. We had to watch out for mean animals. Sometimes, to dodge around them, we had to climb over fences that were eight and ten rails high and go through woodlands. I went to school with the Drawdies, Bowens, Asques, the Parks, and the Stones. My girlfriend was an Asque girl who went my way as we left school. Fred Stone was another of my favorite companions. He'd give me his knife to whittle with. Sometimes he'd carry me on his back, and sometimes he'd shoot marbles with me.

During recess, we played games such as round town ball. We made our own balls starting with an old sock, such as the ones that Mother made of sheep wool, with the heels or toes worn out. We could ravel them out starting from the end of the string of yarn. When we wanted a ball that was hard enough to hurt when you hit a player to shut him out of a game or to keep him from scoring, we wrapped the yarn around a walnut. He would play close to keep from getting hurt with that hard ball. If we wanted a ball that would bounce, a rubber heel from a shoe was better for the core. Our bats were carved from good solid wood (white ash was a favorite source) that was properly cured.

We chose our players for each side. One of the two captains would take a bat and pitch it in the air. The other captain would catch it near the middle. The first captain would put his hand over the second one's hand, and they would take turns moving over the top hand until they reached the end of the bat. The one who had enough room at the end of the handle to hold it when the other let loose would have the first choice and get the best player. If he couldn't hold the bat for a few seconds, the other captain would have first choice.

We were allowed three tries to hit the ball fair—between the right and left bases. It was a fair ball if someone didn't catch it. If you nicked a ball and the catcher caught it, you were out. If you were running from base to base and the opposite player hit you with the ball, you changed sides. But if the fellow who got hit could get the ball and hit that player back before he could get on a base, then he was on the scoring side. When you hit a player with the ball, you would yell, "Corner up." That meant for everyone to get his or her foot on a base. If you got on first base, you were free to bat. Usually there was only the catcher and the backstop player to knock the ball away so the other players could get home. Those players who cornered up didn't score when they got to home plate. To score, we had to hit the ball and run all bases. Sometimes we had an umpire. When we didn't have one, the captain would sometimes settle a disputed call according to who had the most witnesses. At other times, the argument would get so hot that they would fight. If the teacher saw it, someone would get a whipping. Sometimes a gossip would tell the teacher just to see that happen.

In those days, the teacher often used a rod to whip us. For the smaller children, he used a paddle. I was always so afraid of getting a whipping that I behaved very well, so I escaped such punishment. I felt it would be very embarrassing, and I dreaded what Dad had in store for me when I got home. I don't remember of any of the family getting a whipping, but my teacher sometimes pecked me on the head for whispering over my seat. He had a rule that if he caught you whispering three times over your seat or if you failed on your lessons three times, he would give you a whipping. Sometimes he would make you get your book and stand on the floor facing the other pupils or make you put on a dunce cap and stand in the corner. Parents seldom complained if their children did come home with stripes from a hard whipping.

In the spring of 1903, we moved into a little two-room house at Upper King Shoal Creek in Kanawha County, and we lived there for about six years. We used the attic of the house as bedrooms for us children, and we got along very well. The first year, we hardly raised enough grain for our corn bread and for two cows and several chickens. Other than our large garden, we had only about four acres of ground to farm. Dad was working on a lumber job, and we did very well with what we had. The next spring, we cleaned up an old field, adding about four more acres. We tended it in corn, Irish potatoes, and sweet potatoes, and we raised enough cane to make fifty or seventy-five gallons of sorghum. We also raised some hogs.

There was a food famine that year, and it was pretty bad. We could buy food, but most of it was so spoiled that we could hardly eat it. A few times, we bought oatmeal and other cereals that were so musty we had to feed them to the chickens. Other food was also bad. This was in Theodore Roosevelt's administration. Congress passed the Pure Food and Drug Act, and that helped a lot. We lived in the head of Upper King Shoals Creek, about two and a half miles from the nearest grocery store, and we had to take anything we could get for food. By the time that law became effective, we had a good crop and plenty of feed for our hogs, chickens, and cows, and we had old Maude to plow with, to haul our corn to the crib, and to bring in wood for fuel.

We would get up about 6:00 a.m., eat our breakfast, and go to the field. Mother always got up at 5:00 a.m. She had to build a fire in the cooking stove and get it hot in time to cook us a good warm breakfast. We went to the field at about 6:30, stayed until noon, and then came home for dinner. We'd rest for one hour and then go back to the field to work until 6:00 p.m. We boys helped get the ground ready for the plow by cutting cornstalks out of the way, and then we cut all the sprouts missed by the plow. We usually planted four or five bushels of potatoes in March or early April. We had all of the rest of the ground clean and tilled by the middle of April when we planted corn. When the corn was high enough to support the vines, we planted half runner beans—one or two beans in a hill row after row—in some of it. Dad wouldn't plant too many vines on a stock of corn because that would break down the corn, and it wouldn't yield a good crop. We usually grew just enough beans for our own needs. We kept working in the cornfields until we had hoed all of our corn twice. By the time we finished our second round through the field, the blades of the corn made enough shade to keep down the weeds.

We usually got some rest between the time we got our corn laid by and before it was ready to cut, but picking our beans kept us busy part of that time. We'd gather several bushels of green beans and string them for canning, and we dried several bushels in the hull. They were very good both ways. We'd sometimes string them on thread and hang them against the wall or on boards to dry. The last time we went over the field, we picked all of the beans. By then, some were dry, some were green, and some were yellow. We sorted them into three piles. We hulled the yellow beans and strung the green ones. They could then be mixed for cooking or canning. The dry beans could be shelled and stored in cloth bags.

To shell the dry beans, we piled them in the sunshine to dry until they started popping open and falling out of the hull. Then we put them on a sheet that was spread out on the floor and beat them with sticks until they were all thrashed out. Then we shuffled the hulls to separate them from the beans. We threw the hulls aside and gathered the beans up in baskets and pails and kept them dry until there was enough wind to blow the chaff from the beans. Then we took the beans outdoors and poured them from a pail while holding it as high as we could. The wind carried the chaff away, and the beans fell into a tub or onto a sheet. We poured them into a sack and stored them away for our winter food. We would have a bushel or so of each different kind of shell beans. Most were a little striped bean that we called the ground squirrel bean. Some were soup beans, and there was another variety that we called the October bean. They were all good. We also pickled a twelve- or fifteen-gallon crock of string beans and a barrel of roasting ears. Mother also canned some corn and beans.

We grew enough corn to feed our horse, cows, dogs, and chickens and to fatten two or three head of hogs for our meat in the autumn. We sometimes butchered one or two more in the spring. We'd get four or five new pigs by April. We usually raised them from a brood sow. A young sow didn't usually have good success with her first litter. We usually kept a sow for three or four years. Sometimes she would raise two litters of pigs per year. One spring, our sow had eleven pigs. We fed them well and butchered them in the fall and through the winter.

We killed two or three hogs in the early winter, butchered them, and salted the meat with pure white salt to keep it until spring. At times we butchered some hogs in the spring and cured the meat by smoking it. We hung it over a smoldering fire with just enough heat to keep a smoke going. (If we allowed too much fire, the meat would get so hot that the grease would run out and create a high flame.) Hickory wood was good for holding fire. We kept it smoldering overnight, and we added a little sassafras wood to flavor the meat. It tasted just as good as meat cured with the chemicals that we use these days.

There wasn't any stock law in our section of the country, and one of our neighbors had about thirty head of hogs running where they pleased. In the early part of this century, when people bought their pigs, they either tagged them or marked their ears with notches or a certain-shaped hole and had their mark registered at their county seat. They castrated the males while they were small. In summertime, the hogs were razor thin. That's why we called them razorbacks. They lived on what roots, berries, herbs, and animal carcasses that they found in the woods. They were so slender or lean and hungry that they would get through your fence if they had to root under it. People had to build eight-strand barbed-wire fences around their fields, and that wouldn't always keep the free-running hogs out of our grain.

They could destroy a lot of corn. We finally got a good big shepherd dog that could help some, but we couldn't watch our crops day and night. We finally trained the dog so well that it would smell or hear those hogs for half a mile. He would throw up his head and sniff and bark and take off as fast as we could go. The dog soon learned to handle those hogs. He would catch one by its hind leg and hold it. The harder the hog pulled against the dog's teeth, the worse it hurt. The hog would give up and just sit still. We would get us a strong hickory switch and whip the hogs, but we couldn't catch all of the thirty or more of them. They kept coming back. We never killed any of them, but other people did, and we got accused of it.

In late summer when corn was plentiful, Dad often bought one or two of those razorbacks from a neighbor. He herded them home and penned them up for fattening with a diet of corn, bran mash, and slop from the kitchen. Mother preferred a diet of corn for the fattening hogs because corn-fed hogs yielded nice solid white lard from their fat, whereas lard from mast-fed animals was nearly liquid and slightly colored. Also the meat was difficult to cure. Sometimes, when the mast failed, the hogs would starve to death. The next spring we could locate them by the buzzards flying over them. The dead ones were used to make soap (if we could find them before they thawed out).

To make soap, we hued out a big block of wood to form an oval-shaped hopper. During the winter, we put our hardwood ashes from their fireplace into it. We kept it covered over with boards to keep it dry until it was time to make soap in the spring. We boiled the meat and bones in a big kettle. When it cooled, the grease came to the top. We poured water into our ash hopper and let it soak through the ashes to make a solution of lye, which we stirred into the grease. We boiled the grease and lye mixture. (It was very dangerous to be near a kettle of boiling lye and soap. Mother kept us children away from the kettle, but I have known people to get scalded so badly it would take the flesh off. People have been scalded to death making soap.) When it cooled, the soap floated to the top of our water and formed a layer about two to four inches thick. We could cut it into any size of bar we wished, usually about four inches square or four by six inches. Sometimes we made enough soap that we wouldn't need to buy any except the milder soaps we used for a bath or for the face. We could use the homemade soap for our hands.

After a few years, we finally encouraged the people to vote in a stock law to make people responsible for damage their animals did to their neighbors. When they wouldn't pay damage, you could pen their stock and keep it until they paid for damages and for the feed you furnished for their animals. If they didn't, we could sell the animal to pay damages. After we got the stock law passed, mostly everybody acknowledged that it was a fine agreement. The ones who had fought it the most said it was a good law. They could make more money at farming. It no longer cost so much to keep up our fences, and people finally began to improve their stock and farm more systematically. In those days, we didn't have any agricultural organizations. We finally got a county agent in each area, and they began teaching agriculture in our public schools. My family had always been in a farming section, and we encouraged the enactment of those laws.

The cattle in our neighborhood were about as scrubby and rundown as the hogs. Dad bought a registered Hereford bull and started the first good beef breed in our section of the county. Dad also improved the hogs in our area. He got a registered OIC (Ohio Improved Chesters) male and kept it for about four years. People from all around us brought their sows to get them bred. They gave us one weanling pig from each litter to pay for the stud service. When we butchered our registered boar, it weighed nearly eight hundred pounds.

It's late in June, time to pick berries. In Roane County, we had a clean pasture field. We left clumps of blackberry vines when we mowed the field by hand. It was easy to pick the fruit, and they were big and round. After we moved to Kanawha County, we often picked berries in cut-over timberland. It was steep and rough where the timber had been cut. The logs had been hauled over the ground, and trash timber and log dumps were left behind. After two years' growth along the creek, there would be a lot of mature vines with lots of berries. It took more time to get the berries from the rough terrain, but we could usually pick and can from thirty to seventy-five gallons of blackberries and up to fifteen gallon of huckleberries (or blueberries). We always had to watch for snakes, and we saw many of them. Ray was picking berries below the road one day. The berries were high up, and he was standing on a banking log and reaching out to pick berries when a big black snake jumped out at his hand. That scared the stuffings out of him!

Most of us children started working in the fields and doing their little odd jobs when we were eight and nine years old. We took weekly turns at our chores. One would feed corn and roughage to the horse, and the other fed the cows. Another fed the hogs and chickens. Mother and the smaller children gathered the eggs and caught the old mother hen and her little chicks to get them in their coops overnight. (There were plenty of possums, minks, foxes, weasels, and wildcats to steal them when they were not in their coops.) One day, Mother heard the chickens squawking. She rushed out and saw a big wildcat carrying off one of our biggest Plymouth Rock hens. When Mother ran after it, the cat was rather slow about dropping its eight-pound dinner, but it finally let loose and ran away. The hen wasn't hurt much, and she ran back to her coop. We named her the wildcat hen, and we kept her for some few years.

One winter, wild animals caught several of our chickens. We set a string of steel traps and deadfalls for a mile or so and looked over them every day or two. We tried for several years to catch the predators, but they were pretty foxy and hard to snare. Occasionally we found an opossum or a coon in one of the traps. A coon is hard to capture. If you didn't get to him soon after he gets into the steel trap, he would gnaw off his own foot to escape. His foot will be paralyzed from the pressure of the trap. You won't find anything but his foot. A rabbit will twist its leg off. We would set a box trap where we ran a rabbit into a hole. We put wire on the outer end of a box that was large enough to hold the rabbit. The other end had a lid that opened inward. We placed that end over the hole. We propped the lid up and then packed dirt around the box. When the rabbit came out, he would trip the lid, and it would drop behind him and latch.

The ole sly fox is the hardest animal to trap. You don't dare leave a track, sign, or scent. After setting traps, to avoid leaving any signs, we wouldn't go any closer than necessary to see whether we had caught anything. The ole bobcat (or wildcat) is another sly animal, but after a few years, we finally caught one. (We hoped it was the one that caught the wildcat hen.) Cornelius and Ray went to the trap on that day. They were so excited that I heard them from a long distance and ran to see what caused all of the commotion. (I can still see them!) They were afraid to get close enough to kill the cat. It would dodge a stone. The whole family went with Dad to get the cat out of the trap. It shied away as far from Dad as it could, and it looked over its shoulder and growled viciously. Dad hit it in the head with a stick that was about five feet long. The cat fell over "after a little lick." (I remember Dad commenting about how easy it was to kill, but I suspect Dad was a little scared to get so close to it and that he hit it harder than he thought.) Dad took the cat by its hind legs and carried it over his shoulder and on his back. Its head almost touched the ground. It was a huge wildcat, as big as a shepherd dog, but it was very lean and so old that some of its teeth were broken off. Some were missing.

I never had a gun until I was about twelve. Dad wouldn't allow us to handle a gun until about that age, and I had three older brothers to help me handle one. One of the best hunts I ever had was when I was about nine years old. One morning, Uncle Burton Cook came to hunt with us. There was about four inches of snow on the ground, and it was a splendid time to hunt. It was still snowing a little, but not enough to cover the tracks made during the night. When we rousted a rabbit, we could see his fresh tracks. In that kind of weather, a rabbit won't often go to his hole, especially if you don't have a fast dog to chase it. (A rabbit will go to a hole easier when it's clear and not favoring any bad weather because he knows he will have more time to fill his stomach later before the storm comes.) For this hunt, we didn't have a dog, so when we rousted a rabbit (if Uncle Burton didn't get to shoot it before it got out of range), Alvah, Guy, Ray, and I would start after it, each of us barking like a dog all at the same time. We four made a lot of noise! Uncle Burton took a stand right where we rousted the rabbit, and he waited there for it to come back.

If a rabbit doesn't want to go to hole, he will run about a quarter of a mile, then circle and course back on his tracks, trying to get you frustrated by losing his tracks. They would often run on a log and then jump as far as they can. Sometimes we almost lost a rabbit's tracks while he played with us and rested. Uncle Burton knew when the rabbit was getting close to him, and he'd be ready to shoot when it came back in his direction. We would hear his gun go *boom*, and we'd say, "There's another rabbit in our hands."

We would go a little ways further and find another rabbit track made during the night. We would keep tracking it, sometimes for a half hour, until we found him. We usually sensed about where he would be. One of us would say, "There's a good place for him under that log or in that bunch of broom sage. I'll bet he is snuggled up in a good warm bed there." Sometimes, we would be almost within an arm's reach of one before he jumped out of his good warm bed where he was sleeping to get his rest for another night out foraging for his food. Uncle Burton would follow us until we rousted him. We didn't always get our game, but we always chased him for a long time before we gave up.

Uncle Burton nearly always shot the rabbit—if none of us boys were in his way. Sometimes we dropped to the ground when one jumped up, and Uncle Burton could shoot over our heads. Sometimes, there was so much brush in the way that none of us could see the rabbit jump out, but we could see his fresh tracks in the snow and take off after him barking. We made a lot of noise—all four of us barking and howling like a gang of foxhounds. Uncle Burton would take his stand on a log or stand where he could see well. We'd listen for his gun to crack. "There's another rabbit," we would say.

Uncle Burton said, "When I got him, that one was standing on a log straight up on his hind feet looking for those slow dogs." The rabbit had his fun too with those slow dogs, tricking them and watching them chase after him. But he didn't live long!

"Well, it's about dinnertime. We had better go eat and warm up a little."

"I'm not hungry."

"I'm not cold," some of us would say. We would rather hunt than eat, but we went to dinner. We sat by the fire while talking about our exciting hunt and about the tricks the rabbits played on us to get their rest while we were busy trying to follow their tracks.

One day, after we had all warmed up and filled our stomachs with a good mess of rabbit with some of Mother's good fried potatoes, stewed brown beans, some of our sorghum, and some of Molly Bryan's sweet milk, I said, "I know where we can find plenty of rabbits. Let's go over in Granddad's field where he planted his new apple orchard."

"Granddad would be glad for us to get those rabbits. They are gnawing the bark off his trees. There are lots of weeds there, so the rabbit can find a good warm nest." (When there is a snow on the ground, a rabbit will gnaw on sprouts, eating the twigs. Young apple trees are their favorite winter forage. They even eat the bark of mature trees.) We all agreed to go over to Granddad's house, about one mile, and Granddad got out his old double-barreled shotgun and went with us to the orchard.

We lined out up and down the hill for about two hundred yards and started walking through the grass and weeds. Somebody yelled out, "There comes one down the hill! He's jumping high!"

Granddad said, "I'll get him. You ole snoop! Eating the bark off my apple trees until they may die." *Boom!* went one barrel of Granddad's gun. (If that didn't get him, Granddad could let loose with the other barrel.)

"There he is, Ira, just below you in the weeds, kicking."

"Now," said Granddad, "I'll eat on you awhile. You have eaten on my apple trees and got fat."

We killed ten rabbits that day. It was one of the best hunts of my life, but I had a lot more good ventures like that. It was my favorite sport.

At the end of another week, we were looking for Uncle Burton to come over to our house to go hunting again. "There comes Uncle Burton and Mr. Levy Cook." (Mr. Cook was Uncle Burton's dad.) This wasn't a good day to hunt; there wasn't any snow on the ground, and the sun was shining. It didn't favor falling weather, but they had a dog that was well trained for tracking rabbits in any kind of weather. (Unlike us two-legged hunters, he could smell them out.) We went up on the hill and across into Twin Oaks Hollow. When we crossed the hill, we ran into a flock of pheasants. They flew up from a grove of laurel or rhododendron. Mr. Cook shot at them but didn't get one. He said, "I'd like to have one of them birds." We tried to roust them again, but we couldn't find any. They are pretty hard to kill when they are flying across your path, but when they are flying straight away from you, and if they don't spread too fast, they are easier to kill. At times they have a little trouble getting out of the brush, and that gives you more time to shoot. We didn't do well that time. It wasn't a good day for hunting. We killed two rabbits and one squirrel. Squirrels were scarce there. The timber had been cut over, and there wasn't much mast for them. There weren't any game laws for rabbits, and people didn't give the squirrel law much consideration.

We lived about two and one-half miles from the schoolhouse where we had Sunday school in the summer. The church house was about five miles away, and we didn't have Sunday school (or go there often) during the wintertime. In those days, there weren't enough people (who lived close enough to the church) to gather a congregation when the elements were bad. People had to walk or ride a horse. A lot of the winters were so harsh that we didn't even get to go to school much of the time. (There was a schoolhouse in Roane County where we could have gone to school handily, but they didn't allow us to attend it because it was out of our county or district.) Schools started about September the first. We attended pretty regularly for two or three months, but in the winter, we had to go along a creek that was difficult to cross at times. There weren't any bridges for about two miles.

After moving to Kanawha County, we didn't raise sheep. There were too many dogs to kill them. We kept several chickens, and we had more eggs than we could eat. We would carry them to the store and sell them as low as 12 or 15 cents per dozen, and we sold chickens throughout the summer months.

After growing our crops and selling what we could spare, Dad sometimes took a job to make enough cash to buy part of our school clothes. Money was hard to earn, and most of the time, we saw very little of it, especially in the farming sections. But we could buy things at about one-tenth of what it costs now.

We grew most of our food and didn't go to the store more often than twice a month. We had to ask a neighbor to set us across Elk River, and then we had to yell for him to bring us back after we finished shopping. For some time, John Gandy had the nearest store. Then Jim Walker opened one. The first store we went to after moving to Kanawha County was about a mile further down the river at Rand Post Office, where we traded with Pat Samples. I was scared to get into a boat. Until I was about eight years old—that's when we moved from Roane County—I had never seen a river. (We lived near the head of Pocatalico River, which was just a creek about three miles long. It ran about forty miles further before it ambled into the Kanawha River.)

That was also where I saw my first train. It was coming down Elk River with a few boxcars and several flatcars, carrying sawlogs for a big band mill at the mouth of Porter. We could hear it far off, but it came around a bend near us before we could see it. Mother knew it would scare me, so she warned me that it would look like it was going to run over me, but that it would stay on the track. All I had to do was to stand free of the tracks; it wouldn't come after me. On our side of Elk River, there were a lot of places where one couldn't travel with a horse or wagon, so the rails on the opposite side of the river provided the only access to the outside. There was no other way to travel. The train also hauled coal, cattle, sheep, and chickens—all by the carload. There was a lumber mill on our side of the river at the mouth of King Shoals, so they had to haul wagon loads of lumber across Elk River by ferryboat and load the lumber onto railroad cars to ship it out. (Some winters, the river froze over with ice eighteen inches thick, and for two months or longer, they could send lumber across on horse-drawn wagons.) The whole Porter bottom on that side of the river, near the train station, was full of lumber stacks awaiting shipment. There were a few dwelling houses and a big general store and post office near the railroad and train station.

The first time I ever rode a train was from Aper, which was then called King Shoals. That was in 1903, when Theodore Roosevelt was president. He assumed the office when William McKinley was assassinated. Roosevelt was McKinley's vice president. (The next election, William Jennings Bryan ran for president on the Democratic ticket, but he was defeated.) I remember a flat freight car carrying a load of men to hear the presidential nominees speak at Charleston. I think that Dad rode that car to hear Bryan speak.

We had to work hard when we lived on Upper King Shoals Creek, especially during the farming season. All poor children worked daily in the summertime while on the farm and raised enough grain and food to live on. When I was nine or ten years old, I went to the field and worked eight or ten hours per day, hoeing corn, making hay, picking berries, gathering fruit of apples and peaches, and helping Mother peel and can them. We dug fifty or seventy-five bushels of Irish potatoes and eighteen or twenty bushels of sweet potatoes, picked bushels of beans off of the corn, brought in the pumpkins, and gathered tomatoes for canning.

We grew an acre or more of cane (for sorghum molasses), and we sometimes made as much as one hundred gallons of sorghums. Cane begins as a very small plant, and it is very tedious to hoe. We cut the weeds clean between the hills and very carefully scraped the dirt off of the cane plants where the horse trampled them into the ground or covered them with the plow. We had to pull the weeds away from the plants and thin the cane to four to six plants per hill. At times, during a rainy season, the weeds and sprouts grew so fast that they covered the plants so that they didn't get any sunshine. The tiny cane plants often turned yellow and almost perished before we could work out all of the weeds. We usually planted it in newly cleared land where lots of sprouts were growing. In places, the ground was so rough and rugged that we couldn't get a horse over it to plow properly. We had to cut all of the weeds and sprouts and loosen the soil with our hoe. On new ground, we used a grubbing hoe that was made in the blacksmith shop. (It was about half as heavy as a mattock and a lot stronger than the store-bought gooseneck garden hoes that we use today.) We pounded out the cutting edge and filed it almost as sharp as an ax. That was necessary to cut the sprouts that shot up almost overnight from live roots and stumps that were left in the ground when we cleared the land. It took several years of cultivation to kill off all of those sprouts, and new ones were always popping up from seeds that survived our fires.

About 1905, Dad leased a twelve-acre piece of cut-over forest land from Uncle George Estep, and we had to clear it in time for the next crops. We started to work on the new ground soon after we finished cultivating our corn. We cut a lot of the brush while the leaves were still on it, and we just let it lay where it fell. The leaves were so thick on the brush that we didn't need to pile it to burn. We hacked about all of the brush and bad timber before winter set in. In those days, it was a much bigger job to clear land than it is with all the new machinery we now have for jobs like that. The timber had been cut about six or eight years earlier, but people didn't cut timber that was less than eight or ten inches in diameter in those days. They also left a lot of the big trees that were crooked or hollow, and they cut only the best of the hickory, gum, and beech timber. We had to dispose of big decaying trees three to five feet in diameter that were left on the ground because they weren't fit for lumber. We cut them into logs six or eight feet long and rolled them out of their bed with cane hooks and spikes with long handles made of strong white oak or dogwood.

Schools closed about the first or middle of March the next spring, and that gave us quite a bit of time to get the ground cleared for corn. We watched for a spell of dry weather that lasted a week or so. We hacked a clear road around the field to make it safe to burn, raked the ground clean of leaves, and took all the rotten wood out of the raked area. We cut and cleared away any logs that might burn over the road, and we felled all the old dead trees that might drop pieces of fiery branches over our road. Sometimes, where there was little chance that the flames would get too high, we just raked around the trees at the edge of our cleared area to keep the fire from getting into them and burning out of control. For lighting the brush heaps, we made torches from black pine knots. They had rosin in them, and they would flame for quite a while before they burned up. That helped to kindle the damper wood so that it would spread the fire to the bigger pieces, drying them out as they got hotter and hotter. (I still have a scar on my thumb where I cut it with an ax while splitting a pine knot for a torch when we were burning those twelve acres.) It was quite exciting to see the dry brush burn. It flamed as high as fifty feet where a brush heap was five or six feet high and more.

Plowing newly cleared land is very hard work. There are many stumps and, at times, tight rocks on the ground. Some rocks or stumps are covered over with trash or earth, and you can't see to guide your plow away from them, especially if you have a fast horse, which we did. Ole Maude was frisky and fast, and when she ran into a rock or stump, it stopped her with a sudden jolt. Sometimes, we would run into the plow handles and almost break a rib. To avoid too many sudden stops, Dad used a root cutter on the plow. He braced the strong plow stock with iron on each side to make it strong enough to hold the root cutter, which was made of a piece of tempered steel about three inches wide and about eighteen inches long. It set about two inches ahead of the plow and just an inch or two lower than the blade. It cut the roots and ripped a path for the plow to go deep without stalling.

That spring, we were so far behind with our work that Dad just plowed two furies close together in rows about three and a half foot apart, and we seeded it with a corn planter. When the corn had grown to about three or four inches high, he ran the plow through the balk between the corn rows two or three times on each side of the plants. Where the ground was rough, the plow wouldn't always throw enough dirt, so we had to dig around the corn to loosen the dirt and aerate the soil. Sometimes, the plow would catch a root and guide the plow into a hill of corn and tear it out of the ground. If it wasn't too late in the season, we would replant the empty spaces left by the plow.

Crows and chipmunks also caused empty spaces in our corn rows. They would follow the rows for several hills and dig the corn out for their dinner. Also, snails sometimes found the tender sprouts and ate them. We carried seed corn in our pockets to replant it. At times, after the seedlings came out of the ground, the pests would dig out so much of the seed that we had to take the planter and replant it before it was time to hoe the corn. We often planted about an acre of late corn. It was good for fattening hogs (if we didn't gather it for roastnears).

As soon as we got all of our corn hoed over the last time, we started picking blackberries and huckleberries (blueberries). We also worked in our garden, gathering and canning whatever was left for the winter. We picked green beans and canned the ones that were still tender, and we dried and shelled (or threshed) the mature ones. Sometimes the neighbors picked several bushels of beans, and we would gather in the evening and have a bean-stringing session. There were always some comical, jolly neighbors there. Some mischievous person would catch a friend's head turned and pop him with a bean. We kept him guessing about who did it. After we got the beans strung, we played games, told jokes, etc. We had a lot of fun.

By the time we finished harvesting our beans, we were ready to start school, but that didn't end our farmwork. We would come home from school, get our corn cutter (it looked like a machete), and start for the field to cut corn. If the stocks were heavy, we would take a swath of eight rows for a corn shock; if they were light, we would take ten rows. One of us, usually the oldest one (Alvah or Guy), took the two middle rows and cut them on each side of him until he had a load. He made a horse by putting the load between four hills of corn and bending the tops over and pulling them together to form a pyramid shape. Then we crunched the big end of a well-ripened stalk and wrapped it around the tops to bind them. We wrapped the big end of the tie stock over the little end to hold it in place. This made a nice horse, or stand, to hold the stalks straight up. One would follow on the left and one on the right of the shock row and cut a load and carry it to where we set it around the horse. We leaned the shock uphill or to face the usual direction of the winds. We kept adding loads until, according to the weight or size of the corn, we got from eighty to ninety hills in a shock. We squeezed the shock together and wrapped a tie stock around it just above the ears. We tied it by lapping the ends in a kind of a half hitch. Then we'd get another tie stalk (you could let loose of your shock when you got the first stalk tied) and pull the top closer together and bind it again. That kept the wind from catching the shock. Also, it would protect the corn from water. It kept as well as if it were in our corncrib. If there were no severe storms or heavy snows to break them down, the shocks would stand for months.

Cutting corn was also hard work—and a little disagreeable. If the stocks got too ripe and dry and we didn't wear gloves and tie a cloth around our necks to protect us some, the blades would saw our faces and hands. Early on, before our crop finished growing, I got pretty tired of hoeing corn and cutting weeds, but I didn't mind cutting corn and shucking it. When we finally finished cutting corn and shucking it, we shucked just enough to feed our hogs to fatten them for pork and bacon while we waited for the weather to get cool. We let the rest of the corn cure enough to pile it in the crib. Farmers usually built cribs with three- or four-inch slats or boards, placing them just far enough apart to keep the ears from falling through. That kept the air circulating through it so well that it stayed sound until we had another crop.

We weren't often bothered much with insect pests, but sometimes a little worm called a weevil would eat the heart of the corn. We had more trouble with birds, such as starlings and cardinals, and animals, such as rats, squirrels, and chipmunks. If pests got too bad, people would shell the corn. A mechanical sheller with a wheel about four or five feet in diameter could be used to shell a large crib of corn. We would stick the small end of the ear down through the hopper and turn the wheel, which had teeth that would rake the grain off. One man turned the wheel by a handle on the rim, and another man fed the ears into the hopper. It shelled the corn about as fast as we could feed it.

We children came directly home from school to husk our corn and haul in as much of it as we could before dark. We didn't shuck corn when the fodder was too dry because the leaves would crumble and waste so that it wasn't worth much as feed for our livestock. When properly cured, the fodder made good bulk feed for the cows, but it was not so good for horses. Even though we didn't work the horse much during that season, we usually fed her some grain during the winter. We used her to haul our corn and wood and to take our corn to the mill for our bread. (We had to buy our flour because there was no roller mill in our neighborhood suitable for making flour. The nearest one was at Newton in Roane County.)

During the week, we shelled one and one half bushels of corn, poured it into a nice strong white sack long enough to balance over the saddle, and we took it to the mill on Saturday. We carried it about seven miles to Henry Snider's water-driven mill at Queen Shoals, about one half mile below Queen Shoals Bridge. It was almost a day's job to get there and back. The miller kept a gallon of our corn per bushel to pay for grinding it. (We called that the toll meal.)

The weather didn't always cooperate with us for our trip to the mill. Sometimes it was too cold to ride a horse so far, and at other times, it rained and we would have to take something to put over our corn to keep it dry. On rare occasions, the corn got so wet that we had to dry it by spreading it out thinly near a fire. A few times, I've started to the mill and found that a hill had slid in along the narrows below Barren Creek, blocking the road so that we couldn't get a horse over it. I would have to go back home. Maybe they wouldn't get the slide out of the road until after the spring thaw in April.

When we couldn't get to Henry Snider's mill, we went about the same distance to a different one at Amy. We often had to stay there for an hour or two, waiting for our corn to be ground. The boys at the mill would look our horses over, size them up, judge them for speed, and banter one another for a horse race. Ole Maude was a very fast runner, and I often won the event. One time, when I went to the mill in the summertime, Dad had me take Ole Maude to the blacksmith and have her shod at the Geary Blacksmith Shop. (The owner was a relative of the Geary brothers in Clendenin who are in the furniture business and are related to my grandmother Boggs.)

The blacksmith looked at my horse's feet and told me what size of shoes to get and how many nails he would need, and then he sent me to the store just across the road to get them for Ole Maude. The clerk handed me the shoes, tied together, and the nails were in a paper sack. I was barefooted, and I had on long-legged overalls. I caught my toe in my pants leg and fell down—with the nails in my hand. I ran three of them into my hand. One ran nearly clear through it. I went to the doctor there, and he dressed it and put some disinfectant medicine on it. It left scars on my hand for several years, but it didn't give me too much trouble. If we didn't whip her a little, Ole Maude would poke along on her way home, but when she got within a mile or two of home, she would think of her dinner and her rest and step up to double-time without any more coaxing. I managed to get back home in a reasonable time with my grist of meal.

Late in the autumn, before the cold wind and the snow began to blow, we took Ole Maude up the hill above the house to haul in logs for fuel. Ole Maude weighed about twelve hundred pounds, and she was very strong. There was a short dip in the path to our house, and she would keep going fast down the hill to get a good start up the next bank. She could take a pretty large log up it before she lost momentum. We rolled the logs up on skids a foot or so off of the ground and sawed through them about every three feet to make them fit in the old black cast-iron stove.

We split those blocks small enough to fit five or six pieces into the stove, and that stove could throw out a lot of heat from that hickory wood. Before we went to bed, we threw in two or three big sticks and turned the damper just enough to allow some air to circulate and keep the fire smoldering. When we arose the next morning, there were usually some hot coals of fire that flamed up soon after we put more wood on it.

Dad kept up on current events by taking a good newspaper such as *The Commoner* or the *Charleston Gazette* and a few magazines, and he read about every book he could get. He had a good number one grammar school education, and he was an excellent reader. He often sat by that hot woodstove and read to the family from the *New York World* stories, *The Indian Men of Ohio* and other Scout stories, the *Late World Report,* "Granddad's Old Clock Ran Down Never to Run Again," and Robinson Crusoe stories. He also told us a lot of other popular tales that I can't recall. He knew some interesting hunting stories about bears, tigers, and other wild animals. Just imagining them as he talked made them very interesting. At the end of the story, he would say, "Boo!" and jump at us to frighten us. At bedtime, we often pulled our shoes off and ran around the dwelling barefooted in the snow. We then came in and dried our feet before going to bed. We thought that the exercise would help us to sleep better.

During the winter, we cut enough fuel wood on Saturday to last through the week while we went to school. Sundays were the Lord's day, and we didn't have to work. We had hardly any place to go to church or Sunday school, so we often congregated and played with our peers. We called one game called Fox and Geese. We first made a large circular path in the snow about twenty to thirty feet in diameter, with a smaller ring inside it. We trampled eight lanes across the diameter (like the spokes of a wheel). Two "foxes" were chosen—one for the inner circle and one for the outer circle. The others were the "geese." They stayed in the inner circle, and the foxes chased them through the lanes. When a fox tagged one of the geese, that one became a fox and was moved to the outer circle. The game was over when all of the geese were caught by one of the foxes (or geese-turned-foxes). The first ones tagged were chosen to be the foxes in the next game.

When the weather was too bad to play in the open spaces, we would often get our ax and some matches and go about a quarter mile to a rock cliff that ran around a point at the break of a steep hill. We would find some pine knots for kindling and build a fire in a dry space under the cliff. We sang, told stories, played games, climbed trees, hunted wood rats, played in the sand, etc. The highest place in the cliff was about sixty feet. There were some trees growing up to the ceiling from a ledge under the cliff, and there was one we could get into from above the cliff. We climbed out a limb of that tree and slid down the trunk, searching the face of the cliff for holes, bird nests, etc. We found one big cave about fifteen to twenty feet long, ten feet wide, and eight feet high. We called it the bear den. (No doubt, bears and other wild animals had used it.)

We didn't often play around rock cliffs in the summertime because there was danger from rattlesnakes and copperheads, but there was one occasion when we carefully ventured back to our old winter playground. As we neared the bear den, we heard a rumbling noise coming from the cave. We were very scared. Then we saw a large buzzard flapping his long wings to get away from us. As we ventured nearer and nearer to the big black hole under the cliff, we heard a hissing sound, but we kept venturing nearer and nearer until we could see something white. We finally got close enough to the white object to find two young buzzards blowing at us like a gander guarding its babies. We caught them and brought them out to daylight. They vomited the rotting food that their mother and father had fed them. Their odor was so strong that we had trouble washing the smell away. That, no doubt, was the way the buzzards protected themselves from hungry predators. We visited our game until they were old enough to fly. The mother vulture quit feeding them, and they shed their down and grew feathers in their wings. The buzzards returned the next year, raising another pair of young ones. (They say that when two are of the one sex, they will kill them. If they are male and female and one dies, they kill the one that is left.)

We hunted for hawk and crow nests, and we would destroy all of them that we found. We didn't know that some hawks are useful. As far as we knew, they were game and bird predators. Some hawks are useful for catching snakes, rats, and mice, but to us farmers, they were all enemies. They would catch our chickens, squirrels, and rabbits.

We caught baby rabbits, squirrels, chipmunks, groundhogs, and polecats, and we tried to tame some of them. We never raised a rabbit. They would live a few days, but we couldn't get the right kind of food to make them grow. A squirrel is a hardy animal and easy to raise. They will climb all over you, and they seem to thrive well on nuts or bread. They make a nice pet but will bite you at times. If you let them out around timber, they will finally wander away and never come back. Chipmunks are very cute pets, but you have to keep them in a cage or they won't stay around long. A groundhog is another interesting pet. They will stay and follow you like a dog. They hole up (hibernate) in winter. They emerge about the first of February, but they won't stay out if the weather is too cold. A polecat (skunk) is about like a cat and is very pretty. To keep one, you have to cut its stink bag off.

Some little redhead summer sparrows ventured near our house to pick up breadcrumbs. We noticed that when they were feeding on the crumbs, they would let us walk almost within reach of them. We decided we might tame some of them. We lay flat on the ground and flipped crumbs toward them. As we continued to reward them day after day, they kept coming closer and closer until they finally got close enough to pick crumbs from our hands. We would lie still and never move. Then we raised an arm a few inches at a time until one or two would fly into our hand. They'd pick a few crumbs and fly away to eat them. Finally they would sit on our hand while eating the crumbs. Then they'd fill their beaks and carry some to their young ones. The sparrows raised two litters during the summer. For three years, they came back in the spring. We knew they must be the same birds because we had to coax them for only a week or two before they would eat from our hands again. It surprised people to see a bird fly from a tree and pick crumbs from our hands. I have never known of any other family training them.

One time, we caught a dryland tarpon (or tortoise) and brought it to the dwelling. Our cat got to boxing at it and playing cat and mouse with it. Finally, the tarpon got the cat's paw in its mouth and closed its shell on the cat's foot. The squalling cat ran all over the house, going *bumpety-bump* with the tarpon holding tight. We had to use a hammer and beat the tarpon to pieces before it let loose.

If you catch them while they are young, coons (raccoons) also make nice pets. Their bushy ringed tails and the black masks across the eyes easily identify them. They are very pretty, and they will follow you like a dog. They will eat meat, bread, corn, vegetables, nuts, and some weeds. Some of our neighbors kept black snakes (racers) around their barns until they tamed them. They are good to catch rats, but they will eat little chickens and hen eggs (swallowing them whole). After swallowing an egg, a racer will wrap tightly around a pole or other object to crush the shell of the egg. They can move as fast as an adult moving at a brisk pace. If cornered, one will strike repeatedly while vibrating its tail. But they are nonpoisonous. We never made friends with a snake. We killed every one we saw around our place.

I once killed a big rattlesnake within about fifty yards of our dwelling. I was plowing with ole Maude when I noticed one coiled up under a rock that jutted out about four or five feet from the hill that ran alongside our field. I was afraid that if I startled it, it would go further under the rock. I cut a sprout about six feet long and left a small branch near the big end of it. I sharpened the smaller branch about two or three inches from the stock of the main branch. I eased the fork of the stick down behind the coiled snake and jerked it toward me, hooking the sharpened branch into its skin. I pulled the snake away from the rock and jumped back.

I wounded it and listened to it rattle for a few minutes, and then I killed it. It was over four feet long and two and one half inches across its belly. It had sixteen rattlers on it. You can hear one of his many rattlers for a hundred yards or further. They are said to grow a new segment each time they shed their skin, an average of three times a year. So the one I killed must have been five or six years old. The rattlers are easily broken off, so they don't always tell the age of the snake. They are more poisonous than a copperhead snake, possibly because they are larger and inject more poison into you. The rattler and the copperhead are the only severely poisonous snakes we have in West Virginia. There is a big fly called a jar fly that looks like a locust (cicada) and makes a noise like a rattler, but if you hear a rattlesnake close by, you will identify it at once.

The black widow is the only poisonous spider in West Virginia. I have seen them as big as the end of an average man's thumb. They are found mostly anywhere you will find other spiders. Your basement is a place you will often find them. The largest one I found was in my garden. It was an inch across the body. They are black, with a red hourglass-shaped spot on their body. The brown recluse spider is a nuisance in the South, but I don't believe that they have spread this far north. Spiders have eight legs and a two-part body.

We have many native birds in West Virginia. The cardinal is a familiar one. They stay here all their lives. The rooster bird is red. The hen is brown or a mouse color, with a red back and some red on its tail, neck, and head. They are nearly as large as a robin. The robin usually goes south in winter, but if the winter is mild, they stay in West Virginia about all year. Some other native birds are the chickadee, oriole, crow, hawks, some sparrows (with the exception of the little redhead sparrow), starlings, and some owls. The hoot owl hibernates in the worst of winter. If you hear one during a bad spell in the wintertime, you may say that the storm has broken. The screech owl is another native bird. They holler at night and make a noise that will chill your spine. If you find one in the daytime, you can step on it or catch it because they can't see well in the daytime. Screech owls and hoot owls are good rat and mouse eaters. Hoot owls will catch grown chickens. They grow as large as four feet from wing tip to wing tip.

Another night bird is the snipe. At dusk they will fly straight up and make a chattering noise until they land back where they started. The little wren (house wren) and big wren birds are native to West Virginia They stay near the ground, flying through dense brush heaps and over decaying logs, hunting worms. They will readily nest in man-made birdhouses. The whip-poor-will is another ground bird. Some people call them bullbats. They stay here only during the warm months. About September, they sail around in flocks by the thousands before they fly south. When you hear one holler "whip-poor-will," you may know the spring weather is here, but you are still liable to see some snow or frost after they come from the south.

The little hummingbirds thrive here. They are beautiful and will dart and fly so fast you can hardly see them. There are several other birds I might mention, such as a brown bird with a dotted neck and breast that I call the hess bird. They are a little smaller than the robin. They lay their eggs in another bird's nest to be hatched. (By the time I was nine years old, I knew or had a name for almost all of our native birds.)

When we lived in or near the forest, I could identify about every tree in the woods. My favorite trees in winter were evergreens, such as hemlocks and spruce. The hemlock grows on the bluffs near a stream or anywhere in the valley. (The needles and the branches on it look a lot like those on the redwood trees of California, but hemlock trees don't grow as tall as the redwoods.) They are beautiful in winter when the snow is on them. I still cut the hemlock for Christmas trees. The long-needle spruce pine grows on the hilltop and on the thin soil on the points. They are pretty, more so when the snow is on them. The white oak, black walnut, and poplar (tulip) trees are favorite lumber trees in West Virginia. They grow very large. Some trees have been cut that have as much as four thousand board feet of lumber in them.

Some white oak trees that were cut down cut in Fayette County in 1960 were over five feet in diameter. They were over five hundred years old. (We could tell the age by counting the growth rings on the stump.) They used that lumber to make molding. It has a beautiful grain in it, and the lumber is hard and strong. The yellow poplar is a valuable tree to grow. It gets as large as the oak. They are a softwood tree and are used mostly for siding.

When there was a light moon in June and when the sap was right, it was a great sport and pleasure to go to the woods and follow a stream until we found a birch tree to cut down (in those days there wasn't much concern about destroying timber). Sometimes we'd chop for an hour to get one down. If it fell across a hollow, we walked out on it and chopped it in two to get it on the ground where we could peel the bark off. We would have to jump off the log and out of the way when the log broke and fell. We realized the risk of it falling on us. If we made a misstep and slid under it, there was great danger, but we would take that chance to get some good birch sap. We cut a ring around the log about every two feet and then split the bark two ways while peeling it from the log. We scraped off the inner bark and sap with a spoon. It was as tasty and sweet as candy with a strong birch flavor. It was really delicious! We used Mother's spoons, and sometimes we got a scolding for losing them. We often took a big slab of bark to Dad and Mother. They loved it too.

The chestnut was my favorite tree in summer and autumn. They made good timber to hunt squirrel in because they grew nearly as large as the oak and they bore nuts that the squirrel loved more than any other timber forage. So did people. I have seen so much mast, or nuts, fall from them that you could rake them up by the handfuls where they fell and lodged against poles and where they rolled into sinkholes. Chestnut hunting was one of my favorite pastimes. I have gathered as much as three or four gallons in a day. They grew in a big burr, some as large as a man's fist. There would be as many as four nuts in a burr. Some of the nuts grew to be one inch thick and an inch and a quarter long or larger. They were sweeter and tasted better after they had seasoned and dried out for a month or more. You could keep them all winter, but worms often got into them and destroyed the kernels.

Mounter (mountain laurel) was one of the favorite plants that I encountered while going through the forest. It has shiny evergreen leaves that look like bay leaves, and it grows as a shrub. In the spring, its large cup-shaped blooms make show flower clusters. Birch was my favorite spring tree. I loved the flavor of birch. I would break off a young, tender spring growth of a birch twig and either strip the bark and chew it or just take the ends of the twig and chew it. They have a sweet, tasty flavor.

Our dog usually came along, and when he treed a groundhog, we would throw at it until someone knocked it out of the tree. Sometimes we cut the tree. The dog and groundhog would have a good fight. A dog has strength beyond imagination. They can hold on with their teeth and pull a tremendous load, but a big groundhog is strong enough to injure a dog. A small dog that knows how to deal with a groundhog can take hold of it at just the right place (just over or in front of the shoulder) to break it in two (or crush its heart) very quickly. I realized how strong they are when I once caught a nearly fullgrown groundhog in a trap and he pulled the trap into his hole. When I attempted to pull him from the hole by his hind leg, he hung on by his front paws and braced his back until I could hardly pull him out—even if I was about as strong as a mature man.

In the same size range, a coon is about the hardest animal for a dog to handle. They are very strong and tricky and intelligent. You usually find a coon near a stream. They like fish and crayfish and will follow a stream and turn over rocks so large you would think it unreasonable for them to move. A coon will run for a deep hole of water, and if the dog doesn't know how to fight it, it will drown the dog. If you cut down a tree with one, a dog has to be intelligent to find it. At times, they will jump into another tree and go up. They can jump from that one and be gone before the dog can find its traces. They will go for their den or to a hole in the ground or find a hole of water to put up a fight. Sometimes we would shoot one out of the tree with a spotlight, but we preferred to see a fight—if we had time. Other times, if the tree was too large to cut, we would stay by it until daytime and then shoot the coon (or climb the tree and chase it out to see a fight).

It's coming on spring now, and school is over at the first of March. That's when we had a little time to play. Unless we were clearing land, we didn't have much farmwork to do until about the first or middle of April. We liked to go to a place in the forest where there wasn't any mud. It was nicer to play in the clean leaves. We sometimes hunted for a thicket of small trees and climbed to the tops of them. We'd get them to weaving and ride them to the ground as they sprung back and forth. When we dropped from it, the tree would flip straight back.

Sometimes we would climb a tree and bend it to the top of another tree. We'd catch onto that one and let go of the first tree. We kept traveling in that way to see who could travel the furthest from one treetop to another. We also had a lot of fun swinging on grapevines. We would hunt for a tree that had a grapevine in it and cut the vine close to the ground. Two or three of us would pull on the vine to see if it was strong enough to carry us. If it was strong and well anchored in the treetop, we could swing out fifteen or twenty feet or more back and forth over streams or ravines.

One time, my brother Cornelius, just eighteen months younger than I, lost his grip and slipped from a grapevine. He fell to the ground and broke his arm at the wrist. We didn't have a doctor anywhere near our home, so we took him to Granddad Estep. Granddad examined his arm and set it back in place the best he could. He splinted it to hold it straight (about as well as any doctor could do). We put his arm in a sling, and he kept it there until his arm grew strong again. We took many chances at getting hurt at our play—climbing trees and rock cliffs, bending trees over to the tops of the cliffs, sliding down the trees, etc., but we were pretty strong and accurate, and we avoided many potential accidents. Sometimes we chased one another through the forest and hills acting like foxes and dogs until we were exhausted, and then we would regain our reserve strength and keep going.

Occasionally, when we were exhausted from all of that running, we cleaned out a place to play—usually under a big beech tree. Then we would gather moss and flowers to decorate our playground.

Sometimes we played on rock-bottom streams, floating sticks for logs and making water mills and dams. Then we'd tear the dams apart and make little floods. "It's getting late. Let's take Mother a nice bundle of flowers for her vase." We would gather honeysuckle, rhododendron, ivy, laurel, dogwood, sweet williams, blue violets, arbutus, wild iris, and other spring flowers. That was one of my favorite activities in the spring. I loved flowers. Mother was getting worried about us. It was getting late, but when we took her the pretty flowers and all of us accounted for ourselves, she was happy that the day was over and we didn't get hurt. We were all together again.

By this time, we were getting to be a big family. I often told people that we each had one sister. They would be astonished before they caught onto my trick. There was Alvah Vandal, Guy Burl, Ray Emerson, Ira Irvin, Cornelius Thomas, Roy Cecil, Dennis Burl, Ona Izora, and Scott. In 1903, there was an epidemic of an infectious diarrhea that killed children throughout the country. Scott died in July of that year. His was the first death in our family. That was a very sad thing for all of us. We buried him on Pigeon Creek in the Pigeon cemetery, where Grandfather and Grandmother Estep and some of my cousins, uncles, and aunts are buried. Clarence Lee was born in 1904, and Waitman Burnard was born in 1907.

We had about seven acres of land cleared at that time. Dad helped us get the spring crop planted, and then he went away to work on a log job. There were four boys big enough to work on the farm. We could do a little work, but none of us were strong enough to plow with Ole Maude. That summer, Granddad was farming and logging some. He had hired some young men who were large enough to plow with a horse. So Alvah and Guy worked a day for Granddad, and Granddad sent one of his men, Waitman or Ben Ashley—both were large enough to plow with ole Maude—to help for a day to pay for Alva and Guy's work.

We had long rows of corn, and after we hoed a round-trip in the field (two rows each), we would sit down and take five. We called it five, but we usually rested fifteen minutes or longer. Sometimes we would sit and talk and tell stories while we rested. At other times, we played while we relaxed from the hard work. Waitman Ashley liked to throw rocks over trees and down the hill. He could pitch a rock much farther than I had ever seen anyone else throw one. I suppose he was the first grown man I ever saw throw a rock. He got acquainted with my aunt Florence Estep while he worked and boarded with my granddad. My brothers and I would call him Uncle Waitman and giggle about it. That embarrassed him.

Everybody worked six days a week and ten hours per day, but on Sundays, all of us often got together and had a good time playing ball and base. When they got behind in their work, some people worked from daylight until dark. The year we cleared the twelve-acre field, we got behind on our fieldwork, and we were very tired before we got our crop laid by. We cleared the twelve-acre field for five dollars per acre. Mother needed a sewing machine. There was quite a family of us to keep in clothing, and she had been going to Granddad's to sew on Grandmother's machine. That took all of the sixty dollars we made by clearing the big twelve-acre field, but all of us were very proud to help Mother get one. Mother was very proud of her new Singer sewing machine. She used it for many years. Those days, Mother made about all of our clothes—except overalls (we usually bought them ready-made).

The next spring, we sharecropped the twelve-acre field that we had cleared. We grew and shucked the corn and gave one-third of it for the use of the ground. We grew some fine big corn and beans on it the first year. It was easier than normal to tend because the ground was loose and easy to plow. The plow would root out and cover almost all of the weeds except the tree sprouts that grew on the stumps and roots (some of the roots were too big to plow through.)

The year after we moved to Upper King Shoals Creek, after we got the crop finished, Dad, Mother, and the baby, Scott, went to Looneyville to visit Granddad and Grandmother and family. Alvah and I were in the peach orchard, and some of the peaches were turning a little red where the sun shined on them. I thought they were ripe, and I pulled one or two and ate some. They didn't taste too bad, and I liked fruit, but they were very green. I ate only a few bites, but late that evening, I got a headache and got very sick. I went to bed, and that was the last I remembered until sometime the next day. I had convulsions (something like a fit). They said that one of my hands didn't move when I thrashed about. One side seemed to be paralyzed. I thought it was from eating those green peaches with that fuzz on them, but they said that I had what they called cholera morbus. Aunt Florence was staying with us children while Dad and Mother were visiting at Looneyville. One of my brothers walked about two and one half miles to the mouth of King Shoals to get a doctor. The doctor came and stayed all night with me. My eyes set, and I came so close to dying that they thought they couldn't save my life. The next day, I wasn't able to be on my feet. Dad and Mother had ridden ole Maude when they went to Looneyville to see Granddad, so Alvah and Guy had to walk about fifteen miles to get them. They found Mother and Dad and brought them back the next morning. My sickness ruined their vacation and visit. I wasn't able to move around for a week or more.

After we moved to Upper King Shoals, I didn't get to see Granddad and Grandmother again for two years. That was a long time for me to be away from my lovely grandparents and my uncles and aunts, and I also missed my old neighborhood friends and playmates. About 1904, Alvah and Guy were old enough to work in public works. (There wasn't any law against children working those days.) Alvah was twelve, and Guy was eleven. They went to Richwood and stayed with Uncle Elmer Estep while they worked in a clothespin factory for a few weeks. They made a little money, but that helped a lot in buying clothes to go to school. There were nine children in the family at that time.

A few years later, some men were cutting stave timber and hauling it from Granny's Creek about four miles across three hills on a wagon. They split the stave blocks into three-by-six-inch staves four feet in length for making oil and whiskey barrels. Pless McCune and Charley Jarvis had the contract. They hauled them to the top of a rock cliff where we often played, at a site that I have mentioned heretofore. After we got our corn hoed over, Mr. Jarvis and Mr. McCune gave us a contract throwing and pitching these staves down the hill to King Shoals Creek. I worked for fifty cents a day. That was the first money I made with a day's work. There were several hundred of the staves, and we learned to handle them pretty well. We would lay them on our shoulders and give them a sling, bouncing them end over end for a long way down the hill. We worked them to the creek, and they lay there until the creek flooded enough to float them to near the river where somebody had stretched a net across the mouth of the creek to catch them. That saved a lot of time and labor that would have been required to haul them twenty miles. After loading them onto a wagon and taking them across the river on a ferryboat, they shipped the staves to Charleston, where they sold them.

Alvah and Guy were almost young men at this time (1905). They were getting along pretty well in school and growing to know a lot about life. The neighborhood held a revival meeting at the schoolhouse. (Their nearest church was at Barren Creek, about five miles from our home, and it was about half that far to the schoolhouse.) They held the meetings at night because there was school during the day. The revival continued for about three weeks, and there were several conversions. Alvah and Guy went to the altar and prayed. Alvah made such a bright testimony that the preacher told him he ought to be a minister. Everybody talked a lot about the meeting. I liked to hear them talking about people repenting of their sins, but I didn't quite understand what it was all about or how to get saved. I was about nine or ten years old then. When the weather was bad and we couldn't very well go to church, we children would stay at home, and some of our neighborhood youngsters would take our songbooks and go to a shelter at an outbuilding, such as the crib or barn and sometimes to our playhouse at the rock cliff, to hold our own meetings. We would sing a song, and then someone—usually Alvah, Guy, or my cousin Harley Belcher—would lead the meeting. He would talk for a while and then call on someone to pray. Some of my brothers and cousins kept talking to me and explaining Christianity. I began to understand more about what I needed to do to be saved. I was eleven years old and had gone to Sunday school and church as long as I could remember. I knew what death meant, and I had often thought about how awful it would be to die and never be anymore. From the time I could remember, I already knew how to pray. I knew that everybody should be good and that it was a terribly bad thing to swear and use bad words or to steal, fight, or break one of the Ten Commandments. So I began to appreciate the forgiveness of our sins and what an awful thing it was to sin. My older brothers, including Ray (the older brother next to me), and my cousins were all saved. I got uneasy about my soul and being saved like the rest of them. So I got to praying that I might get saved. Alvah was my oldest brother, about four years older than I. I asked him if I would be saved if I were to die.

Alvah told me that unless I was "born again," I might be lost, but I don't think he understood. The Bible says in Acts 2:38, "Then Peter said unto them, Repent, and be baptized every one of you in the name of Jesus Christ for the remission of sins, and ye shall receive the gift of the Holy Ghost."

I think that anyone who is seeking salvation and is trying to live right, according to the Bible, is saved already. But I hadn't felt the real blessings of salvation, so I kept praying that I might be like my brothers and cousins. One day, Cornelius, Harley, and I were praying in the woods near Granddad's lumber stack. We climbed to the top of the stack, and Harley suggested that we sing and have a prayer. So Harley prayed with Cornelius and me. We kept praying, and I was blessed in the forgiveness of my sins. I was very happy. Cornelius prayed through too. Then I realized what it meant to be saved from our sins. For sometime, or as long as we lived on King Shoals, we would either go to church and

Sunday school or have our own prayer sessions and meetings. I prayed with a new understanding, and I enjoyed our meetings more. Alvah and Harley could pray like a minister. I was younger than three of my brothers and about the same age as my cousin Harley. They would sometimes call on me to pray. I was always a little timid, but I never refused to pray orally when they called on me. We had some really good meetings and were often blessed by the spirit of God. I couldn't think of much to say when I prayed, not as much as some of the older ones, but what we say when we pray is not as important as the meaning and our faith in what we do pray about. I always liked to go to church and Sunday school, and I went every time I could.

Some people in our community decided to build a church near the mouth of Porter Creek. The site was about a mile beyond our schoolhouse, but two miles closer than Barren Creek Church. The church was organized by the Methodist denomination, and they named it the Bedo Church after the elder of the Methodist congregation. We attended meetings there for sometime. Usually in the spring of the year or in the autumn before the weather got bad (the winters were very long and cold at that time), they would have a revival. The church was on the opposite side of the river from where we lived. We would call for a boat, and some of our neighbors would row us across the river and back. Although my family was Baptist, the Methodists were glad to have us attend their church, and when spring came, we could gather with our own fellowship at Barren Creek. (Some people wouldn't attend another denomination, but we didn't believe that was right.) The Methodists had a good congregation, and they had some lively revivals there. When we went there, we boys walked seven miles to Barren Creek Church, and Mother would ride ole Maude. The women had a special saddle to keep from straddling the horse's back. The saddle had a horn, or an offset, on it. A woman could throw her leg over it and ride on one side of the horse holding onto the saddle. We had to adjust the saddle very tight around the horse, or it might roll over the side of the horse and slide a person off. (Later on, they made a split skirt so the women could ride astride the horse.)

We went over the hill from the river by Dave Smith's farm, out the ridge, and off the hill to the church—a shorter way than following the river. We usually came back the same way as we went, and Brother Smith would often invite us to stop at his house and stay for dinner. We usually got home before dark, but it took most of the day to travel fourteen miles for the round-trip. The circuit riders would start to their churches on Saturday and ride (or walk) several miles. Then they came back and went to their farms on Wednesday morning.

In the spring of 1907, we decided to leave King Shoals and move back to Wallback in Roane County, near where Dad and Mother had lived before and for a few years after they were married. (This was where I was born about a year before we moved to Looneyville.) We leased a farm from Mike Underwood, Mother's first cousin. It had a bigger house, and the ground was very fertile, so we could grow lots of grain and have good pasture for our horse and cows. We were also closer to school and church and to the post office. It was about two miles to the Baptist church and about one mile to the schoolhouse and the Methodist church, which were located on one fork of Big Sandy Creek (which empties into the river at Clendenin). There were three forks of Big Sandy within a half mile of our home, and there were churches and schools on each fork. We now had plenty of places to go to church and a neighborhood of very friendly people.

The nearest route to Wallback from King Shoals was about seven miles. We moved in the spring (in March), hauling our furniture on a wagon. We still had some feed for our cattle at King Shoals, so we took only one cow to Wallback. I stayed at King Shoals with my granddad and uncle Burton Cook to finish doling out the feed to the cattle. During my stay, Uncle Burton chopped his leg with an ax. He cut it pretty badly. I helped Aunt Lula with the work, feeding the farm animals and getting wood for fuel. The cattle consumed all of the winter feed within about a month, and by that time, the grass was ready to pasture the cattle at our new home. Some of my brothers came back to help me drive the cattle to Wallback.

We fed the cattle and started early in the morning. We drove them through the hills by Granny's Creek, then over the hill to the right-hand fork of Sandy Creek. We got home in the afternoon. We left some of our shelled corn in a big box at Granddad's. We depended on that grain for our bread, so about every two weeks, we had to take ole Maude back to King Shoals and get about two bushels of the corn. We put it into a big, long sack and slung the load over ole Maude's back, and we rode on top of it all the way back to Wallback. After several trips for our bread corn, we finally got it all home.

There was a corn mill at Wallback, so we didn't have to go as far to the mill as we did at King Shoals. We got our cornmeal ground there, but we had to go to Newton to get our wheat rolled into flour. Newton was about four miles down Sandy to another of the three forks of Big Sandy. Big Sandy spreads out over quite a territory in Roane, Kanawha, and Clay counties. It heads at Ivydale about forty-five miles from where it empties into Elk River at Clendenin. Like most rivers or creeks in this mountain state, Sandy winds through the hills. It drains one of the principal farming sections of West Virginia. The pretty rolling bluegrass hills are especially beautiful around Newton and Wallback. There are some valuable oil and gas wells throughout the Sandy Creek area, but there has been very little coal mining in that vicinity.

Alvah and Guy worked on lumbering jobs and sometimes on neighboring farms. They also helped with the busy part of the farming at home. Alvah, Guy, Ray, and I were now mature enough to do a lot of work. In those days, poor people's children didn't always get time from their chores to attend school. But people got along better without an education than they can now. If a person was a good manager of his time and was able to work, there wasn't any reason that he couldn't make a good living. If a person could read and write and work with figures a little, it was considered an average education—equivalent to fifth or sixth grade. Eight grades were as good as, or better than, a high school education is today, but not quite as broad.

Mother always wanted a Jersey cow, but Dad preferred Hereford cattle. We could get more money for a beef-type calf. The stock (cattle and hogs) that we sold provided about all the cash income that we had in those days. We didn't raise sheep. Dad said it didn't pay out. People's dogs killed too many of them, and that caused a lot of trouble between neighbors. There wasn't any law against shooting a sheep-killing dog, but Dad always avoided trouble with anyone.

Mother finally got her Jersey cow. Uncle Smith Boggs had a nice-looking yellow Jersey heifer, and Aunt Ann told Mother that the mother cow was a very good butter producer, so Mother encouraged Dad to buy the heifer. We didn't have the money to pay for it, but Uncle Smith needed some ground cleared to grow corn, and Dad agreed to clear the brush from four acres of ground. We just hacked it down and cut the logs short enough to pile up and burn them. There was such an abundance of choice timber that just to get them out of the way, people would often cut and burn big trees that could saw out a thousand feet of lumber. Sometimes we piled them in a rough dreen, left them to rot, and filled the holes in the land to make it smooth and easier to work over and cultivate.

Dad, Ray, and I got our ax, crosscut saw, and mattocks and went to work. Dad was a good axman, and he did most of the chopping. After Dad notched them in the right direction, Ray and I sawed the trees down and cut them into short logs. We cut the brush into sections small enough to handle and piled it into large heaps to burn. Uncle Smith lived about five miles from our dwelling. We would leave home on Sunday or Wednesday and hike across three hills through the forest to stay with Uncle Smith and family until the last of the week. We came back home to spend our Sundays with our family and returned to our job for the rest of the week.

It took the three of us (Dad, Ray, and I) about six weeks to get the ground cleared. The logs were too large for Uncle Smith to pile up to burn, so his neighbors joined in and helped him. That was the custom those days. The neighbors would get together and decide when to have a log-rolling day. Some would bring a team of strong horses, and some had cane hooks to roll the logs together. There were usually fifteen or twenty men to move the large logs, and the boys picked up the small timbers and brush.

It took a lot of additional work to get a piece of land ready for the plow. When they got everything all piled up in shape to burn, we waited for a dry day to set fire to the brush heaps, and after they burned out, we had to pick up the parts that didn't burn on the first try and pile them onto the log heaps. After we got all of the ground cleared of the leafy brush, we set fire to the remaining logs and branches. It sometimes took a week or more for those big green logs to burn. After they burned in two, we moved the logs and rolled them together in a new spot, with the biggest logs on the ground and the smaller ones on top of them. We burned them again, and after that fire burned out, we picked up the remaining pieces (or chunks) of wood and chucked them onto new heaps. We repeated this process several times before all of the wood was burned clean, leaving only the ashes.

If we weren't careful, we could have such big heaps that the heat from the fire would scorch the ground so badly that we couldn't grow corn where we burned the logs. so we always moved the logs onto other ground as soon as they were about half-burned. That saved the ground. Also, if we pulled the piles of logs and brush and chunks of wood onto stumps, we could burn them out of the way of the plow, and we could grow two or three hills of corn where the stump would have been. If the ground wasn't scorched too much, we could grow the best corn in the burned spots. There, the corn grew the biggest and tallest stocks and produced the largest ears. Spreading the burns helped the soil and also made it easier for us to cultivate the crops. The ashes from the timbers contained fertilizer that provided nutrients for growing grain, and the fire destroyed the wild seeds and killed the stumps. Where we spread the burns, there weren't so many weeds and sprouts to smother our plants, and when there weren't so many of them in our way, it didn't take so long to cultivate the field.

We had to work pretty hard to get the job done on schedule so that Uncle Smith could get the ground cleaned up and ready for them to plant corn on it in the spring, but we finally got to take our pretty yellow heifer home. We were very proud of our calf, and it became a very gentle pet. We would take it by the neck and lead it around with a child on its back. It seemed to delight in our rubbing it and playing with it. About a year after we bought it, it bore a calf. Because she was normally so gentle, we expected the heifer to be easy to milk, but we soon learned a different story. When we tried to milk her, she kicked and ran until Dad was about ready to sell her. Finally, he put a halter on her head and tied her to a stall, and he tied a rope on her legs so she couldn't kick. She still tried to kick the pail over and spill the milk, but we kept coaxing her to be calm. She eventually understood that it wasn't going to hurt, so she became a good gentle cow.

When we moved to Wallback, there wasn't enough cleared ground on Mike Underwood's farm for us to grow our crops. The spring we moved there, we went to work on about four acres. We didn't have time to clear more than that and get corn in it. To grow big corn, we had to get it planted by May 15. We could have planted 100-day corn, but 120-day corn is bigger and has much more grain per ear. (There's a 90-day corn we could plant about June 15, but it doesn't grow very large and doesn't make much grain per ear.)

About July 4, after we got our field corn laid by (or finished cultivating), we planted some sweet corn. It was a variety that wouldn't get ripe before frost, but it would get mature enough to eat. We found a fertile piece of land and cleared it and piled the brush off of it. We didn't have time to let it dry to burn, so we piled the brush all around the edges of the fertile piece of ground. We just took ole Maude and furried the ground with a sharp root-cutter plow and planted. If the ground is about right (damp or just wet enough that it won't hurt it to stir the soil), corn will sprout and be peeping out of the soil within about four days.

The quails and chipmunks would be pretty hungry for some of our good sweet corn, so we had to watch it pretty close and see that they didn't dig it up. In about four days, I went back to see how it was coming along. I found a little round hole dug in the row where we had planted the corn, and I could see that it had been freshly dug. That's the work of a chipmunk. Quails don't dig a little round hole; they scratch it out. "I'll get you this evening or early in the morning." I was about twelve years old now, and I had learned to handle a gun fairly well. I went to the store and bought me some shotgun shells with birdshot (about number six shot). There are more small shots in a number six shell than a number four or five. It will scatter more when you shoot it, and you are more apt to hit your target with at least one pellet.

I got up early enough the next morning to get out there at about daybreak. The chipmunks and quails knew that the early bird gets the worm, but I was an early riser too. They are very cunning, and they watch for you while they are stealing your corn. It was a great sport for me to kill those chipmunks and the quails that were digging out the corn that I had planted. I wanted to eat it myself instead of letting them have it.

I slipped around behind the trees and bushes. When I heard a chirp, I said, "I'll get you, you striped little thief!" Chipmunks are brown and hard to spot. You don't often see them except when they run. I pulled the shotgun to my shoulder and pulled the trigger on him. He rolled end over end. I didn't stir, as I didn't want to be seen. I stood there quiet a few minutes. Then I heard a bird chirping *bob-bob-white*. I knew that was a quail. They are cunning and very difficult to slip up on to get close enough to shoot them. I thought he was coming after my good sweet corn, so I just kept really quiet. I could hear him calling for his mate. It kept coming nearer until I spied it scratching out some seed corn. He didn't get more than one hill before I got him with the birdshot. I picked up my chipmunk and my quail and got back home in time for breakfast. I asked Mother to put some water in the teakettle and heat it so I could scald my bird and skin the chipmunk. The quail has about the best fowl meat you can find, but few people know that a chipmunk is good to eat. They have the sweetest meat that I have tasted. I could eat a half dozen of them at one meal.

People grew wheat and other small grain crops, and there was enough waste left on the ground that small game could live on it for some time after we cut our harvest. Late in the autumn, after they had hatched their eggs—two litters of them—there would be numerous flocks of quail. It was a great sport to hunt them (and chipmunks), especially when they were stealing my corn.

I watched the corn patch pretty closely. After the fowls and chipmunks got through with it, there was still enough corn left to grow a good crop of roastnears. It was too late to replant it, so if the quails and chipmunks got my seed, we wouldn't have had any good, sweet ears of corn to roast, pickle, or can. After it grows for two weeks or so, the fowls and chipmunks won't dig the corn up. (The grain is dissolved to feed the growing shoot, and it disappears.) As soon as the seedlings were high enough to cultivate, we took ole Maude and ran two or three furriers between the rows with the plow. We hoed the corn and cut all of the weeds. The weather was very hot at that time of the year, and there was plenty of moisture, so the plants grew very fast. They didn't need very much time to mature.

Well, it's now July 20—turnip day. Mother hunted for the old birthday almanac to see what the signs were and if it was a good time to plant. "Well, anyway, Mother, I'm going to plant some turnips today. I don't plant turnips in the signs. I plant them in the ground."

Ha-ha! I didn't believe so much in that old almanac. We had already dug up the ground just deep enough for the plants to take root. It was in good shape for planting, and the prospects were good for rain within a day or two. Dad usually sowed the turnips, and he was a good judge of how to regulate the seed by mixing it with sand or ashes. He would go to the store and buy about a half pint of turnip seed and mix it with a gallon or so of sand or ashes. Ashes were better. They are more fertile than creek sand, and the insects wouldn't eat the seed with lye (potash) coating it. Dad got his sand (or ashes) and put the seed in it. He stirred it well to work the seed evenly into the mix. He started sowing it, and I followed him with an armload of stalks. Watching the seed fall on the loose soil, I set the stalks so that Dad could see how far the seed was scattered. We went back and forth over the field until it was all covered with the mix.

We used two kinds of turnip seed. If the ground had been tended and the soil was loose, we planted globe turnip seeds. Very often, the ground was too steep and rough to cultivate with ole Maude, and we just dug it up with hand tools. If the ground was just recently cleared and hadn't been plowed, we planted a flat turnip—one that would grow on top of the ground. (With just a little room, the root would grow deep enough into the soil to bring up enough nutrients and water to grow a big turnip.) It was shaped like a saucer and would get as big as a breakfast plate. I have seen them grow to six inches in diameter and bigger. The globe turnip was oval shaped, and it was usually heavier than the flat turnip. Some of them would weigh four pounds or more. Boy! Those turnips were good when they were about half-grown. While walking through the turnip patch, we'd pull one up, brush the dirt off of it, and peel it. We sliced it or scraped it with our jacket knife or just peeled one end of the turnip and scraped it with our knife or a teaspoon. When I was hungry, I could eat a whole turnip while going through the turnip patch after looking over our corn and beans and other vegetable and grain crops.

After he got his turnip seed into the ground, Dad sewed some bluegrass seed on top of it. The grass would sprout and take root well enough to stand the winter freeze. That made good pasture for the cattle and sheep. There would also be a few little turnips left for them to eat. The next spring, those turnip tops would sprout up nice and tender, and Mother would pick them and cook a big pot of fresh greens to eat. They were tender and sweet and very good. She also used them in a salad.

Sometimes, when coming back from a squirrel hunt or from cutting corn shocks, I'd say, "Let's get some of those roastnears and some of those tomatoes." Mother sliced those big yellow tomatoes, and I husked that sweet corn and silked it. It will cook in about fifteen minutes. "Boy, I'm hungry from that hunt!" Mother usually had a big dish of green beans, seasoned well and cooked good and tender, and some boiled or mashed potatoes. After filling my stomach, I'd say, "Well, since we have eaten our dinner and taken a good rest, we had better skin and dress those squirrels so Mother can put them in some saltwater and soak the blood out of them. We will have them for dinner tomorrow." Mother would cook them well done and tender in gravy or fry them after cooking some. They made delicious fresh meat. I could eat a whole squirrel. "Well, it's getting late in the autumn, and we had better get our beans picked off of that corn and get it ready to cut. There's going to be some frost soon."

The first time I went squirrel hunting or rabbit hunting, I started up the hill to a patch of timber where I had seen some squirrels. I wasn't more than two hundred yards from our house when two rabbits jumped up and started up the hill. I whistled like a hawk. One stopped. I shot it. The other one ran on a few yards before it stopped. I shot it too. Those were the first rabbits I ever killed. I called for my brother Cecil to come and get the rabbits. I wanted to go on to the hickory grove and see if I could get a squirrel. I went on up the hill and around the ridge through the cornfield to where I'd been observing them. I slipped into the forest and listened. I heard some nuts fall from a tall hickory tree. I kept going quietly until I was almost under the tree. Then I kept still for a few minutes. A squirrel saw me, and he started barking, "Squack! Squack! Squack!"

I got nervous. (I took the buckaroos, as we called it.) My knees trembled. It was a little exciting to shoot my first squirrel. I hesitated too much, and when I cut down on him, I missed because he was running. When the gun popped, it scared the squirrel, and it ran back up the tree. I walked around above the tree and got behind some brush. I kept quiet for about a half hour until the squirrel thought I had gone. It ran out a branch of the tree and started cutting more nuts. I could see flickers of it through the leaves. I shot at its shadow where the leaves moved. The squirrel jumped (or fell) from the tree. It was crippled so that it couldn't climb back up the tree. It started running down the hill. I thought I could catch it and save using another shell, as I didn't have money to buy more. I ran it down the hill, and it darted around some trees. I kept up with it and finally got a stick. I knocked it out and grabbed it. It wasn't dead. It bit right through my finger. I slung it loose, and it started running and tumbling down the steep hill over rocks and logs. I fell down and skinned patches of hide off my legs and arms, but I finally caught my squirrel. It wasn't able to bite me again. Before I got back up the hill to where I left my gun, another squirrel jumped out of a tree and ran away. I could have shot it too—if I had taken my gun with me. It was getting late. The sun had gone down, and I knew Mother would be worried if I didn't get home before dark.

It was almost dark before I finally found my gun and started home. When I got near, I heard Mother holler for me. I answered her and went on in with my game. "Well," Mother said, "you had a pretty good hunt—for a first timer." When I had been home for a few minutes, I became aware that my cousin Harley Belcher had come from King Shoals and brought Granddad's big double-barreled shotgun to hunt with me. but he had arrived too late to accompany me on my first hunt.

We went up to Aunt Liddy's, which was nearby, to see our cousins. They were all girls. Two were a little older than I was, and two were about my age. They were just like sisters to me. (I had only one sister at that time, and she was small.) We played games for a while, and then the girls and Uncle Filmore, Aunt Lidia, Dad, Mother, Guy, and Alvah got the old hymn songbooks and started singing some of those old hymns. Guy sang soprano. Mother and Aunt Ledia sang alto. The girls—Gertrude, Amy, and Zelma—sang alto and soprano. Alva and Dad sang tenor, and Harley sang bass. They didn't quit singing until eleven o'clock. They really could make music! I did love to hear those sweet melodies.

I could follow a tune somewhat, but I was bashful, and for some few years, I just didn't try to join the others in singing. When there was enough noise that I thought I couldn't be heard, I finally started picking up courage to try. I would get back in another room or in the back of the church and sing softly. When he discovered that I was singing, Dad said, "You have a good bass voice." He advised me to sing bass. I would take the courage to try for a while, and I finally learned that I could sing some. There were enough voices in our family for a choir. Alvah sang bass or tenor; Dad usually sang tenor; Guy, soprano; and Mother, alto. Ona was also beginning to sing at this time. She sang alto or soprano. Cornelius and Cecil could sing bass, tenor, or soprano. We would get our hymnbooks and sing and sing—sometimes until we got hoarse and had to quit. Ray wouldn't make much effort to sing, but he could have done well if had tried.

Harley and I got out early the next morning and started up Taterhole Mountain to hunt squirrels. We went far up the hill and around through a hickory grove. I had my ivory Johnson shotgun, single barrel. Harley had Granddad's big double-barreled shotgun. Granddad called it Ole Boker. We were both hardly young men, and there were lots of squirrels those days, but neither of us knew much about hunting. When we finally got to some of those big tall hickory trees, Harley spotted a squirrel. It ran around a tree, and he followed it to the other side. I stood still. The squirrel ran back around the tree to me. Each time Harley went after a squirrel, I shot it out of the tree. I killed four, and Harley killed one. Harley was discouraged by not getting as many squirrels as I did. After we got home, I told him why he wasn't getting the squirrels. Then I told him the next time he went hunting with anyone to let that person run the squirrel around the tree to him. We skinned our squirrels and ate supper.

After supper, we went to Uncle Filmore's with Dad and Mother. Several of us boys were there, and we had a great time. Uncle Filmore gathered up the songbooks, and he said, "Well, you youngsters have had a good time, and now we will all join together and sing." Someone picked up a book and started humming some of our choice tunes. We lined the chairs and selected places for the soprano, alto, tenor, and bass. We chose some favorite songs and started singing. (Those ladies could really sing too.) We sang for an hour or more and then rested for a few minutes while we ate some apples or sandwiches. Everyone gathered back into their seats and started up again. We sang until eleven o'clock before breaking up and going home.

The next morning, we went to Sunday school at the Baptist church below Wallback. Then we came home for dinner. In the afternoon, we went to the White Pilgrim Schoolhouse to singing and preaching. In the evening, there was singing on Summer's Fork of Sandy, or the Middle Fork, as we sometimes called it. (We lived within a mile of the two schoolhouses where the services were held and about a mile and a half of the Baptist church.) So everybody decided to go to the singing. There was always a big crowd, and we had lively and interesting services at these events. We really, really enjoyed the meetings.

We lived on Mike Underwood's farm for about six years. Before we left Wallback, we cleared mostly all the tillable land on his sixty acres. The spring of 1910, we tended about twenty acres of corn. Ray and I were the only ones there to plow, and Ray fell and broke his arm. That left all of those twenty acres for me to plow, but I was hardy and strong at fifteen years of age. (Alvah and Guy worked on lumber jobs during the winter until about March, April, or May. After we got the corn planted and it was ready to cultivate, they came home and helped us farm through the summer.)

On about April 1, I got ole Maude and my tools lined up and started plowing. I continued until May and planted some of the field to start it growing while I finished preparing the rest of the ground for the balance of the twenty acres. Cornelius could plant some while I furried the rows. Ole Maude went fast through those long rows, and Cornelius couldn't plant it as fast as I could furry it. I would prepare several rows and then stop to help him for a while. We had a hand planter that held about three pints of seed. We walked along the furrow with the planter, taking two short steps (or one long step) and then jabbing the planter into the ground, opening it while it was still in the ground. When we pulled the planter up, it left three or so kernels of corn, and the dirt would fall back and cover them.

Sometimes, the kernels didn't get covered up good with dirt (and some would jolt out of the planter box), leaving it exposed where the chipmunks or birds could get it. A crow could learn the planter track and follow the row and scratch the corn out and eat it before it sprouted out of the ground. If the fowl or the chipmunks took up very much of it, we would go over it again with our planter, and when we started to hoe the corn, we would have some seed in our pockets and replant it again as we hoed. The second time we weeded the corn, the new seedlings would be grown enough that we could hoe them at the same time that we tilled the larger plants.

Because of the roots, stumps, and rocks, the new ground was hard to plow through. We got Uncle Filmore to help us plow some of the field, and we paid him back by helping him hoe his corn. Our cousins, Uncle Filmore's girls, would get their hoes and hoe about as much corn as any of us. (In those days, the women also helped with the farmwork when there weren't enough men.) It was very ordinary to see women working on a farm. One of my neighbor's women was once mowing hay with a team of horses when they ran into a hornet's nest. The hornets stung the horses, and the horses ran away with her and crippled her for life.

I worked some for my uncle Joseph Boggs. He had only one boy, who was about my age, and they did quite a bit of farming. I hoed corn ten hours per day, and he paid me 50 cents per day. (In that time, people paid boys 50 cents and men 75 cents per day.) We were glad to get the work and make a little money. Sometimes people had more hay than they could gather and stack without help, and they usually paid a few cents more for making hay.

We finally got our big field of corn hoed out. We grew a lot of good corn on the twenty acres in 1910. I wasn't very large and didn't grow much until I was sixteen or seventeen years old. I weighed about one hundred twelve pounds at age fifteen, but I was strong and could do about as much hard work as the average man.

A new church sprung up here in about 1910—the Advent Church. Their theme included a short hell. Your soul would be cast away, and you just wouldn't be any more. There was a big stir about this doctrine of a short hell (or no hell at all) that said you just disappeared forever. You didn't often hear one of those preachers deliver a sermon when he didn't mention his short hell. Very few people believed in that doctrine, and a lot of people wouldn't attend their meetings at all.

There was an interesting morale about it. They were holding a revival in a schoolhouse here at Porter. Some people attended just to be amused. The preacher asked everybody who wanted to go to heaven to stand up. There was one man in attendance who was ignorant about salvation, and he didn't stand up. The preacher noticed him and walked back to the rear of the church. He said, "Sir, don't you want to go to heaven?"

"Huntuh, Huntuh, West Virginia is good enough for me." That's a true story! The mischievous people would encourage this fellow to make a political speech. They'd put him on a stump or box and get him started. He would get so involved in his subject that his speech went on and on. He could say some interesting things, but they would have trouble getting him to stop speaking. (It doesn't necessarily take all kinds of people to make a world, but we do have all kinds of people in this world.)

There were also places for the devil's works, as there is mostly anywhere. There was a place on Rush Fork on Otter Creek that was just about as bad as in some of the cities. Dad and Mother saw that none of us children got mixed with the gang that went there. They gathered there to have their round dances—bringing moonshine and having some tearing-down, rough times. They would dance and fight and drink. There was always a bully in each neighborhood, but people fought with their fists in those days, and you never heard of a murder.

Most of the men were very strong. People did hard labor and were tough and hardy. They worked either on the farm or on timber and lumber works, and that's all manual labor—chopping and sawing timber with a six- or seven-foot crosscut saw, rolling big sawlogs with a cane hook or spikes, and turning a team or two of horses. I have seen logs six feet in diameter and maybe twenty feet long. It would take several teams of horses or yoke of cattle to handle that kind of a log. People worked hard ten hours per day, and they didn't consider it as burdensome as we would today. There weren't any power saws to cut timber until about 1950, when there were a few here and there.

Some people there at Wallback farmed on a grand scale. Crough Tatman owned about three hundred acres. (His was the farm that my granddad Boggs owned before he and Dad moved to Looneyville.) He hired out quite a bit of work, such as making hay and cutting the brush, sprouts, and weeds that would have smothered out the grass. My brothers and I took a contract cleaning two years of growth off about fifty acres of pastureland on that farm. Some of the brush was higher than our heads; other parts of the field had very little filth. Alvah, Guy, Ray, Cornelius, and I worked on that project for about six weeks. We got $20 for the job. That was a lot of money when you worked for fifty cents or less per day.

After we finished the job one Saturday evening, we went to Mr. Tallman's farm where they were playing baseball. In front of some of those ballplayers, he pulled a twenty-dollar bill out his pocketbook and handed it to Ray as he commended us for the good job we had done. They looked at us like we were rich! Mr. Tallman usually kept about three hundred head of fine Hereford and polled Angus cattle. He pastured the cattle on the hill land and grew corn and hay on the bottomland. He rotated his hay and corn year by year. He would cut fifty or seventy-five haystacks, and he took the hay to his bottomland to feed his cattle during the winter months. They left waste and

manure where they were fed, and that kept his ground fertile. Mr.
Tallman could grow big corn on the fertile bottomland. He usually
grew corn on it for two years and then sowed it in timothy and clover
grass (for hay) for two years or more. People didn't use commercial
fertilizers in those days.

Mr. Tallman had a special big horse to ride over his farm. (He
weighed a little over three hundred pounds, and it took a very
strong animal to carry such a huge man.) In June, he built a six-
strand barbed-wire fence on his line next to Mike Underwood's
farm. He had left several small trees to tack his fence to, instead of
posts. He stretched his wire and drove his staples into one of the
trees. By evening, the leaves wilted, and the next day, the tree was
dying. There's a day or two in June, when, if you stick an ax in a big
tree, it will be dead the next day. Not many know when that day is
in June. Mr. Tallman lived in the house where my grandfather Boggs
lived before he moved his family to Looneyville. His was one of the
best farms in Sandy Creek Valley.

In 1911, the Baptist built a church on Ralph Tallman's farm. He
provided about an acre of land on top of a point by the Pleasant Hill
Cemetery. They built a nice country church, which is still being used.
Mr. Tallman oversaw the job, and he said, "I'm going to get some
sixty penny nails to put in the foundation. I haven't forgotten the
cyclone that went through here in 1899."

Everybody gathered in and helped with the project, and we all
chipped in to pay for the building material. The project was finished
it in about four months. They announced a time to dedicate the
building, and a large crowd of people came from far and near to
attend the service. There were many people in attendance that
hadn't met in several years. Granddad and Grandmother Boggs and
Granddad and Grandmother Estep were among those who hadn't
seen each other for several years. (They lived about fifteen miles
apart.) I believe Rev. Herbert Smith preached the dedication and
sermon. Everybody made great preparations for such gatherings in
those days, and we all had a joyful time meeting old friends. I had

gotten away from my grandparents and my aunt Florence. She was only four years older than I, and we used to play together a lot. I loved to be with her.

Granddad Estep was a good wood craftsman. He could make mostly anything for the farm and the home, such as chairs and other furniture, plow stalks, and tool handles. He was also a good blacksmith. He made tools such as hoes, shovels, sharp plows, and root cutters, and he could shoe horses and repair wagons. He worked until he was very old. He took glaucoma and was almost blind for several years before he died, at age 85. (Grandmother Estep died in 1918, during the World War I, while I was in France. She was about 68. Granddad and Grandmother Boggs also died at about 68.)

We finally got our big field of corn hoed out. I wasn't very large and didn't grow much until I was 16 or 17 years old. I weighed about 112 pounds at age 15, but I was strong and could do about as much hard work as the average man.

Ina Fay (born on May 11, 1909) and Victor Clyde (born on Sept 26, 1910) were born while we lived at Wallback. Ina drowned in Sandy Creek when she was about 18 months old and was buried in the Big Pigeon Cemetery by the side of our little brother Scott. That was a very sad time for our family.

2

My First Job

Uncle Filmore Belcher (Aunt Lidia's husband) moved to a log and stave job in Braxton County at Gross on Steer Creek, where he supervised a timber cutting crew and kept their crosscut saws sharp. He needed a water boy to carry drinking water for his crew, and he wrote a letter to Dad to see if one of us boys could come and work for him. I felt that it would be a good start for me. I was fifteen years old, and I had never worked in public works. Dad decided to let me go there.

The job site was about twenty-five miles from where we lived, and it was seven miles from our house to the railroad (at Ivydale). There, I could take a tram to Frametown, and from there, I would have to walk five miles to Uncle Filmore's place. I decided to walk all of the way. I went through the hills to Uncle Burn Boggs's place on Big Otter (at the post office). That was about halfway to Gross. I stayed there overnight, and the next morning, my cousin Andrew Boggs walked with me as far as Hallburg, where he got me lined out on the way to Gross. I walked to Serbia, a little village down on Steer Creek below Rosedale within six miles of Gross. There, I inquired about the best way to go through the forest to my destination. Someone directed me to the walking paths over the hills, and I finished the trip without much trouble. I arrived at Uncle Filmore's at about three o'clock on Sunday afternoon, and after a short discussion with them, I decided to board with Uncle Filmore.

I started my new job the next morning, Monday. When I first appeared on the job, Uncle Filmore had just filed a saw. He handed one end of the saw to me and said, "Let's try cutting one, Ira." We started sawing at the same time the other two men started cutting their block. Uncle Filmore and I finished first. Uncle Filmore looked at the other team and smiled. They were astonished that a boy as young as I was could work that fast, but I had used a crosscut saw ever since I was large enough to carry one. Ray and I could cut several big blocks of wood for fuel about as fast as any grown men could.

Uncle Filmore gave me a gallon jug and asked me to carry water to his men, and I soon got acquainted with the crew. They realized that I hadn't been away from home much, and they would kid me a lot, and I kidded them back. They told me big yarns (or embellished stories) while I listened attentively and pretended to believe them. I liked everybody on the job, and I enjoyed working with all of them. They would take care that I didn't get hurt, and they taught me how to avoid danger. I had to watch closely to keep blocks from rolling over me. They were four and a half to five foot long and eight inches or more in diameter. When I heard one coming down the hill at me, I would jump behind a big tree. Sometimes it would jump clear over my head as it passed me. A fast-rolling block could knock down a small tree or start a big stone to rolling. Cutting timber or being around where trees are falling is very dangerous, but I had cut timber before I went to Steer Creek, and the crew soon realized that I could take care of myself.

I worked ten hours per day at $1.15 per day. That was much more than the fifty cents per day I had been earning on the farm, but I had to pay for my board and room. I paid fifty cents per day at Uncle Filmore's. I worked six days per week, but most of the time, I paid board for seven days. When I didn't stay there for Sunday dinner, I would tell Aunt Lidia, and she wouldn't charge me for the meal. Uncle Filmore and family were very good to me. I had known them all of my life, and being with his family was almost like being at home.

The weather was hot and dry throughout the summer. At times, I had to go almost a mile to get a jug of water, and by the time I could get around to all of them, the crew would drink about all of the gallon. Sometimes, after I had gotten around to all of the men and given them a drink, I had some water left in my jug. I would set it in the shade behind a big tree (or a big stump), where it wouldn't get broken by a falling tree or a stave block, so that I could keep busy (by rolling stave blocks) until they needed more water.

Uncle Filmore gave me a pick and showed me how to stick it into a block to turn it around or to pull it from behind a tree, rock, or stump, or out of a sinkhole. The boss would fire anyone that didn't turn out a good day's work, and there weren't many workers who didn't mind losing their jobs. Uncle Filmore was a good man to work for, and he wouldn't discharge a man that would work hard and not raise trouble among the crew.

I soon started helping the men cut down big trees. We cut a few that were six feet across the stump. The job was more complicated than I would have imagined if I hadn't tried it. It required a lot of skill and good judgment. To start on a new tree, we cut a notch by first sawing a foot or eighteen inches into one side of the tree and then taking an ax and chipping it down to the stump. If the tree stood up straight, we didn't need to cut a big notch. If it leaned straight down the hill, we would aim it around the hill to keep it from falling too soon and splitting.

After cutting our notch, we'd start sawing on the opposite side of the tree, just an inch or two higher. We cut until it was nearly ready to fall or within one or two inches of the first notch. Sometimes we sawed on the lower side of the tree first. We would stop there while we cut the heart, or center of the tree. If the tree was very large, we would cut a break notch (just about the size of our ax) on the upper side about two inches above the main notch. We'd sink the ax as far as it would reach. That would hold the tree until we cut nearly through the heart. That way, the tree would break evenly. It wouldn't split and ruin a log. (If a man split many trees, he would lose his job or be transferred to an easier task such as rolling stave blocks or driving a mule or horse for pulling the blocks down the dreens.)

When the tree started breaking, we would jerk the saw through it as fast as we could. We tried to cut all the way through it. That would keep it from splitting or pulling splinters from the heart of the tree. When we heard the tree popping and saw it starting to fall, we would holler out big and loud, "Ti-m-b-e-r f-a-l-l-i-n-g!" (There could have been someone near enough to get hurt.) I can hear big Bill Loushe squalling out in his loud rough voice; if the tree didn't fall just right, he made a big fuss about it. Bill was about six feet two inches tall and weighed about two hundred twenty-five pounds, and he made a strong impression when he wasn't happy with a job. If a tree fell into or across a dreen (ravine or gulch), he often shouted out some cussing words about it—no matter what caused it to fall that way.

Sometimes a big tree would fall against another tree and break it down, and anyone as far as a hundred yards down the hill could be in danger. There was also a lot of danger for the men cutting the tree. We had to be careful to have a good footing and jump back quickly out of the way of the falling tree. We had to look up the tree as it fell because it might fall against another tree and bend it to the ground. As that tree flew back up, it would drag a limb or branch off the falling tree and flip the tree limb or bush toward us. I once saw Uncle Filmore come within an inch of getting killed. He was sitting above a tree when it fell. It broke off a seventy-five pound limb and threw it just a few inches over his head. He had on a broad-rimmed hat, and he just forgot to look up. It hit the ground behind him with a force that would have smashed him if it had hit him.

I went to Steer Creek in July and took my first leave in October. Prior to that, I had never been away from home more than four or five days. This time—after three months—I was pretty homesick. Uncle Filmore and family and I went to Frametown and caught a train to Ivydale. From there, we walked seven miles to Wallback. I sure was glad to be home again.

The next morning, I said to Uncle Filmore, "Get your old mountain rifle, and we will go hunting. I'll beat you at killing squirrels."

Uncle Filmore said, "I don't know if I have any bullets made for my mountain rifle. I have some lead and a ladle to melt it in. I'll hunt for it and get my bullet molds and make me some bullets and fill my powder horn with some of that smoky powder, and I'll kill more squirrels than you might think of." He molded some bullets and put some powder in his gun. Then he took his ramrod, tamped the powder in it, and put a bullet in. Then he got a firing cap and put it on his firing pin and said, "Let's go."

We went to a hickory and chestnut grove where there were usually lots of squirrels. It was a fine day to hunt. The leaves were damp enough that we could walk through the woods without making much noise by crunching them—as long as we were careful to not step on sticks and make them pop by breaking them.

If he could find one sitting still long enough for him to get a bead sight on it, Uncle Filmore could kill a squirrel a hundred yards away. He got one about every time that old mountain rifle cracked. With my shotgun, I couldn't kill a squirrel more than sixty or seventy yards away, but I could kill one that was moving pretty fast. I had about one hundred pellets or shot in a shell, and it would scatter about eighteen inches to two feet and kill a squirrel within that target area. If I didn't kill the squirrel with the first shot, I could soon get a shell in my gun and shoot again. Before Uncle Filmore shot another round, he would have to take the lid (or top) off of his powder horn, pour the powder in his gun, take out his ramrod, and tamp the powder. After putting a bullet in his gun and putting a cap on the firing pin, he had to put his ramrod back in its holder. Then he had to pull his hammer back and cock the gun before it was ready for firing.

We separated when we got to the forest. I went on up to the top of the hill to some big hickory trees, and Uncle Filmore went on around the hill to where there were some chestnut trees. Uncle Filmore said, "Now we will have to be careful and not shoot one another and be sure we see where we are shooting."

"Yes," I said, "I'll whistle if I come down the hill in front of you. A squirrel will think it's a bird." I went on up the hill, and in about fifteen minutes, I heard that old mountain rifle crack big and loud. I thought, *He's going to beat me even by just killing one one at a time as he doesn't often miss getting his squirrel.* I slipped on up the hill and heard some nuts falling out of a big, tall hickory tree. I looked right at the top of the tree and saw a squirrel sitting on a limb, gnawing on a hickory nut. I pulled my gun to my shoulder and pulled the hammer back. I aimed the gun and pulled the trigger. The gun went *bang*, and the squirrel dropped about halfway down the tree. It caught on a limb and ran toward the trunk of the tree. He was on the other side of the tree and out of sight before I could get another shell into my gun. I slipped on around above the tree and sat still for a few minutes.

I picked up a little stone and tossed it on the other side of the tree. The squirrel slipped around to where I could see it. I shot it again, and it fell about halfway down the tree and caught on a limb. I got another shell in my gun before it could hide behind the tree again. It moved slowly because it was hurt. I shot again, and it fell to the ground dead. I picked up my squirrel and put it in my hunting bag. (When I got home and skinned that squirrel, it must have had twenty-five shots just under the skin. That tree was so tall that the first two shots didn't hit it with much power.)

I went on around the ridge and shot another one on the ground. I heard Uncle Filmore shoot again, so I decided to join him. On my way, I saw another squirrel run out onto a limb of a big chestnut tree, and it was taking the nut out of a big burr when I shot it. I scared another squirrel around the tree. Uncle Filmore was also watching that tree, and his gun cracked when the squirrel ran around the tree from me. "Well," I said, "you have three, and I have three, and it's getting late. Maybe we had better go home."

"Yes," Uncle Filmore said, "you have three, but you shot five times, and I only shot three times to get my three."

I said, "You are the best shot, and you have the best gun."

We went out of the forest into a wheat field. I said, "This wheat is getting ripe. There ought to be some quail here." I put a birdshot shell in my gun so I would be ready for them. I hadn't gone more than a hundred yards when a bevy of about twenty quail flew up. I put my gun to my shoulder and pulled the trigger. They had just gotten into the air and were still close enough together that when I shot, four of them fell to the ground. Uncle Filmore didn't shoot. He had only one bullet in his rifle, and if he had shot one with it, the large bullet behind a powerful charge would have torn the bird in two. "Well," I said, "I've got you beat, after all. I have three squirrels and four quails. Even if I did shoot six times, I have one extra game. I have seven for six shots." But Uncle Filmore was almost a sure shot when he pulled that old mountain rifle to his shoulder. I had seen him shoot a squirrel at a hundred yards and hit it in the head.

We had left Steer Creek on Saturday, and we started back from Wallback the next Wednesday. To start our return trip, we had to walk about seven miles to Ivydale, where we could catch the morning train to Frametown. I said, "Maybe Cornelius can go with us to Ivydale so Aunt Lidia can ride ole Maude. Cornelius can then bring ole Maude back home." Cornelius caught ole Maude, put the sidesaddle on her, and led her up to the stepping block. Aunt Lidia stepped upon it and got into the saddle. She rode the horse to Ivydale and to where we caught the morning train at 10:30 a.m. We arrived at Frametown at noon, and from there, we walked across the hill to Steer Creek and then on to Gross, which was about four miles. We got there at about 2:00 p.m.

The next morning, we got up at about five o'clock and started for the forest to cut stave blocks. We went to work at 7:00 a.m. and rested for an hour at noon. Then we worked until six o'clock (ten hours per day). I carried water to the men in Uncle Filmore's crew. When I wasn't busy carrying water, I got a pickax and rolled stave blocks. I liked to start a big stave block over the hill and watch it roll. Sometimes the blocks would roll beside a tree and wedge between the tree and a steep hill; other times, it would wedge between two trees. Sometimes one would roll into a root hole behind an uprooted tree, and it took some lifting and pulling to get it out. When someone hollered, "Water boy!" I took my jug around and gave everybody a good drink of cool water.

At the end of my first summer at Steer Creek, Ray and Alvah came there to work during the winter. Ray worked in the forest, and Alvah worked on the railroad as a road repairman. In the winter, I didn't have to carry much water because there was plenty of water handy. I rolled stave blocks and sometimes helped another man on the saw to cut a few blocks from a log.

The next spring, I worked some on a stave mill. I washed blocks to get the mud off of them so it wouldn't dull the saw, and I would do mostly anything I noticed that needed to be done. I took the waste strips that were culled from the staves and loaded them on a wheelbarrow and wheeled them to the steam boiler for fuel. I learned how to sort staves and cut (or trim) their edges smooth and also how to catch staves as they fell from the saw. I was working at that task one day when the superintendent came by. He said, "That's right, Boggs. Learn all you can about this work. I'm leaving." (I guess that he thought I might learn enough to get his job someday.)

Once in a while, I landed a stave in the wrong place. This gave the fellow opposite me an excuse to give me a little trouble. He was afraid that I might take his job later on, so if I didn't land one just right, he would throw the stave back at me. I got hit once or twice, and I saw that he aimed to hit me. I didn't say a word. I picked up a strong strip of wood and hit the end of it on the ground to see if it was sound enough that it wouldn't break over his head too easily if I hit him with it, and I laid it within my reach. He saw that he had hurt me and that I was angry about it. So he took care not to hit me again.

Gross was a new village that had just sprung up in a year or so, and there wasn't much going on there for amusement. There was a church and a store across the hill at the post office (Belmont Post

Office). We would go there on Saturday evenings and to church on Sunday mornings. We organized a baseball team and played ball on Sunday evenings, and we had some interesting games.

Sometimes there were arguments and fights over calls of the rules. One time, a Fitswater boy about my size was playing opposite from me on the other team. He was a little high-strung and thought he was important. (His dad was boss at the stave mill where I worked.) He got smart with me and called me a bad name. Then he came at me to give me a whipping. He tackled me, but I got free. We hit a few licks, and he clinched me. I tripped him and was able to land on top. He started scratching me in the face. I got hold of his arms and held on to them, then I came down on his throat with my elbow. That choked him. He saw that I could handle him. (I had worked hard and was strong. He didn't work.) He said, "Let me up, or I will kill you." He was really angry. I didn't try to hurt him much, but when I did finally let him up, he grabbed a big rock and was going to hit me with it. An older man grabbed him, and that ended the fight. The next day at work, right in the presence of my boss (the boy's father), a man asked me what scratched my face.

I answered, "A wildcat." The boss knew about the fight, and he just chuckled a little about it.

We had parties where the boys and girls played games together, and we enjoyed ourselves quite a bit. One time, there was to be a party at the boardinghouse or hotel. My friend (Evert Vaughn), a man who boarded with me, said, "Let's go to the party." He knew what was going on, but I didn't. He didn't tell me that they were having a round dance. I went with him, but when I saw it was a dance, I didn't go in. I didn't want Mother or Aunt Lidia to know that I had been to a dance, but Uncle Filmore learned about it. I think he knew before I went to the event that it was going to include dancing, but he didn't tell me. Mother never did find out that I had gone to a dancing party.

A great uncle (Uncle Pate Boggs) whom I had never met had a farm on Sugar Creek (near Belmont). I stopped at his house for just a little while. He was getting old then. My great grandfather (James Anderson Boggs) once owned about three thousand acres of land near there. He was the original owner of all the land where the city of Gassaway now stands. Just after the Civil War, when the railroad was built up Elk River to Gassaway, he talked about going into the general merchandise business. There was quite a bit of timbering (and some mining) going on there, and Grandfather Boggs thought he could make a go of it. My great uncle Mart Boggs (brother to Henry Clay Boggs), told his father (James Anderson Boggs) that he would not advise anyone go into that business because he would be obliged to let some people buy on credit. (Uncle Mart had a college education, and he was one of the most intelligent businessmen in the county.) Grandfather did not follow Uncle Mart's advice. He ran the store for a few years, and as Uncle Mart predicted, he did finally go broke.

Because of his failure in that business, my great grandfather (James Anderson Boggs) didn't have the money to pay the taxes on all of his land, and he was going to lose it. His son, Uncle Mart, decided he could take over the land and pay the taxes by cutting the timber and selling it. So Uncle Mart went into the timber business and became wealthy through saving this land and the virgin timber. He later moved to Clay County, where he owned one of the best farms in the county and raised some of the finest Hereford cattle in the state. He made a lot of money and became one of the wealthiest men in Clay County. I understand that Uncle Mart was quite a sport at times. He was a pretty good poker player, and I hear that he liked his whiskey pretty well.

Uncle Mart had a son whom he was sending to college to be a doctor. (That son, Andrew Boggs, later opened an office on Summers Street in Charleston, and before that he had a hospital at Gassaway.) Uncle Mart wanted my dad (James Curtis Boggs) to go to college with Andrew. (Dad was about the same age as Andrew.) Uncle Mart told Dad that he would pay his expenses and help him through college if he would go. Dad wouldn't venture. (Dad said he didn't want to be a doctor as they become dope fiends, but I think that Granddad Boggs and all of Uncle Mart's other brothers had hard feelings toward Uncle Mart because of his taking over all of the land.) I think that his people envied him a lot and were just plain jealous of him. I met Uncle Mart only once. I was at his home on Otter Creek a few years before he died. Uncle Mart told me a lot about his business and just how he came to acquire all of the land. I feel that it is very likely that the rest of the family just didn't take any interest in helping him save it. Yet they resented Uncle Mart for getting it.

My great uncle Ike Boggs lived at Wallback where he had a big farm adjoining Granddad Boggs's place, and he kept it until he died. He raised cattle, and he hired several people to help him make hay. He was a good worker. I've heard my uncle Filmore talk about working for him. Uncle Ike would bring the crew in and have dinner with them and then get right up from the table and go back to work. Uncle Filmore said Uncle Ike would say, "I have rheumatism, and when I sit down, I get so stiff I can hardly move. I'm going back to work. You men have your rest." I got acquainted with another brother of Uncle Mart and Grandfather Boggs, Uncle Johnce Boggs. (I met him at his son's home at Dundon, just across the river from Clay town.) All of them were small men—about five feet six inches tall.

I worked at Gross until winter. A thirty-inch snow fell that winter, and everything shut down for two weeks. This was the coldest weather I ever experienced. The temperature dropped to thirty below zero, and it stayed below zero for over a week. The lumber company had built temporary buildings out of rough lumber and just put batting over the cracks between the boards. If you didn't cover the cracks with heavy paper, plenty of air got in. Uncle Filmore's house was lined inside, and we were in fairly good shape for that arctic winter. We cut plenty of wood and kept warm by keeping a big fire going in his big Burnside stove during that zero weather. I went to a neighbor's house to help him cut wood. He didn't have his house sealed, and they couldn't keep warm at all. You couldn't turn around by the stove fast enough to keep warm on both sides.

When the winter broke, the snow was so deep people couldn't work in the forest to furnish logs or stave blocks for the mill. The superintendent, Tile Dunckle, gathered up a crew and went to the millpond and cut ice blocks to put away for the summer. There was about a half an acre of water there, and it had frozen eighteen inches thick. We cut those ice blocks two feet long (twenty-four by eighteen by eighteen) and hauled them on a wagon to a big building. We used our crosscut saws to cut the ice. (We took one handle off each saw and used it as a one-man handsaw.) They laid about six inches of sawdust on the floor, and we put a layer of those ice blocks on it and poured sawdust over them. We stacked layers of ice blocks to the ceiling. We had ice tongs to handle the ice, and we used cane hooks that were made for rolling logs to scoot the blocks over a board onto the wagon. We had several tons of ice, and it lasted until midsummer. Without it, we would have done without any refrigeration for keeping our iceboxes cold. There wasn't another source of ice nearer than Charleston. They paid us our regular wages and sold enough ice that summer to cover their expenses in harvesting and storing it.

When the winter was so bad we couldn't get into the forest, we worked a bit at getting our staves ready for shipment. We piled four or five staves to the layer and crisscrossed them until the stacks were about six feet high. To load them for shipment, we lined up, facing each other, and passed five staves at a time to stack them on the railroad cars. We would load several cars, and then the train would hook onto them and haul them to Gassaway to the Coal & Coke Railroad. They had a railroad bridge at Gassaway, but they had to reload the staves because the train we loaded was on narrow gauged tracks, and the C&C (as it was called at that time) was a standard gauged road. That spring, I got a raise from $1.15 per day to $1.35.

One day, Big Bill Loush said to me, "Boggs, what makes you so late? Eating chestnuts?"

"Maybe so," I answered, "and I have a good place to board, and this hard work makes you have a good appetite." I was just a boy, and they all liked to joke with me. I didn't start to grow into a man until after I was sixteen years old. There were a lot of chestnuts that autumn, and I could handily pick them up as I was going through the forest carrying water. I did eat a lot of chestnuts. They were very good. Sometimes, I would find a grove of hazelnuts too and put some of them in my pockets. When I went home, I'd get a hammer and shell the nuts and eat some of those tasty kernels, and I would lay some of the nuts away to dry. They are fine and sweet when they dry out good. Aunt Lida and my cousins Gertrude, Zelma, and Amy would make candy with them or put them on a cake. They were good either way. (People worked hard in those days, but I believe they enjoyed themselves as well or better than we do today.)

We would roll those stave blocks into the dreen, and a man would haul them out with a mule or horse to the stave mill. A mule is tougher and quicker than a horse, and it can go in rougher and narrower places. They are cunning and intelligent, and they don't get hurt so easily. My uncle Elmer Estep had a mule that he used to pull a log truck along a tram road. Tram road tracks are mounted on crossties like they use for railroads—with wooden rails instead of steel railings. They would take two two-by-fours and put one on the other so as to hold the flange of the truck wheels up off the ground. They made the boards out of hardwood (usually beech or gumwood) that wasn't so good for lumber but would stand lots of wear. They would lay this kind of track up into those long rough hollows and haul trucks loaded with several tons of logs over them.

They'd pile the logs onto the truck and tie them with chains near each end of the truck bed, around and under the truck floor, and over the logs. Someone would take a strong, tough stick (usually of hickory or white oak) and twist the chain until it clamped the logs tight so they wouldn't shuffle about and fall off of the truck. A man would climb on top or on the end of the truck and take hold of the lever (or handle) on the brake. They would have a scotch (a wedge to block the wheels) under the wheels of the truck to keep the truck from rolling out of control. "Okay, I have the brake in control, you may kick those scotches from under the wheel, and I'll be on my way down this steep, rough hollow." In places, the road was elevated so steep that it took a strong man to hold the brake. Once in a while, they'd have a runaway turning over and throwing those logs and tearing the truck to pieces. A man could get killed in such a wreck. He was usually in a place where he could jump free from danger, but the truck would be going so fast that the man would be lucky if he didn't get a serious injury.

Uncle Elmer used his mule to pull the truck back up the track to the head of the hollow to get the logs. I've heard Uncle Elmer say he had seen his mule walk on a four-inch rail to stay out of a mudhole. Uncle Elmer thought so much of that mule that he had several fights over people abusing him. He would scold a man if he saw one handle it roughly, or even if he only heard him curse at it. Uncle Elmer was a small man (he was about five feet six inches and weighed only about one hundred twenty pounds), but he was very active. It would have taken a very strong and alert man to handle him.

To haul them down the hollow, we attached a short chain on each end of the stave blocks by driving a spike through a link of it into the center of the block. We linked the blocks together in tandem to form a string of as many blocks as the mule could pull. Then we hooked our singletree to the free end of the chain on the first block and started our mule down the hollow. Once we got those blocks moving, a mule could pull a long train of them. The mule soon learned how to maneuver his load, and he could do a better job handling it than a man knew about it. Where the decline of the path was very steep, the mule knew just how fast to go to keep those blocks from rolling on his heels. He kept the traces of his harness tight enough that the blocks wouldn't catch his heels. We hauled those blocks to a bolting yard where, after they split them in quarters (from three to ten inches wide—the right size for making staves) with a steel wedge or a wooden gluton (wedge), a tram or a wagon could get to them.

Those staves were used for making barrels to hold oil, wine, or whiskey. To have anything to do with the liquor business bothered some of us, but Uncle George said, "Well, they would be made by somebody if I don't make them. They need some of the barrels or kegs for oil, nails, spikes, and other things, and the Bible said to take a little wine for the stomach's sake." There wasn't anything else to do to support his family, so Uncle George decided that he had no excuse for not working at this trade. Everybody liked Uncle George. They commended him, and he would say things that, in his reasoning or without reasoning, were comical. He said, "A possum got his name, didn't he?" Uncle Robert Estep was a good neighbor, but he wasn't so religious as Uncle George or Granddad Estep. Uncle Bob would backslide sometimes, and the church would have quite a bit of trouble getting him back without churching him (taking his name off of the church register).

Through December (1911) and January (1912), I didn't get to work very steadily at Steer Creek because of the hard winter, and in those days, we got paid (to the half hour) for just what time we worked. In the spring, when the weather opened up so we could work, there was a lot to do. Sometimes, we would work ten hours and go home and have our supper, and then Tile Dunkle, the superintendent, would call us back. He would say, "I have a big order for several thousand staves, and my loading crew can't keep my cars going. My stave yard is filling up, and my crew is so busy I can't get those staves out. I would like for you to work two to four hours tonight." Working long hours made a little extra money for us, but we didn't get higher wages for overtime. We just got what hours we made, even when we did work twelve or fourteen hours per day.

I went back to Steer Creek in the following spring, and I had worked there for only about a month when my brother, Guy, who was working at Cresmont on a timber job, wrote me that he had a job for me at $1.50 per day. That was fifteen cents more than I was then getting, and it was considerably closer to home. I decided to go back to Wallback and try that job. So I bid everybody good-bye and went home the next weekend.

I went to Cresmont and started working in the forest—sawing logs, cutting roads for a team, bumping knots, and trimming the branches off logs. I wasn't a man yet, but I tackled the job and made a go of it. Our boss, Dan Shaw, was a strict man to work for. You had to do a good day's work to get by, and I wasn't an expert with an ax. I went to work with two other men in my crew. They'd sit down and have me go on the hill and look for trees suitable for logs. The timber was scattered there. On one occasion, when I came back to report that I had found a few little logs that were just large enough to pay to get out, I learned that Dan had fired those two men. He caught them sitting down on the job. Somehow he didn't fire me, even if I did barely earn my money. I suppose he thought, "He is just a boy, and he is at least trying to do something."

I had worked at the timber job for about a month when their lobby boy got dooless (lax) about his job. They fired him and gave me the job. I had to work pretty hard for the first week or so, but once I got the lobby clean, I didn't need to work so hard to keep it that way. I had to make about twenty beds during the week. On Sunday morning, mostly everybody had gone home, and I didn't have much to do. I had to be on the job for an hour or two Sunday without Sunday pay. I got everything in fairly good shape on Saturday so that I didn't need to do much on Sunday or Monday, when a lot of the men didn't go back to camp until after they finished their day's work.

The bunks (or beds) were on each side of the lobby, about two feet apart with about four feet of aisle between them. After making the beds, I would sweep around them and then sweep the lobby. It was about twenty by thirty, with a big Burnside stove in the center of it. I kept wood handy for the stove, and anyone could put wood in the stove to keep a good, hot fire. We had some benches made of rough lumber to sit on, and everybody seemed to fare fairly well. I mopped the aisles and the lobby three or four times per week, and I cleaned what few windows we had about once a month.

I also had to cut wood to fuel the cookstove. The company furnished me a light truck, which I used on a tram road. I would push it up the hollow, cut a load of wood, and push it back to the boardinghouse. I had to carry the wood to where it would be handy for the cooks. I got on the good side of the ladies running the boardinghouse. I saw that they got wood that would heat up that big cooking stove, and they prepared some delicious meals. One said to me, "You cut good wood, much better than the other boy."

I answered, "Yes, there was a big family of boys at our home, and my mother insisted that we cut wood that would burn well." The ladies often called me in and gave me a big piece of pie or cake or a good sandwich.

We often sat around that big wood-fueled stove until bedtime playing dominos, checkers, and cards while telling stories and jokes. There was usually some comical friend in the gang that everybody would pick at, and we played jokes and tricks on each other. We had a lively time and a lot of fun, and we really enjoyed ourselves. The older ones usually went to bed by nine o'clock, and about everyone was in bed by ten or ten thirty.

Dan Shaw was a roughneck and a very wicked man. (I don't know what became of him. Most people there liked him as a boss. When he was in good humor, he could be as jolly as anyone.) He would get so angry when something didn't suit him that he would take what I called a mad fit. He could curse the wickedest oaths; you would shudder to hear him. He would call on the Almighty and wish He would strike something with lightning and tear it to pieces. He took one of those mad fits one day when there was an electric storm on, and he was in the forest near a creek. He wished God Almighty would strike something. He had hardly got the oath out of his wicked mouth and mind when lightning hit a big beech tree near enough to shock him. Lightning doesn't often strike beech timber. Neither does it often strike on a creek. On the hills of West

Virginia, lightning usually hits black oak, hickory, locust, or white oak. It seldom hits softwood such as poplar, pine, lin, or cucumber trees, and it seldom hit chestnut trees (before they died out).

Guy, my brother, worked in the woods, driving grabs into the logs so that the teamster could hook his team to the grab links and pull the logs to where they could load them onto the train with a steam-powered crane. The operator of the crane was very accurate with his tongs. He could throw them for several feet and hit so close to the middle of the log that it would balance when he picked it up. He would lift the load and swing the crane around in a position to lay the log onto a freight car. He could soon load several cars. They hauled the logs to the mill, where they dumped them into a pond of water to wash the grit and dirt off of them. Before sawing the logs, someone would take a hot water pipe and hose with a strong steam pressure and wash off all of the remaining dirt. That saved the teeth on the band-saw blade. (In those days, we would do well to cut twenty thousand board feet of lumber in ten hours. Now they can cut forty thousand board feet in eight hours.)

We were logging and cutting lumber about fifteen miles up Buffalo Creek at that time. The railroad came to Dundon at Elk River. The Buffalo Creek and Gauley RR connected to the Coal & Coke Railway. It hauled the lumber to Charleston and other cities, where they dressed it and finished it for building purposes. At that time, they didn't have a passenger train, so when we came to the C&C road, we would ride the lumber train. On evenings when there wasn't a train going out, we could get on our lever car after we finished our day's work. We could get about eight men on it and ride it to Dundon, pumping a lever by hand.

There was a gear in the middle of this flatcar, and the lever bar ran up about four feet. There was a crossbar on the end of the rod, and handlebars ran each way from it to each end of the car. Four men, two on each end of the car, facing each other, would pump this handle, and we could make about twenty miles per hour. So if we had no other way, we could go to Dundon on the lever car and get back to camp at Cresmont before midnight. We also used the handcars to go from the camp to the woods for the log job. (When we got too far away from the boardinghouse, they would move and build another camp.)

Guy had an accident, and I left when he did. The lever car that they ran to work and back wrecked and broke his leg. There were about eight men on it. All of them were hurt to some extent, but Guy was hurt the worst. They left Guy at the camp for about a week, and the doctor visited him there. (The company retained a doctor, and we paid a monthly doctor's fee.) The company left a man with Guy to take care of him. One morning Guy was suffering so badly that his caretaker knew something was pretty seriously wrong, so he called the doctor. The doctor came and examined Guy. Gangrene had set in. We had to get him to the hospital at Charleston at once.

They unhooked the tram from the cars, and we started to Dundon to catch the C&C train to Charleston. We were about twenty minutes late for the train, but they got word to the station operator, and he held up the train until we got there. Dad met the train at Porters Station and went with Guy. I got off there and went home with Mother. They got Guy to the hospital just in time to save his life. If that train had not waited for Guy, he would have died. The hospital doctor said that if he had been an hour later, they couldn't have saved him. They didn't have the techniques or the medicine to take care of people as they do now.

Guy was in the hospital for several weeks, and he had to visit the hospital for some time after he was released to go home. His leg was left in a bad shape. It was broken about halfway between his knee and ankle. One of his leg bones splintered so badly that pieces came out for two or three years. That leg is shorter than the other, and he has to wear a special heel on his shoe about three inches higher than the natural heel. In those days, people didn't carry hospital insurance, neither did the corporation carry insurance for you. The company did pay his hospital bill, but they didn't pay his wages for the time he lost from work. Guy said that lawyers came to the hospital and begged him to sue the company, but in those days, people didn't often bring suits against their neighbor.

In the spring of 1912, we moved from Wallback to Porter Creek. Aunt Julia and Uncle Charley Foreman lived here, and one of Uncle Charley's brothers-in-law, Enos Matheny, had a sixty-acre farm that he wanted to sell. Dad looked at it and decided to buy it. Dad went to Looneyville to see Granddad Boggs to get the down payment for the farm. He got $250. Granddad (Henry Clay) said to Dad, "Now you keep this a secret, and I won't ask you to pay it back." Granddad gave him the money, and Dad agreed to pay $750 for the farm. Ray was working on a planing mill at Elkhurst, and I got a timber job near there working for William Evans and Elby Hinkle. Mother later told me that Ray and I paid for the farm and home. We provided $25 per month until it was paid for. This was the first home that Dad ever owned. Dad and Mother had a family of fourteen, and Dad couldn't pay for a home while managing to take care of such a big family. He wasn't strong and couldn't venture to buy himself a home.

The farm had a four-room house on it. It was built of rough lumber (unpainted), double-walled, with matched flooring. The walls weren't sealed, so we bought wallpaper and papered it. It looked pretty good. It had a double chimney, with one fireplace in the sitting room and one bedroom behind the fireplace. It had a large dining room and about a ten-by-ten-foot kitchen. We built two more bedrooms and a cellar with a large bedroom over it. It was a good stone cellar. There was a good spring of water near the house, and for a year or two, we got our water from it. We later dug a good water well.

Evans and Hinkle had a contract for logging the steep river hill just a mile or two above Elkhurst. Mr. Evans said, "That boy can sure handle a crosscut saw—for a boy." I was seventeen years old but hadn't gotten my growth. I really was just a boy. (I wasn't completely grown until I was about nineteen.) That job didn't last long. We commenced cutting timber out of a little dreen, where we could cut the timber and bruit it into a dreen to where the teams could get to it. (Bruiting is a logger man's name for handling logs by personal skill and strength.) Much of the hill was so steep and rough that a team of horses couldn't get over it. We cleared room to make a road for the team to brute the logs. There was a short flat area about halfway up the hill where we could let the logs pile up until we were ready to get them the rest of the way off the mountain.

We would cut timber for a day or two, and then we would take time to trim the branches and knots off of the logs. It took some skill and strength to handle some of those big red oak logs. Using cane hooks and spikes, we would start them scooting down the mountain. Sometimes one would jam into or under a boulder so deep in the ground that we had to cut it off before we could get it started again. Sometimes one would run into a tree and glance around the hill or hit another tree and stop. It would lay there until we could get it moving again. We would have to keep working at it until we could skid it out. Sometimes we had to cut a tree or stump to the ground before we could get the log started down the hill again. It was a brutish job. People did hard work those days, but we didn't get impatient about it—just kept at it.

We had to be careful not to skid the logs into the railroad, but sometimes one would get away from us, not going the way we wanted it to go. Once we cut a big red oak tree near the top of the hill. The hill was so steep that the tree jumped from the stump and landed about twenty feet down the hill. It fell against the opposite steep bank and rolled into the dreen. The dreen had a solid smooth rock bed in it. The tree skidded over those rocks so fast that they stripped limbs off it from bottom to top. It rolled clear to the foot of the hill and to the railroad before it stopped. We thought we were in serious trouble. We got off that hill almost as fast as that log did. By chance, the railroad bed had been built up about four or five feet at that spot, and the log jammed into the bank under the railroad. It didn't do any damage to the track. We didn't need to strip that tree!

All the bark was stripped off going down that hill, limbs and all. We cut the tree into logs, and while the trains weren't running, we hauled them along a path by the railroad track to the sawmill.

Spring soon came (1912), and the sap came up in the timber. A blacksmith made some sharp spudding tools for us, and we used the opportunity (while the sap softened the layers) to bark our logs. We would take an ax and split the bark on top of the log. The spudding tool had about a five-foot handle on it. One man would get on each side of the log. They would start prying the bark apart from the top of the log and continue to the end. During the summer, when the sap was up, skilled spudders could slip all the bark off of a log within a few minutes.

The weather was getting hot, and the river was warm enough to go swimming. We went down the river a mile or so along the railroad. There weren't any dwellings nearby, and there wasn't often anyone walking along the track. One fellow stripped off his clothes and jumped in. The water was eight or ten feet deep. He went to the bottom and came up and couldn't swim (or he didn't get his balance to swim). He was going down the third time when another fellow, who had already stripped off his clothes, jumped in and got his arm around the sinking man and got him out before he went down again. That fellow seemed to know how to handle a drowning person. He took the victim by the hair and kept him in front until he got him to the bank. The riverbank was very steep at that spot, so all of us helped to pull them out of the river.

I stayed on that job only about two months. Something went wrong, and they shut down. There was some fine timber on that rough hillside, but it was very difficult to get it off. I don't know if the job started up again or not. Working against that steep hill was so rough and dangerous and such hard work that I didn't intend to stay there long in the first place. At the best, I couldn't see much future in the lumber works. I don't see how anyone could make any money at such a difficult job.

I went home and stayed for a few days before going somewhere to hunt for another job. I went to see Mr. Evans here at Bomont and got my pay for what he owed me. I learned that the United Fuel Gas Company was preparing to drill some wells on Little Blue Creek, so I decided to see about a job there. I went over to King Shoals to Uncle George Estep's, about three miles from where the gas company was working. I left Uncle George's place early the next morning. Along the way, I met Ed Westfall, and I walked the rest of the way with him. He already had a job with United Fuel. Ed said, "Now, Ira, when we get there, you just pick up a mattock and a shovel and start working." (Ed wanted a buddy to work with him.)

We arrived at the job site just before work time. There was a pile of tools laying there. I picked up the tools and started working, and I worked like fire until about noon. The timekeeper came along and asked me my name. He wrote it on his book and went on. (I thought he would ask who hired me, but I suppose he thought the boss had told me to go to work.) I finished my day's work, and Ed and I started for King Shoals. (Ed lived about one mile up the creek from Uncle George on top of the hill.) I decided to board at Uncle George's. He said he could keep me, and I imagine he was glad to have me board with him. He was out of a job and wasn't really able to work. He had two boys and a girl and was trying to send them to school while he was short of money. I was glad to stay there because it was about five miles from our home at Porter. I could have made it on foot to my job from home, even if we did work ten hours per day, but that wasn't necessary.

Aunt Arebell called me the next morning. She said, "Breakfast is ready, and Ed will be along in a few minutes." I ate my breakfast while Aunt Arebell fixed me a pail of good food to take with me. Boy, could she cook! I would be mighty hungry by noon after getting up at five o'clock in the morning and walking three miles and then putting in a half day's work, and that good food really hit the spot. Ed came along, and we started before daybreak. I soon learned why Ed wanted company. There were wildcats in the three-mile stretch of woodland that we walked through, and some black bears had been seen in that section of King Shoals. We went down King Shoals about a mile, and then up Adkins Fork of King Shoals, and then over the hill onto Little Blue Creek, and followed that stream almost to Big Sandy River. That was a rough thick forestland with big rock cliffs, rhododendron thickets, and plenty of good places for wildcats and bear dens. I didn't blame Ed for wanting a friend along. I wasn't very brave either! While I didn't sanction them, by any means, I wasn't much scared of wildcats, but those bears terrified me. They didn't often bother anybody, but they would tackle a man if they had a cub or if they were real hungry. They are ferocious if you hem them in for a fight. We didn't have any gun with us, and we didn't want any fight with a bear.

We got to our job a few minutes before work time, so we sat down to rest for a few minutes. The boss hollered, "It's seven o'clock. Work time, boys." We went to the toolbox, where the boss handed out axes, crosscut saws, mattocks, shovels, and cane hooks. I got in line and took a crosscut saw. I liked to saw logs. We started cutting a new right-of-way for a road up a steep hill to a gas well location. We finished cutting the roadway and started to clear about one half acre for a well site. We cut the brush and built a fire in some dry chestnut poles. We piled the brush on the fire and let it burn while we cut the timber. We trashed some trees that would have made good lumber, but when we couldn't get the logs out of the way pretty handily, we burned the good timber along with the bad. It would have presented a danger from fire that might burn down a derrick.

My crew got the brush and trees out of the way and burned it while another crew started digging the road up that steep hill with their mattocks and shovels. It was pretty slow work, but altogether, there were about thirty-five men on that job. Normally after our crew cleared the brush, the other crew could dig a lot of road in ten hours, but they ran onto some big rocks, so I dropped back and joined the shooting crew. We got some four-foot drills and an eight-pound hammer and started drilling holes in those solid, hard rocks.

There were three of us on each drill team. Two men would take a hammer, and one would turn the drill. We had to be careful not to hit the man turning the drill, especially until we got used to our hammer and learned to handle it carefully. The man who turned that drill had to hold it straight and not let it wobble, or the hammer might miss the drill and hit his hand or arm. We didn't need to grip the drill very tight. I never knew of anyone that got a broken arm or hand, but I did know of a man almost losing an eye from a particle of steel flying from the head of the drill. (There's danger in mostly anything you do. I have seen people that were so careless or awkward that they couldn't risk working on a job like that one.)

We hammered away with the four-foot drill until we sunk it into the stone so far that we no longer had a handle on it. To drill deeper, we had to get an eight-foot drill. One man would hit the drill, and the turner would rotate it real quick while the other man was drawing for his lick. After fifteen minutes or so, the turner would holler, "Mud!" The hammer men would stop striking while the drill turner got a stick with a cloth on the end of it and swabbed the hole clean of the stone cuttings. Then he poured water in the hole and wrapped a cloth around the drill (at the base of the hole) to keep the water from splashing in our faces. When we started hammering again to test the nerves of the drill turner, we would sing a short song—"this old hammer killed my buddy, but it won't kill me"—while we drilled away. Sometimes, according to the hardness of the stone, it would take three or four hours to drill one hole. After we finished a hole, we would pour some coarse-grained black powder into it. Sometimes we used from a pint to a half gallon, according to the depth of a hole. We would put split each end of the fuse (so it would ignite easily) before we put it into the hole with the powder.

The crews drilled several holes in a half day, and when the people stopped working in the area to eat or go home, we would holler out big and loud, "Fire in a hole!" Everybody would take cover. They all knew what that meant. We sometimes had twenty or more charges ready to fire. Two men would start firing around the middle of the string of holes, and one would go each way with a torch or matches. They'd light the fuses and run for cover. I can hear those blasts, *Bang! Bang! Bang!* When the elements are just right, people could hear the explosions for twenty miles or more. Sometimes we would get under a rock cliff, and sometimes we got behind a big tree. Occasionally, we stayed right out in the open and dodged those stones as they shattered all around us, but I have known of people getting hit by those flying stones. We had to be very alert!

One evening, I lit one end of a fuse right at quitting time. I was already on my way home when the rocks stopped falling, so I hurried out of their range and continued on my way. The first thing we did when we went back the next morning was to look over our blasting area. One charge had failed to go off. I suppose we didn't get the hole dried out properly and some water had leaked into it. We cleaned out the hole, dried it thoroughly, and lined it with paper, then we loaded it again and blew it into smidgens.

In a few days, we got some dynamite. A stick of dynamite is more powerful than a load of powder, but it is more dangerous to handle. (The force of dynamite goes downward when it explodes, and a powder charge goes upward when it goes off.) There were two ways to shoot dynamite. One way is in a hole, and the other way is without a hole.

Shooting with a hole goes like this: After you got your hole ready (before you put your dynamite in it), you would first put a fuse and a blasting cap on a stick of dynamite, or you could put the cap on one end of the fuse. A blasting cap is a little bigger than a .22 rifle cartridge, and you would slip it over the end of the fuse and put that in a stick of dynamite (or a piece of a stick). You put the stick and fuse in the middle of your load. (You may use more than one stick of dynamite in one hole, but you need only one cap and fuse to ignite the whole load.) After loading the hole, you light the fuse as you would a powder shot. The cap makes a forty-pound jar when it goes off. That fires the dynamite. Another way to shoot dynamite is to run a wire in your cap. You do it carefully. Don't scratch it. It might go off, and that little cap can blow your hand off or kill you. You put the cap in the hole with the dynamite (as you did your loaded blasting holes) and attach two wires. You attach the end of one wire to a battery (or two flashlight batteries) and get ready. To set off the charge, you just touch the other pole of the battery to the other wire, and the load will explode. You can rig a battery to explode several loads at the same time in one shot.

Shooting without a hole: The second way to use dynamite is called an adobe shot or shooting without a hole. (You use it to break a rock that's too large to move otherwise.) You mix some mud with water and make it thick enough that it won't run. You lay your dynamite on top of the rock and plaster it with the mud, then lay a heavy flat rock or two on it. You can fire it with a cap and fuse (or wire and battery) just as you would any other load. Four or five sticks of dynamite (with an adobe shot) will blow a very large rock into many pieces. The downward explosion of the dynamite tears up the rock underneath it.

One day, I said, "Ed, it doesn't look very favorable for work today, but maybe we might as well start. If it starts raining, we can come back. Those clouds look pretty heavy, but I don't hear any thunder or see any lightning flashing. I hate to see that hole in my time sheet. I would like to get a straight month. This job won't last long. At the best, I judge about two or three months." It rained some, but we finished our day. We drilled several holes that day, and that completed the shooting on that road.

Each day, we got out of bed at five o'clock and left home base at about 5:30 a.m. We reported for work at 7:00 a.m., worked five hours, and then ate our dinner (lunch). That good solid grub—potatoes, beans, meat, fruit, and usually a piece of cream or fruit pie or a piece of cake—was really satisfying. This was hard work. We got hungry enough to eat a full meal. (I paid 50 cents per day for that good food. They grew almost all of their food on the farm, so they didn't buy much—just sugar, salt, and a few food that didn't cost much.) We rested an hour at noon and went back to work at one o'clock. We continued working until 6:00 p.m. We worked pretty hard, but the company paid us $2 per day, and that was the best wages in the area, except for digging coal, but I would never work in the coal mines.

"Well, Ed, we'll pry out a few of those big rocks. Maybe we won't have to shoot them. That shot yesterday tore that stone apart in good shape for us to handle. There's no rush for this job, so I don't suppose they will ask us to work Sunday. I'll welcome a day of rest. We work ten hours a day and six days per week, and it is a pleasure to see a day of rest come around."

Sunday morning, I got up at about eight o'clock. I ate my breakfast and sat around a few minutes. My cousins Charles and Bessie and I got out and passed a baseball back and forth. We batted it some and entertained ourselves. We had a jolly good time that day.

My granddad and grandmother and my cousin Harley Belcher lived just a few hundred yards above Uncle George. (Granddad and Grandmother raised Harley. Aunt Nana died when he was born.) Also, Aunt Florence was still living at home, and I got to see her. We hadn't met often during the seven years since my family had left King Shoals Creek, so we had a nice visit when we did get together. She was about four years older than me, but she didn't get married until she was about twenty-five.

Uncle Robert Estep lived a few hundred yards farther up the creek, and while I was in the neighborhood, I went to see him and Aunt Allie (and my cousins Harry, Oral, Carl, Forest, and Opal). Harley went with me, and Charles and Bessie came up later. Harley was about my age, and my other cousins were five or more years younger than I. We had a good time playing ball. Aunt Florence played too, so we all passed the day happily—together once more.

I went back down to their house and had supper with Aunt Florence, Harley, Granddad, and Grandmother. Granddad got his Bible and read some. Then we talked about the Civil War. He knew that I liked to hear him talk about that. He was only sixteen or seventeen when the South came and got him. He told me about some of his exciting adventures and about the Battle of Fredericksburg. He wasn't in the army much longer than three years before it was over (when they surrendered to General Grant). Granddad said he was scheduled to go to a prison camp after the surrender, but he didn't have to go. He had a brother-in-law on the Union side who was a colonel. The officer heard about Granddad's retention and influenced his command to release Granddad. Being the only boy in his family, Granddad was needed at home, and he may have starved if he had to go to prison for any length of time. Everybody was short of food. I said, "Granddad, you sure were lucky to have such a high-ranking soldier to help you, to keep you from suffering like some of those other prisoners did." Yet I don't think any of them stayed in prison very long after the war ended. All the able men needed to get to work and rebuild, to farm and grow some food to get ready for winter.

Ed and I went back to work on Monday morning and finished the road to that drilling site. We were told that we would be moving on down Blue Creek, about a mile further away from Uncle George's place. I went back and told Aunt Arebell that we were moving further away and that it would be too far to walk. I would have to hunt for a place closer to my job. I thanked her for helping me and paid her what I still owed for my board and room.

Some of the men on the new location were boarding with a family by the name of Adkins near where we were working, and they told me they thought I could stay there. When I stopped and inquired about board and room, they first said that they had about all they could take care of. Then Mr. Adkins asked me my name, and I told him. He asked, "Are you Curt Boggs's son?"

I said, "Yes."

"Well, I know your dad." He said, "We're not very well fixed to keep you, but if you can put up with our service, we'll do the best we can for you."

I said, "I'm not very hard to please, and no doubt we'll get along fine." They showed me my room, and I washed and got ready for supper. They soon called us all to the table. There were six of us boarding there. They served a very good meal, but the food wasn't fixed as well as that which Aunt Arebell cooked.

We started cutting a right-of-way for a road to the next well site, which was near the top of a hill. We had about a half mile of right-of-way to cut and a lot of digging to do. We expected that it would take about a month to dig the road and get the location ready for a rig. As we began digging, we soon ran onto some huge rocks. Me and the buddies I had been with on other sites got our drills and hammers and went to work. We drilled one or two holes ten feet deep. That stone was so hard that it took us half of a day to drill one hole.

"Well," I asked, "did you ever notice some of those big rock cliffs where they drilled for the C&O Railway up Elk River? Some of those holes were twenty feet deep. You can still see the imprint of one side of the drill where they made those cuts in the rocks along the railroad. They did that with handheld drills, just like we are doing it. I know some of the men who helped build that road. When we moved to Kanawha County in 1903, it was complete only as far as Ivydale. They extended it on to Gassaway during the next year or so."

The job at Blue Creek was finished in about two months. Then I went home, and Ray got me a job at Elkhurst, where he was working. That paid $1.75 per day for ten hours. I worked there at the planing mill for a few months. I began the job by loading lumber on a truck for kiln drying. It was not the kind of hard work that I was used to. It was inside work, and it was straight time. We started with green lumber freshly sawed from the logs. We unloaded it from a railroad car and moved it to smaller cars, which we pushed into a kiln dryer. There were two tracks in the building, and steam lines ran on each side and under the cars. That kept the temperature at about 130 degrees. We would push one carload in and another out as they dried. We kept the lumber in the oven dryer for about five days, and then it was ready to be planed.

We lifted it up out of a pit and loaded it onto trucks that were on the floor where they had their planing machines. Erve Simons and I worked together for quite a while. We would take turnabout, handing it up out of the pit. The lumber was so hot for some time after it was out of the drying bin that we couldn't handle it. Each evening, we would shove some trucks out and let them set overnight to cool. We needed help for pushing those trucks to where we could unload them, and the men working on the plaining floor were supposed to help. They didn't like to quit their work to push those trucks, and we had so much trouble that we had to go hunt for the boss to get help.

One day, we called on help, and those men just got so stubborn or independent about helping us that they wouldn't come. I said, "Erve, I'm tired of having to hunt for the boss every time we need help. Let's just sit down until the boss gets here." We sat there for about an hour. I said, "Erve, I see the boss coming. Just pretend you don't see him."

The boss said, "What's the matter, boys? We've got to have that lumber up here or shut the mill down." Erve and I told him that we couldn't get any help and that we were tired of having to hunt for the boss every time we needed help. He said to the foreman, "You get down there when they need you and help move that truck." We worked for about a week without having any more trouble about help. Then one morning, they wouldn't help us when we called. I became a bit angry.

I said, "If we can't get you to help us, I know who can."

I found the boss before they had to shut the planers down. The boss was angry. He said, "If you men can't cooperate here with this job, I'll have to get men who can." We never had any more trouble getting help to move those trucks.

Later, Erve said, "I had to laugh at how you spoke to those contrary men."

After I had worked at the kiln dryers for about three months, the boss needed a man to help in the storing rooms where they held the lumber for shipping. He said, "Boggs, you come with me. I have a better job for you. You help Ray with this dressed lumber. He will show you what to do." I helped push the trucks of lumber away from the machines after it was dressed and shaped into flooring, siding, and other building material. We loaded it off of the truck into the storing bins. Later, we loaded it onto trucks for shipping. From the trucks, we would load it onto railroad cars to ship to Charleston. From there, it was sometimes shipped to cities in Ohio, New York, Pennsylvania, and other states. We had a big planing mill. It could handle several thousand feet of lumber per day. They made everything for dwellings and other buildings. They made all sizes and kinds of moldings for houses, picture frames, and just about everything that's made of lumber, some furniture too. They also had a demolition mill that made handles for tools. That mill operated until about 1920, when for some reason, it was shut down.

Our work (at Elkhurst) got slack, and they laid off a lot of men, including me. I came home and stayed a few days, then I decided to go back to the gas fields. A big oil boom was going on at Big Blue Creek. (That became one of the most valuable fields in this country.) It started near the mouth of Blue Creek. They drilled wells that made some of those poor farmers millionaires overnight. The farmers got one-eighth of the oil without touching the work. Their land was leased under those terms. I went to work at Coca, about eight miles up Blue Creek. Alvah and I worked for the Sun Oil Company. We cut right-of-ways and made roads (as I had done before). James Ross was our boss, and we boarded with the Millard Ross family. (We knew them from Wallback, where we had formerly lived.) Millard had three girls and two boys at home. The two boys worked with Alvah and me. We had a good time with our old friends from Wallback. Coca was a lively place. That was a wealthy oil field, and there was always a lot of money in circulation. We could go to parties or somewhere interesting almost every night.

At that time, open saloons were legal in West Virginia, but there weren't any bars in our area that served hard liquor. However, there was plenty of bootleg whiskey. I had never drunk any intoxicating drinks, but some of the boys got some cider, and we all had a drink of it. I didn't know it had fermented enough to intoxicate anyone, but some of the boys got pretty intoxicated. I got enough to feel it, and

I quit at that stage. We also got us a deck of cards. This was my first game of cards. We didn't gamble for money; we picked up beechnuts and used them for money. The next day, we didn't feel much like working, and we didn't get much accomplished. We were too busy otherwise! Somehow, Dad found out that we had been playing cards, and he called our attention to it when we went home. He said that he was worried that we would be arrested. In those days, the law was pretty strict on gambling. We always stayed hidden in the brush to play any kind of card game.

We did some work on a site up Laurel Creek, where they were drilling some very productive oil wells. They produced a very fine grade of oil—about the most valuable oil found anywhere. A poor and ignorant family lived there in a shack that looked like it would fall apart anytime, but they did own their land. The oil company drilled some good-producing wells on it. I later heard that some slick, shyster of a lawyer wrote up a contract that was supposed to be for a lease on part of their land, but somehow, he tricked them into signing over all of the land. That kind of thing happened to a lot of poor, ignorant people.

One Sunday, we took a notion to go to a revival meeting at Odessa, which is over the hill about six or seven miles. Some of the boys had some whiskey, and they were already a little lit up. They sat at the back of the church, where some of them got to talking and making a little extra noise. Lee Young came back and said, "I think I heard some of you boys using some profane language." (Lee Young is Carl, Clarence, and John Young's father.) We all went outside. Some of the boys who were drinking wanted to go back inside to drag Lee Young out and give him a whipping. The ones who weren't drunk encouraged them to leave and get on their way back to Coca.

We labored on the Laurel Creek site until we got that road finished across the hill to Hackberry Creek, where a flowing well came in with such a gusher that it spurted oil for a hundred yards. It created a mist of oil and gas that was dangerous to be near. One of the major stockholders was present when the well came in so strong. He was so excited that he pulled a big cigar out of his pocket to celebrate. He was reaching for a match when one of the well workers noticed him just in time to knock the match out of the man's hand (without taking time to call his attention to it). If he had struck that match, it would have set a fire one hundred yards in diameter. It would have burned us all to death. That well was gushing oil with so much force that it caused the flow lines to vibrate so hard that it looked like they would blow apart. A four-inch line carried the black gold into a holding tank. That kept the pumps busy, moving it to big storage tanks. It was only one of several hundred wells within the few miles surrounding us at that time (1912).

That weekend we took a notion to go to Charleston. I was seventeen years old, and Alvah was twenty-one, but neither of us had ever been there. Most of the gang with us was from Roane, Clay, or Kanawha Counties, and only one or two of them had ever been in the capital city. We walked to the mouth of Blue Creek and caught the evening train into the big city. We got off the train where the B&O station is now located and walked from there over to the main part of Charleston. Most of the streets were paved with brick, but some were dirt. There were very few automobiles there, and there wasn't a concrete sidewalk or street anywhere in the city at that time. We stayed at a hotel on Kanawha Street, which is now Kanawha Boulevard. There were a few nice commercial buildings on Kanawha Street then, but mostly farmhouses lined each side of the street. At that time, there were big farms where most of Charleston is now settled solid.

We went into a barbershop on Virginia and Summers Street to get our hair cut. At age seventeen, I was the youngest of the gang, and this was the first time that I—and most of the others— was ever in a barbershop. The others got their hair cut and walked out, saying they would wait outside until I was through. They waited quite a while! After the barber cut my hair, he asked me if I wanted a massage, then everything else he could think of. I would ask a few questions about it and then give in to whatever he asked. I must have been in the chair for an hour and a half. My buddies knew what I was accepting from that barber, and they were just letting me take it all. A haircut was twenty-five cents, and I thought he was accommodating me with all of this extra doting on my hair. I finally got out of the chair and asked him what I owed him, and he answered, "Two dollars, sir."

When I went outside and rejoined my gang, they were all laughing at me. I said, "A day's work for a haircut!" We started walking on down the street, and I saw a well-dressed man coming toward us. I said, "Boys, why are you walking so slow? If we are going to stay overnight, it's time we find a room." I lined out straight toward this big sport, and Phil Ross was right behind me. I got almost face-to-face with the well-dressed dude, then I quickly stepped aside. Phil ran head-on into him! The fellow looked at Phil like he was going to sock him a hard blow, and then we all mustered up to him. He walked on. That was my turn to laugh. I said to Phil, "Can't you see such a big man as that one is? You'll get us all put in the brig. We had better get to our room before we are arrested. Come on, let's get out of here."

The others, however, ignored me and ambled over to the nearest saloon.

I said, "No, leave that saloon alone. Don't you know when you've had enough of that stuff?"

He answered, "I've just had only three or four drinks of whiskey and beer."

I pleaded, "Yes, but it doesn't take much beer and whiskey mixed to make you sot-drunk."

"Come on with me. Don't you see that policeman watching us?"

"Come on! I'm the younger of us. You ought to be looking after me. If you are going to drink anymore, get it and take it home with you."

"Let's get out of here!"

We got two rooms at the Washington Hotel. I hid all of the whiskey, and I told the gang that they had drunk it. Some of them were so drunk that they couldn't tell their left hand from their right. The next morning, I set the whiskey out where they could see it.

"I thought we drank all of that bottle."

I answered, "You were so drunk you couldn't see a bottle."

"Well, it's a good thing we have a little to sober up on."

"Yes," I said, "I imagine you're about broke, as freely as you spent your money. I haven't got much either. I didn't drink with you, but I got a haircut—two dollars for a haircut."

"Well," Phil said, "you were in there long enough to get four haircuts."

"Well, I guess I got the whole works. I'll know that barbershop if I ever come into town for another haircut. I won't forget that!"

We left the hotel at about ten o'clock the next morning and caught the train to Blue Creek station. We walked the rest of the way to Coca. Some of the gang looked pretty sickly, and I'm sure they didn't feel any better than they looked—I'll assure you of that— from drinking that whiskey and beer. Those drinks don't mix well. "Well, this is Monday, blue Monday. Do you think you can do a day's work today?"

"I don't feel too good myself. I'm going to try to earn my money today, but I don't know what kind of a job I'll do at it." We got to work at seven o'clock and started back at digging a road to a location.

The boss said, "Boggs, this looks like a pretty rough place here. We may have some shooting to do today." I was assigned to work with a man who wasn't much interested in his job, and we had a bad section to dig. One would dig while the other shoveled the dirt. We had some stumps to dig out, and we got behind with our section.

Alvah said to me, "The boss is going to can you if you don't do better. He has been complaining about you getting behind with your section."

I said, "I'll get me another buddy and not work with this fellow. He wants to stand and roll too many cigarettes."

(I think that the boss knew who was slacking on the job because a few days before that, someone had reported to me that he heard the boss say, "That little fellow, Boggs, digs more dirt than any man on the job.") I was only seventeen, but I could do as much work as the next man could. We finished our day and went back to the boardinghouse. There was a gas well so near our boardinghouse that we were in danger from it. Before they plugged it, it blew out at such a strong pressure that they took three days to get it under control. I felt lucky when we finished that job without a major disaster.

Dad kept urging us to go back to school, and he said that we should help one another through the eighth grade. (In those days, that was about equal to today's high school education.) Howard White and Howard's brother, Webb, were teaching then, and they both encouraged us to complete our free school—or grammar school, as it was called then. Alvah had quit school at the fifth grade, and Guy was in the fourth grade when they started back in 1912. Ray and I worked through that year to finish paying for our home. I was eighteen years old when I went back to school in September of 1913. Ray continued working at the planing mill job at Elkhurst, and he helped the family while we went to school that year. He didn't make up his mind to go back until the next school year.

I started at a poor third grade. I had been in that grade when I quit school, but I was out for nine years. I could read and write and spell poorly, and I knew a little in figures or arithmetic. I could add, subtract, multiply, and divide some, but very little. As a man, it was pretty embarrassing to go to school with little children who knew more than I did, but I was mature enough to know how much a person needed an education. My teacher, Webb White, put me with the eighth graders. Webb knew how embarrassing it would be for me to be in a class with the little children. The eighth grade books had a few third- and fourth-grade problems in them, and he assigned me the easier ones. Alvah, Guy, and I stayed with it, even if it was awkward. We knew we wouldn't be embarrassed all of our lives. We had one-room schools in those days, and sometimes there were thirty or forty pupils in one school, so at times, our schools were pretty crowded.

During the noon hour, we would choose our players and have a good time playing ball. We had such interesting games that we hardly took time to eat. We would choose our players by the old method. Choose two of the best players and have them stand opposite one another. Someone throws up a bat, and one of the captains grabs it near the middle with one hand. The opposing player clasps one hand above that of the first, and they take turns placing one hand over that of the other person's. The last hand that can hold it gets the first choice for his team. (We played by baseball rules in those days, but some of the rules were different from what they are now.) Some of the players were so absorbed by the game that they would try to change the rules or pretend they were different in order to win. Our leader was one who couldn't take a loss. He was good winner but a poor loser. We had some exciting times, but we often got into such harsh arguments that some players would quit for the day. In the winter, when the weather was too bad for us to play outside, some of us played checkers or dominoes. Sometimes, we would talk and argue on an interesting subject such as politics or other current events. We learned from each other about the rules, the laws, and so on.

When school was closed for the year, some of us worked in public works while the others ran the farm. (At that time, the school term lasted only six months, so we had six months to work while not in school, and all of us worked on Saturdays and holidays during the school year.) Alvah and Guy got jobs in timber and lumber works while school was out, and my younger brothers Cornelius, Cecil, and Dennis worked with me on the farm during the spring and summer of 1914.

We added four to five acres to our grain farm each year until we had all of the best land cleared. We cleared the hillside land and tended it in corn, but we found it didn't pay to plow such steep land. It was so soft and sandy that it wouldn't pack like clay land does, and the heavy stock, such as cattle, horses, or hogs, trampled the soft soil so that it didn't hold grass well. Almost all of the soil on our former farm at Wallback was clay. It packed well and would hold up well to the cattle, etc., but clay soil washed away worse than the sandy soil, making gullies where the cattle made trails around hillsides.

I did most of the plowing, and Cornelius, Cecil, and Dennis hoed the corn. One day, I was plowing with old Maude on a pretty rough and steep hillside. It was very hot that day, and old Maude was very fast, especially on rough ground. I got too hot, but I didn't notice it until after I stopped. (Old Maude went so fast that the air kept me cool while I was going.) The heat made me so sick that it affected me for most of the summer. Cornelius relieved me once in a while during the week, and Alvah and Guy helped with the plowing on Saturdays. They were going to a summer school that year to Howard White. This was their second year. As soon as they finished the eighth grade, they intended to teach public school. By going to school for six to eight weeks during the summer, they would be able to get number two certificates to teach.

I worked in the cornfield until about the first or middle of July. After we laid by the corn, I found a job with the United Fuel Gas Company here at Porter Creek, where I could board at home for the next six to eight weeks before school started up again. I worked with a crew that recased gas wells. We followed behind a well-cleaning crew. They blow a hard, sharp grade of sand (almost like glass) into the well with several thousand pounds of pressure. That opens up the pours, and the oil or gas is as free to flow about as freely as it did when the well was first drilled. We pulled the casing and reran it to keep out the saltwater that was leaking into it and hindering the flow of gas. I worked out about $80 before school started, and that helped me buy some new clothes and school supplies for my second year. It wasn't so hard or embarrassing to start back this time because I had got straightened out the first year and at least learned just how ignorant I was.

In the autumn, while the weather was nice, we would walk two or three miles each way after school to attend an old-time shouting revival meeting. Some of the revivals lasted for three weeks or more. People didn't have anywhere else to go. There weren't any automobiles or hard roads then, and the young people liked to go to church to meet their friends, and by the second or third week, most of them would be taking an interest in the meeting. There was a lot of interest in the Lord in those days.

I finished my second year in school and tended a crop and cleared some ground. One day, I came within an inch of my life (as we sometimes say). It happened on a Saturday when Alvah and Guy were not in school. About six of us (Alvah, Guy, Ray, Cornelius, Cecil, and I) were rolling logs up in heaps to burn them out of the way. There was an old chestnut log that had lain there so long that we had to dig in the earth to get it sawed in two with our crosscut saw. We finally got it cut into several short logs. It was about three feet in diameter and was hard to handle.

I got upon the middle log with my cane hook. I pulled downhill on it with all of my weight. The log finally came out of its bed and started rolling downhill. I jumped off, and somehow, I didn't get out of the way of the rolling log as quickly as I should have. The hill was pretty steep there, and the log picked up speed pretty fast. It bumped my heels for several steps. I finally gained enough speed to get out of its path. My brothers were so shook up that they didn't say a word. If they had said anything, it might have distracted me enough that I wouldn't have gotten out of the way. I wasn't scared until it was all over with. If I had caught my pant leg over a snag on the ground (or if a snag on the log had hooked in my pants), it would have thrown me to the ground under the log, and that log weighed nearly a ton! The log incident happened when I was eighteen years old. That wasn't the first time that I had such a narrow escape—I had nearly died in convulsions when I was eight years old—and it was not the last time I came so near death, but I am still here at seventy-six years of age. We worked hard from near twilight to dusk and turned out a big day's work. The new ground that we cleared that year produced some of the finest corn in the community.

By March or April 1915, we had a few more acres of new ground ready for corn. After I finished the second year of school and after we got the corn crop laid by, I had a little time to work off the farm. I went to Cabin Creek and helped build one of the first (if not the first) big power plants in the state. The plant built by the Virginia Power Company is still operating.

That was the year the saloons were voted out of West Virginia (the nearest one was at Cabin Creek). The day before the saloons closed, people got their suitcases and lined out for several yards at the saloons. They bought their last legal whiskey in the state—until 1934 when it became legal to buy it in a state-run whiskey store (package store). You had to have a ticket to buy it, and they couldn't sell more than a quart at a time to each person. The nearest saloon to reopen under the new law was at Catlettsburg, Kentucky. People would go there and buy what they were allowed to bring across the state line. When the county was dry, there was a lot of bootlegging going on. A lot of people just couldn't do without their whiskey. So they campaigned for several years for its return. They claimed it was being made illegally and sold to people under age, and that problem was handled worse than when we had saloons. Another argument was that we were losing a lot of tax money from the sale of intoxicating drinks.

I went back to school again in September 1915, and I worked hard at my studies and made fairly good grades. During that winter, when we weren't in school, we continued to clear land for farming. After the corn was laid by that year, Alvah and I and Carl Samples went to Winona, Fayette County, to work until school started again. We worked at building a narrow gauged railroad on a timber job.

We boarded with a coal miner at Winona. He took us into a coal mine there, and we went about a quarter of a mile into it. This was the first time I was ever in a coal mine. It was a big seam of coal, and we could stand up straight and walk in it. I decided I didn't want to work in a coal mine. At that time, they didn't have very good safety procedures, and it looked too dangerous for me. Most of the mines had poor working conditions, and there were frequent slate falls that killed or crippled the miners. At most of the mines, they pulled the loaded trucks out with mules. Later, electric motors were installed in the mines to pull the coal trucks.

I worked there at Winona until school time. On my return trip, I rode a hack (or a closed-in buggy) that carried passengers about five miles to the railroad. (There weren't any automobiles there then.) The hack had three rows of seats in it, and it could carry about nine or ten passengers. After returning home, I started back to school in September for my third and last term. Webb White was still our teacher. As usual, we worked on our farmwork in our spare time or while not in school, starting each day as soon as we would get home from school. We had a fairly good crop of corn that year, about twelve acres of it, and some oats to feed our cows and chickens. We would cut corn, pick beans, dig potatoes, and gather in the truck crops from the garden and field and prepare them for winter. We had to string and can beans, fruit, and vegetables until we had our cellar full.

Alvah and Guy had finished free school the year before and had attended a teachers' school that summer to qualify for teaching. They earned number two certificates. They taught free school this term and made a little money, thirty dollars per month. They taught for six months and went to a teachers' school the next summer. (They continued until they had number one certificates that paid thirty-five to forty-five dollars per month in Clay County.) They had to ride a train from Procious to Clay and back home to attend teachers' school. They got a discount fare for school travels, and they were able to make a little money while learning and teaching, but it was slow progress toward making good wages. They also took high school classes while teaching, and after some few years, they finished high school.

After Alvah taught (in one-room schools) for a few years, the political leaders got him to register for the nomination for county superintendent of schools. He was nominated on the Democrat ticket and ran against one of his old teachers, who ran on the Republican ticket. Alva was elected for a four-year term. He was a good talker and a good school manager, and he continued to work for the schools for the rest of his life. Guy taught until 1917. Ray didn't go back to school until a year after I started, and he only went for two years.

In 1916, Woodrow Wilson ran against Judge Hughes of New York for the office of president of the United States. After the election, news came that Hughes had won the office. He had carried New York by a landslide, and they thought that pushed him over. That night, the Republicans got together to celebrate. They collected some powder and other material and put off some shots to commemorate their victory. (About 75 percent of our schoolmates were Republicans.) They had a happy time celebrating their election.

News came the next morning that Wilson had carried California and that he was elected president (instead of Hughes). My brothers and I (and some few other families) were staunch Democrats. When it came our time to celebrate, some of the Republicans had changed their politics. We had a bigger crowd than we expected, and did we sound off! We got us plenty of good coarse powder and some two-inch steel gas pipes. We cut off about three feet of a pipe and tamped about one-third of one end with clay dirt, good and solid. Then we put about a quart of powder into the pipe, with a good long fuse in it, and tightly packed the rest of the pipe with clay. We placed this pipe bomb in the forks of a tree about head level. We struck a match and lit it and then ran and got behind some trees.

When the shot exploded, it roared so loud that people a half mile away said it sounded like it was right in their yards (especially the Republicans who had set off shots the night before). They were going to have someone arrested for setting off shots in their door. We few Democrats didn't hear anymore about politics for some time. Woodrow Wilson made a fine president and served two terms. He was an educator from New Jersey, but he was born in Lexington, Virginia. He formed a labor cabinet in his administration and appointed a secretary of labor. This was one of the first labor movements by our government.

School closed as usual in March 1917. I had worked hard at my education while still doing farmwork. Starting from the third grade and doing four six-month terms and by studying some between terms (when I had time to study), I had completed six grades in four years, and they let me take the test for a grade school diploma. In those days, you had to make a grade average of 70 percent to pass the test. That qualified one to attend high school. I made an average of 85.5 on my eighth grade diploma test.

3

The War Years

Until June (after I turned twenty-two), I worked on the farm at home and hired out some for my neighbors.

There was war going on in Europe, had been since 1914. I had been reading about the war for three years, and I felt that Germany was far in the wrong. The war could have been prevented in the first place, but Germany was ruled by warlords who thought she could conquer the world. They were waging war on France, Italy, Serbia, Belgium, and some smaller nations. Austria, Hungary, and I believe, Romania were with the German Alliance. Germany expanded the war to take on England, and they almost made war on Norway and Sweden, but those countries wouldn't fight back. (They let Germany interfere with their rights.) Most of the American people were for France, but some were so steadfast for Germany that they were very unpatriotic toward their own government.

France was our best friend in Europe and one of our most favored nations because France had helped us in the Revolutionary War against England. We couldn't afford to stand by and see a warlord nation take over France or England, and Germany was making headway toward taking both of them.

France was pretty well prepared for war, but Germany was better armed. Germany was supposed to be neutral with Belgium, but Belgium was in her way, between Germany and France and the North Sea and the English Channel, so Germany swept through Belgium, brutally murdering women and children. They committed many crimes against helpless nations, such brutal deeds that we could hardly believe it.

It made my blood boil to read about it. It was hard for me to believe until I saw it with my own eyes, as I did later, in the battle of the Argonne and during the Meuse Offensive. (They were as brutal as the Japanese were in the death march when Japan took Corregidor in the Second World War.)

Germany got so bold that she broke international laws as if she owned the world and could do as she pleased with any nation. The United States was shipping food and supplies to Europe—mostly to France and England. Our ships were unarmed, and we were helpless to protect our merchant vessels from armed battleships. According to international law, we were at liberty to ship anything we pleased. Germany had the right to capture our ships and take our cargo, as long as she didn't harm our crews or destroy our ships, but under international law, she was required to turn our ships loose to go home and to pay for our cargo when she did take it.

Germany sank a big passenger liner, the *Lusitania,* and didn't even try to rescue the passengers; they just let them drown. Some American people were aboard the ship. President Wilson called Congress to Washington. The Congress didn't have to declare war on Germany; they just declared that war already existed. We started mobilizing our troops and ships, and our government called all reserves to duty and declared a draft law. We went to war against Germany and her allies (April 6, 1917).

I helped with the crop until we got it worked over once (June 19, 1917), then I told Mother that I might as well volunteer. I would be called soon anyway, so I thought I should go while I could choose my organization.

Mother said, "Granddad said you don't know what you are doing." I told Mother somebody had to go. We couldn't afford to be ruled by such people as the warlords of Germany. Mother was right; I didn't know what I was doing. Until he has been there, no one knows what war is like, that's for sure! I might try to explain it, but that can't be done either. No one knows until he goes through a war. You take a healthy soldier and train him and drill him to every hardship of battle, but until he has seen the battlefield, he still won't know what he is getting into. I said, "A well-trained soldier has more lives than a cat's nine lives."

I went to Charleston and tried to get in the navy. I had been told that the navy was a good place to learn a valuable trade, but I didn't pass their physical examination. The recruiting officer said that only one out of ten passed the navy physical. I went to the army recruiting office on Summers Street. (They still have a recruiting station there.) The army rated me 1-A. I stayed overnight at the Washington Hotel. The date was June 19, 1917. The next morning, along with several other recruits, I boarded a train at the C&O Railway station, and we traveled to Columbus, Ohio, where we were sworn in. They issued us our uniforms, and some other recruits and I stayed there for two days. Then we took a train south.

The next day, we arrived in Chattanooga, Tennessee. There, we got off the train and hiked ten miles to Fort Oglethorpe, Georgia. We got there at about three o'clock that afternoon. That was my first hike in the army. (I had many, many more during the following two years in the service!) Fort Oglethorpe had been an army post since the Civil War. They displayed a lot of old relics such as cannons, wagons, and other guns and material from that war. We were assigned to some barracks, and the ole bugle sounded reveille the next morning. That was my first time to answer to its duty. They led us to the quartermaster's barracks, where they issued each of us another uniform and some underwear. The quartermaster clerk just looked at us and threw each of us a uniform. He said, "Take that, and trade amongst yourselves. Make them fit the best you can." We traded around until some fit and some didn't fit. "Well, you're in the army now. You're in the army now. You sonofagun, you're not behind the plow. You're in the army now."

The bugle sounded again. "What's that call?"

"That's mess call." We went to the mess hall for the first time. It was about two hundred and fifty feet long with a long table on each side. There were board seats on each side of the tables, with an aisle in the middle. I went through the chow line, where they filled my tray. Then I carried it to a table, stepped over the wooden bench, and sat down for my first meal in the mess hall. We had pot roast beef, potatoes, corn on the cob, sliced tomatoes, butter, baked beans, fruit, and a few other vegetables. It was a very hearty meal for people who did hard work.

After dinner, our captain lined us out and gave us a good speech about what it takes to be a good soldier. Then he issued us some manuals containing our general orders about drilling, guard duty, and other activities. The next day, our first sergeant lined us up with the tallest of the platoon at the head of the line on down to the shortest at the other end. He selected us for squads of eight. There were three platoons to a company of one hundred and fifty men. The sergeant took us to the practice field and explained our drill. Then we started practicing. We learned to step off and count time and to do squad right and left, to the rear, and forward march. We soon knew how to soldier.

Each morning, the bugle sounded for reveille, and we hustled out to get our clothes on. We didn't have much time to dress, and if we weren't in line, fully dressed, to account for ourselves, we might have to look out for punishment, such as being put on a nasty or hard labor detail. The experienced officers who led my division knew how to command the recruits. They understood how to handle soldiers, and they knew that we would have to be disciplined and well trained.

Several of our officers were direct from West Point. But some of the lieutenants and captains didn't know the drills as well as some of the sergeants and lower-ranked enlisted men. The old regular divisions had the best soldiers. A lot of them had been in military service for fifteen to twenty years or longer. They had a lot of arguments with some of the newly commissioned officers. They almost fought at times. Often, a commanding officer didn't like to give in, even after he learned where he was wrong.

My company commander, Captain White, was one of those seasoned regular soldiers. He was very strict. Everything had to be done to the point. I've heard him jeer at those West Point officers until a fly would be afraid to light on one of them. He was a strict, rough-going commander, but he did it in a way that mostly every soldier liked him. We enjoyed listening to him argue with those bigheaded West Point officers.

We drilled hard and long hours through the week. After about six or eight weeks of hard work, we could drill fairly well. Sometimes we passed in review before our general-in-command. After training to march, we got our rifles and soon learned the rifle drills. We were quite awkward at times, and it appeared as though some of the soldiers would never learn the drill. A few of those noncommissioned officers got rough with them. If we didn't drill to the point, they would give us a lot of trouble. If a recruit kept making mistakes, they put him in the "awkward squad" and drilled him extra time. Sometimes, they double-timed them until they almost collapsed. The persons who couldn't keep time with the music were the most awkward ones. I don't believe I got put in the awkward squad more than once. It was considered a disgrace.

We practiced until we were pretty sharp at the rifle drill and could handle our guns well to the command. The next thing was the bayonet drill. We practiced at that for quite a while. Then they lined us up, facing each other, to thrust our bayonets toward one another. We used real steel bayonets, not rubber ones. If someone made an awkward thrust or got in the way of another soldier's bayonet, a soldier could get stabbed. I've heard of a few being killed at bayonet drill. We learned to thrust our bayonets in all directions—up, down, to the left, right, and to the rear. We also mastered the use of the shoulder end of our rifle to quickly strike the enemy at close range, getting him into a position where we could stab him with our bayonet.

The next rifle training was on the range shooting at targets. Those .30-30 Springfield rifles shot with power. If you didn't hold one solid to your shoulder, it would spring up or back when it fired, hitting you in the face or bouncing against your shoulder. It could hurt you so badly that your face or shoulder would be sore for a week. I've seen soldiers with bloody faces. Some of them had lived in the cities and had never shot a gun. I was raised on a farm on the edge of a huge forest, and I learned to handle guns when I was just a boy. I made marksman the first and only time that I was on the practice range with a rifle.

Every man had to take a three-day turn at KP (kitchen police) every three months. I didn't mind it, but they always had some rule breakers or some unruly toughs who were getting into trouble with the mess sergeant, and he was as mean as the outlaws were. We had to peel potatoes for about two hours. It took about two bushels or more for one meal. We had good cooks, and our mess sergeant saw that we had plenty to eat. Some of the other outfits didn't put all of their food allowance on the table. They used some of it for parties and other pleasures.

One Saturday morning, the battalion was called to pass in review before one of our commanding officers. I was on kitchen duty, so I didn't get to march that day. The band was on the field, and everyone was marching to the music. I could see them from the kitchen. That was the first large band I ever heard. I realized that their music would be nice to march to. I loved music in general, but I always liked string music the best of all.

I got sick with a pretty high fever. I told my mess sergeant that I had a terrible headache. He said, "You had better go to the infirmary and see the doctor." I just walked off without going to the office to get a relief slip. (I thought my sergeant would look for that.) I had the German measles. The doctor sent me direct to the infirmary, and I had to stay there for about two weeks. He wouldn't let me go back to my barracks because I could give it to the others. One night, my fever ran so high that I was almost unconscious before I got the orderly to my room. I kept ringing the bell for him, and he wouldn't come. There were two more patients in my room at the hospital, and one of them was about well enough to leave the hospital. He went to hunt for the orderly and found him down in the basement playing poker.

The orderly came and said, "My god! You have a terrible fever." I asked him how high it was, and he said 104, but I'll say it was higher than that. He hurried around and got me an ice cap to put on my head. He put a cloth between the ice cap and my scalp. It didn't seem to do me any good. I took the cloth off and put the bare ice cap to my head. (That was dangerous and against the rules, but I was suffering so much that I didn't think of that.) My face broke out so much that it looked almost as red as blood.

When the doctor examined me the next morning, he said, "This is the first case like this I have had in several thousand patients. Your blood has come to your skin."

When the orderly came into my room the next morning, the head nurse said, "I heard the bell ring and ring. Why didn't you answer it?" I had a notion to tell her that he was down in the basement playing poker. I should have reported him, but I always avoided trouble. If I had told her, he could have been court-martialed, and he could have gotten a pretty long sentence. He had made a serious mistake. I could have died if the other patient had not have been in my room to help me. At that time, measles was a severe disease.

I said to my nurse, "If I ever get to Germany, I hope those Germans won't be as hard on me as their measles are."

After about two weeks, when I reported back to my company, my first sergeant said, "I had you marked AWOL for several days before I learned where you were."

I said, "My mess sergeant sent me to the doctor. I had the measles, and my doctor sent me on to the hospital. He didn't want me to spread the measles."

He said, "You should have come to my office first."

I said, "Maybe it's well that I didn't as you might be in the hospital now with the measles." He agreed! I had been pretty sick, and I was still so weak that I had to stay in quarters for a few days before I could go back to work. About all I had to do while convalescing was to keep my bunk and my surroundings neat. I read the news and wrote a few letters, and I fared very well.

Inspection of quarters and equipment was scheduled on Saturday, the day my doctor let me go to work. We were required to have all of our possessions laid out in such order that everything could be seen, and they had to be clean and in proper shape for use. If we were short of any article that was called for, we were supposed to report it to our superior officer. These were just our personal belongings—such as your mess kit, comb, shaving kit, and clothing.

We had arms inspection at least once a month. All of us had rifles at that time, and we had to take them all apart and clean every particle of dirt or rust from anywhere the company commander knew where he might find it. We had to line up with our rifles, and when the officer came by each soldier, he was required to bring his rifle up in both hands. The officer would grab it and look it over, then slam it back at him, and the soldier had better grab it properly and bring it properly to the ground by his side.

One time, I had cleaned my gun in good shape for inspection, but when I put my lock in my gun, I failed to snap it so it wouldn't come off. When I pulled my rifle up for inspection and snapped the lock back so the officer might look through the barrel, I jerked the lock back with so much force that it flew out of my hand and hit the soldier next to me. The commanding officer said to my sergeant, "Take this soldier's name." The next Sunday, I didn't get my day of rest. I had to work in the kitchen. That's the only time that I remember getting disciplined while in military service.

When war started, there was a big German battleship in or near New York harbor. It had been captured. (I remember that its masts were so tall that they had to take them down before they could get them under the Brooklyn Bridge.) The sailors on it were brought to Fort Oglethorpe, and they worked around the camp and marched by my barracks mostly every evening. There must have been five hundred or more of them. They certainly knew how to march. We could hear the sharp cadence of their steps clicking to time.

I was at Fort Oglethorpe for only about three months. About two miles from us, they were building a big new camp that was named after General Nathan Forrest, a leader of the Confederate forces in the Civil War. I soldiered at Camp Forrest for the rest of the year that I was in Georgia. That was the winter of 1917 and 1918, one of the coldest winters we ever had. About the first of September, the temperature dropped to three above zero, and during January and February, it snowed a lot (for that far south).

After three months from the time I enlisted, I got a furlough. Three months was the longest I had ever been away from home. I went straight to Chattanooga and caught a train to Louisville, where I had to stay overnight. I caught a train to Charleston the next morning and got home the same day. I was glad to get back. I told my parents that I was very well satisfied with the army. I liked the training and experience of being a soldier. At that time, I was the only one of the family in military service. (Cornelius tried to enlist, but was turned down because he did not pass the physical. So he went back home and got married, but after a few months, he was drafted. He was on the waters on his way overseas when the armistice was signed. He went to France and was stationed there for about three months before he was sent back home and discharged.)

I certainly enjoyed seeing all of my friends and relatives, and I had a good time while at home. After about ten days, I started back to training camp. I knew I wouldn't return home until after the war was over, but I always felt that I would get back home safely.

I went back to Camp Forest and was there until the next June. Edgar Rogers was the only one person in our battalion that I had known back home. He was from Wallback, and I found him within three buildings of my barrack. Edgar was a good soldier. (After the war, he learned the barber trade. He lived at Miami, near Cabin Creek, until he retired. He died in 1963.)

About six months after I entered the service, several members of our division were transferred to units that were sent to France and soon went into battle. I was left at Camp Forrest to help train troops. Later, I was assigned to a machine gun battalion where I stayed until discharged in June 1918. Edgar Rogers was transferred with me. Edgar and I never got separated, and we were close friends clear through the war. Edgar was an orderly for his company commander—and a runner, as they called it at times. When on the front, a runner sometimes had to take some daring adventures to deliver messages to other officers in active battle. Sometimes, they would have to risk getting into no-man's-land between the enemy and our own troops.

While at Camp Forest, Edgar and I attended Sunday school and singing sessions at a little country church. We would sing with the choir during regular services, but we didn't join them at their singing conventions. Sometimes our chaplain held services at the YMCA or at movie theaters, and at other times he had short services at the library, where we went to do most of our corresponding. Before we went to France, the chaplain gave an invitation for baptism. I had joined the church while we lived at Wallback, but I hadn't been baptized. Another soldier and I responded, and he set a date. We were baptized in the Chickamauga River near Camp Forrest.

The army included all kinds of characters. Some of them caused trouble at times—the same as in any other body of people. They would gamble in playing poker and with other civil games. Sometimes that led to uncivil behavior. If they got into a fight in the barracks, the sergeant would get them a pair of boxing gloves and take them out behind the barracks. He made them fight until one of them gave in. That was exciting for a lot of the soldiers.

We were transferred to Camp Wadsworth, South Carolina, where there was a range suitable for us to practice firing our machine guns. We went to a little town by the name of Spartanburg (which is now a city). While there, we lived in big tents—a squad of eight soldiers to a tent. We lingered there for two or three days, waiting for animals and carts to haul our guns and ammunition to the target range.

We were given fresh mules from the West. They had never had harnesses on them or a bridle in their mouths, and lots of the soldiers were from the city and had never had a thing to do with animals. That caused a lot of excitement. Some of the mules did very well, but some got scared and balked. Some of them ran away. We followed them out through people's farms and over fences until, one by one, we got them back into the road. We eventually got the harnesses on them, loaded our two-wheel carts with ammunition and a machine gun on each cart. and started for the machine gun range. We finally got to the range where we had corrals to hold the beasts. The mules survived, and nobody was seriously injured.

We stayed on the range for about ten days and learned to fire and take care of our machine guns. We had the Vickers machine gun while on the range. (When we got to France, we had to use a French machine gun, which was a little different from the Vickers.)

We left Camp Wadsworth on June 29, 1918, and traveled to Camp Mills, Long Island, New York, where we stayed until July 7, 1918. We went from there to Brooklyn, New York, and crossed the bay to Jersey City, New Jersey, where we loaded onto an English vessel (the *Desney Belfast*) that had been converted from a cargo carrier to a troop transport ship.

We started out through the East River between New York City and Long Island (through the Long Island Sound) and departed from there on our voyage to France. In order to get out of so much danger from German submarines, we sailed into the Atlantic for a few miles—far enough that we couldn't see land for three days. We sailed for Halifax, Nova Scotia, Canada, and stayed there on board the ship right where a spy had blown a shipload of ammunition to bits. (The city was burned, and only tree stubs were left. Several hundred people were killed in that disaster.) We were at the Halifax port for about three days waiting for a fleet of Canadian troops to join us.

This was my first voyage on the waters. I got a bit seasick, but not as bad as some of the other soldiers did; at least, I didn't have to vomit. Our ships were loaded with cold storage rations, but we nearly starved for the duration of our voyage. We got so hungry that some of the soldiers became very cranky and nearly fought over what we did have to eat.

We had twenty-four ships (the largest convoy of the war). It included one cruiser, two cargo ships, and twenty-one transport ships loaded with ninety thousand soldiers. For our protection, several destroyers followed us for the first three days. The cruiser could sail from one side of the convoy to the other in just a few minutes. On the second day of our voyage, we began to fire our big guns. They had spied something sticking up out of the water that they thought was a submarine periscope. We fired about twenty-five shots at it. The water was very calm at this time, and a submarine couldn't get within torpedo firing range. To lose the submarine, our ships increased their speed and changed directions every few minutes. While it was submerged underwater, the submarine couldn't travel as fast as we did, and it didn't dare to come to the surface where the cruiser guns could get it. If the water had been rough, it could have gotten close enough to fire a torpedo at us.

The *Desney Belfast* was one of our biggest transport vessels. The Germans had sunk her sister ship and were always after it. We stayed near the middle of the convoy, where we were safer. The sea was very calm for about five days, but then it got very rough for about two days. I had gotten over my sickness before we left Halifax. I felt a little queasy at times, but I didn't suffer any more seasickness for the rest of the voyage. Some soldiers got very ill. By the seventh day, some Canadian troops had died. They wrapped them in a white cloth and lowered them into the ocean for burial.

On about the ninth day of our voyage, we met ten submarine destroyers that had been sent to protect us. They had run into five subs that were after us, and they sank three of them. We arrived in Europe without any more trouble. Some of our division landed in England for a few days before completing their voyage, but my boat went directly to Le Havre, France.

We were starved and worn-out when we got ashore, but we had to hike about four miles to an English camp. We could hear artillery in distance, so we knew that we weren't far from the front lines. After resting for about four days, we started toward the front. We traveled in a boxcar (or a freight car) for about forty-eight hours. It was supposed to hold twenty men per unit, but there were forty men on each of those cars. Some stood up while the others lay down to rest for about four hours each shift. Before that trip was over, we were about as tired as we had been when we disembarked from the boats. We got off our train at a little town by the name of Clairvaux?

The Eighteenth Machine Gun Battalion was about ten hours ahead of us. (They were on a train that wrecked and killed twenty soldiers.) We hiked eight miles to our camp, where we could drill and maneuver for battle. We stayed there until August 11, preparing to meet the Hun (German enemy). We were billeted in a small town, Dienville, where only old people and a few children were living. The women and the old men worked in the fields on the farms.

One day, we noticed that they were celebrating—drinking and singing. We learned that they were honoring several soldiers from this little town who had been killed. We stayed there until August 27, 10:00 a.m. We loaded onto trucks and traveled until 11:00 p.m. We got off and lay down on the ground, where we rested until 4:00 a.m. We got back on our trucks and traveled until 3:00 p.m. We stopped at a little town by the name of Vagna, which was within about twenty miles of the battle zone. As we were marching to our billets, we saw an air raid some distance away.

Here, we met the first American troops that had come from the front lines. They were a replacement unit from the Forty-Second Division, the Rainbow Division. They participated in more battles than any other Americans. When a division had lost a lot of troops, the Forty-Second Division would replace them.

We left Vagna on September 3 at 7:00 a.m. and marched to a small town by the name of Le Tholy. Here we stayed in pup tents just large enough for two soldiers to lie down in. There were more air raids near us. On September 4 at noon, we struck tents. We rolled our packs and started for the front lines. This time, we rode in American trucks. They were much more comfortable than the French trucks.

We had twenty-seven men on each of them. We traveled about fourteen miles, climbing the Vosges Mountains and arriving at our camp at about midnight.

We drilled there for a few days and saw some more air battles near us. An enemy plane was shot down while we were there. Here we met some strange and miserable company. The French had left us cooties (body lice). The chicken-wire mattresses made us feel at home with the cooties. We had to fight them constantly. One soldier caught two to see if they wouldn't fight each other. They had quite a battle. Jeff beat up Joe pretty badly.

We slept in bunk beds, one over the other. This location was on the border between Germany and France, where the war began. We were near the crown prince of Germany's summer resort. In the surrounding area, there were pretty forests of big and tall pine trees that surrounded some clean and grassy little fields. There were also a few steep hills and gorges within our view.

On September 9, 1918, we ate supper at about 4:00 p.m. Then we unloaded the ammunition from our carts and left camp. Each of us picked up and carried forty-eight pounds of ammunition, one twenty-four-pound box in each hand. We already had on our full field packs, which weighed seventy-five pounds. We hiked around a hill in a narrow path and went as fast as we could, but with that load, we couldn't keep up with the infantry. We would hike for fifty minutes and then rest for ten minutes. I thought my arms would come apart, but in places, I could drag one box along the bank. That helped some.

We got too far behind the infantry to catch up with them, so we laid the ammunition down by the road and waited for the wagons to come and get it. After loading it on the wagons, we hiked along with them until we got to the end of the road. Then we had to unload the ammunition again and carry it about one and a half miles down a steep hill into the narrow valley (like Porter Creek at Bomont, West Virginia). We got to our trenches at about 3:00 a.m.

Some of our crew had to report immediately for guard duty on the front lines. I got to rest for about ten hours. Then we relieved a French division, all but a few French gunners who stayed with us until we were fully armed. We each had a .45-caliber pistol and a knife that we kept at all times, but we didn't get our guns until the next day or two.

The French had driven the Hun back into the mountains about fourteen miles into Lorene State. This was on the southern front, near Mulhouse, France, only a few miles from Switzerland. There didn't seem to be any urgency for either the enemy or us to take this place. So the French and Germans almost mingled together there. There was some farming on both sides, and they had to share access to the water. One side would wash their clothes one day and the other the next day, all in the same place.

There wasn't much need to start a battle, but we didn't have any orders not to fight. The Germans didn't know we had shipped in, so they started showing up on their farms as usual. We scouted around some and did guard duty, but we couldn't consider this a game of friendship or sport. We wanted to get this war over with. So we started something of interest, and we soon had a few close run-ins. We showed them that we came to fight.

After we started war with the Hun, they fired somewhere around us about every day. At intervals, they would open up on our entrenchment lines. The Hun had a one-pound cannon near us (that is, a gun that shoots a one-pound shell.) It will fire about seventy-five rounds per minute, and it is very accurate.) They kept this up for a few days, and it caused us some trouble in getting our supplies. We kept firing artillery at it without success because we didn't know its exact location. When we finally noticed a big rock against the hill about five hundred yards from our hideout, we put some artillery on it, and that was the last trouble we had from that cannon.

We had to go to our kitchen, about a mile back of the lines on or near the top of the hill, to get our food and carry it back it in big cans, ten gallons and larger, to our stationary troops. We would start for that chow at about eleven o'clock, and we didn't usually get more than three hundred yards from our billets before the Hun started shelling the road that we traveled. We usually halted about midway to our kitchen to rest for a few minutes and to wait for the firing to stop. One day, while we waited there, some shells started whizzing close to us. They made a wobbling noise.

We were trained to recognize that sound as a mustard gas alert, but we didn't have to put on our masks because the canisters didn't land quite close enough to expose us to the poison. We went on to get our rations, and when we returned, there was a two-hundred-pound shell, six inches long, lying under the pine tree where we had stopped to rest. It must have glanced off of the trees without hitting on the front point where the explosive trigger was located. It just didn't explode, but it could have been a time bomb, set to explode at any time, in minutes or hours. We didn't tarry long there. We had been taught what to do in such a case, and it didn't take us much time to get out of range of it. The commander sent an experienced squad of soldiers to examine it, and they determined that it was an old shell that had lost its explosive energy.

One day, when we started for our lunch, the Germans opened fire again. A six-inch shell of TNT landed in the road about three hundred yards ahead of us and formed a crater about fifteen feet in diameter and fifteen feet deep. We stopped until they cut out the firing. They were trying hard to get us—for real! Some infantrymen were billeted in a little village by the name of Paree, close to where that shell hit. One day we heard shells falling there. We soon learned that several soldiers were out in their lawn playing ball, and the enemy must have spied them. They landed a shell or two before the infantrymen had time to take cover. They shot one soldier's legs off close up. He said, "Stop the blood!" Then he fainted away. He died while they were carrying him to cover. Another soldier lost his underarm. (We heard from him three days later, and he was still living.) The shell injured six more soldiers, some critically.

They continued trying to get us at our lunchtime. Once, we were on our way to get our chow and heard the shells bang at our kitchen. It was near a little dreen behind a point, but they hit close to it. One soldier was eating his dinner with his mess kit in his lap. The shrapnel knocked a hole about an inch in diameter in it. The enemy struck an American flag up from their trench, and one of our men let loose at him. In turn, an American soldier put his helmet on a stick and pushed it above our trench. It was hit at once by a machine gun. (That was risky because he could have gotten hit by a slug or by a bullet bouncing from the helmet.)

There was a small cannon on the hill in front of us about three hundred yards from our billet. We soldiers usually camouflaged our posts, but sometimes, when things had been quiet for a day or two, a few soldiers would get a little careless, and the enemy could spy them. (The enemy had previously retreated from these trenches, and no doubt, they had maps of every foot of them and of every hideout.) We heard cannons back over the hill about two miles. (We could hear the shells before we heard the gun.) The trees began to blast apart and fall. The soldiers who were in the open jumped into the trench just in time to save themselves. A shell hit their cannon, knocking it into the trench and covering it with dirt.

One day the enemy tried his luck on our billet. They were firing six- and eight-inch cannon shells in rapid order. We were located near the hill. Their shells were coming close and landing behind us. Some flew only a few feet over us. Our shavetail Second Lieutenant Harper was standing in the lawn near our billet, and he shouted, "Soldiers, get out of here before a shell hits our billet and tears it to pieces." We beat it to our trenches.

We stayed up late that night and played cards. We joked with each other about getting killed, and we talked about where we should be buried. Someone asked who would like to be buried next to our commanding officer. One soldier spoke up and said, "Not me! I've already had enough trouble with him here." Who was going to be in heaven? They all agreed they had enough hell here, and everyone thought he deserved a place in heaven.

I asked, "Who are you? A Jap or a Chink? They believe they will go to heaven for sure if they die in battle."

The next night, I was standing guard on our camouflaged line with a rifle. (We rotated positions, with a rifle or a machine gun.) I was posted in a six-by-eight booth that was sticking out where I could see into no-man's-land. It was one or two hundred yards away from any of my soldier friends. The moon wasn't shining, and it was very dark and lonely. Some new German troops had taken over the positions opposite us, and they were young and venturesome. They were also slick and skillful in their maneuvers, and we had been warned to keep a close lookout for them. I kept quiet, listening for any maneuver they might make. They chirped like birds to let their comrades know where they were, and we didn't know enough about the local birds to distinguish which sounds were real. I heard plenty of chirping, and so did the other guards at their rifle or machine gun posts.

I had been on guard for almost an hour, and my time was almost up. (On the front lines, they didn't keep us on guard longer than that. A person might get sleepy, and we had to be very alert.) I was suddenly alerted by a rustling noise. A German had slipped up to within a bayonet's reach of me. I suppose I must have moved when he startled me, and that startled him too. He hurried away from my booth and broke into a run. I opened fire on him and emptied my rifle of six shots. I was reloading it when I got relief and was told to quit firing. I still don't know whether or not I hit that Hun, but if I didn't get him, he must have hit his old mother earth and hugged it closely. Other guards were disturbed that night, and one machine gunner released a burst of fire at the Germans.

The Hun was still disturbing us at chow time. They continued to shell our road about every morning at around eleven o'clock. One time, a six-inch shell hit pretty close by, and the shrapnel sang all around us.

We were stationed in the warm part of France before we went into those mountains, and we were stuck with our summer clothing (mostly khakis). The weather in the mountains was very rainy, and our raincoats were porous. They leaked, and we got wet. At times, it was almost cold enough to snow, and we would almost freeze when we had to stand still. We were supposed to have OD or wool clothing, but it never came. Some soldiers caught colds and pneumonia and had to go to the hospital.

One of our officers was killed while making a scouting trip across no-man's-land. He had some important maps and orders on him, and we didn't want them to fall into enemy hands. His body was on the enemy's side of the lines and up against a hill. Several of us machine gunners fired a box barrage around the lieutenant's body while the infantry rescued his remains. We fired over their heads and on each side of them so that the enemy couldn't get to our troops. (We had drilled and trained for all kinds of maneuvers with our machine guns.) By day, we could see his body and protect those maps on it, but we had to level our guns each time we fired a few blasts because they would vibrate off the target. We couldn't see him at night, so we set up stakes in front of our guns in direct line with the target and leveled our sights to fire over the stake. We lined our machine guns around the hills and fired around the body at different intervals to keep the Germans from getting to the lieutenant. To see the enemy after dark, we shot flares high into the air, and that made the night bright as day.

We got to the officer after he had lain there for eleven days. The detail of soldiers that retrieved the body did not lose even one man. The enemy didn't fire at them. A booby trap set by the enemy had killed the officer, and the electric line that electrocuted him was still touching his body. A sergeant grabbed the officer and tried to pull him loose, but the soldier got shocked and had to let loose and leave the body there. Another soldier put on a rubber suit and gloves to cut the electric line.

A few days later, we captured two German soldiers. They told our officer that we were lucky that all of the rescue detail didn't get killed. Those captives said that they had a gag on the engine that charged the line, but our troops didn't cut the live wire, and that's what saved them. The enemy had machine guns set on the soldier's body, and they intended to open fire when alerted, but our soldiers cut the dead line instead of the live one.

Machine Gun Soldiers on Alert on Western Front

I had one more exciting experience before we left the Gérardmer sector front. We were expecting trouble that night, and to prepare for it, we mounted one of our machine guns about one hundred yards back of our billets. The others were deployed in other strategic positions. It was my turn to guard the guns. I took another soldier with me, and we stationed ourselves in a ready position about one hundred yards up the hill from the field where my machine gun was previously deployed. The weather was getting cold in those five-thousand-foot mountains, and we were in a drizzling rain still wearing our summer clothing (our OD clothing still hadn't arrived). We got miserably chilly, and we had to keep still while on guard. I told my friend we would have to be very quiet, but we did talk some in low voice or whispers. We were expecting the enemy at any time.

We hadn't been posted long before we heard sticks breaking about thirty feet above us. I cracked one of my grenades and counted five. I threw it and immediately grabbed my buddy. We ran around the hill. I was afraid the grenade might roll back and explode on us. It landed a few yards up the hill, just above where I released it. We waited a few seconds, and then I told my buddy to go and alert our lieutenant. He might want to get around the enemy scouts and try to capture them. The grenade didn't explode, and the enemy slipped away quietly. I never heard another move from them. We were using some old grenades that the French had kept there for about five years. They had probably gotten wet. (Our munitions experts tried several of them the next day, and just a few exploded.) A French outfit relieved us at about midnight, and we moved out the next morning. We had been on the Gérardmer front for thirty-two days, but it seemed more like two months. We were the only Americans ever stationed on that sector. We were glad to get out of that miserable, damp, and cold place, as well as out of the danger. We had experienced many narrow escapes.

We went back to the same small town, Vagna, where we had stayed before we left for the front lines. It was great to get back to where we could have a little pleasure and rest in comfort. We drilled some and took it pretty easy for about three weeks. The weather was pretty comfortable down in the valley. (The climate there and about everywhere else we were stationed during the war was much like that we have in West Virginia.)

We needed a little exercise to keep us in shape for service, so I took my squad and gave them a few right-face, left-face, about-face, forward, and to-the-rear-march commands. We didn't expect to be there long because we thought we would soon be in a real battle, but we realized that the war was about to end. We were pressing the enemy on all fronts. General Pershing had been made commander in chief. He took over the French generals Foch and Joffre. The trouble with the French was that they moved from place to place. They would start a battle on one position and give the enemy time to fortify on another front.

General Pershing said, "We'll hit them as hard as we can on all fronts. We will not give them any rest." By that time, we had a big army of about one million American troops. After our unit had stayed at Vagna for about three weeks, we were well rested and in good shape to fight again, and we were anxious to get this war over so we could go back to God's country.

Map of Western Front, 1918

We never knew for sure just where we were going. That was a secret. The enemy might learn what was coming, and the main idea was to take them by surprise to catch them off guard as much as possible. When we finally got orders to move out, we supposed we were going to the Meuse-Argonne front, but nobody confirmed our expectations.

We left Vagna on October 26 at 2:30 a.m. We marched to Remiremont, got there at 5:00 a.m., and loaded our equipment onto the train. We boarded the train and started for the front at about 10:30 a.m., traveling up the Moselle River through Ohnil, Nancy, Toul, Cammay, and Lerouville. We got off of the train at 4:00 a.m. on October 27 and marched about fourteen miles to Belleau Woods before we pitched tents on the hillsides. We were several miles from the Hindenburg Line, where some of the heaviest fighting of the war was going on. Airplanes battled over our heads. They glided like birds below and above the clouds while firing their machine guns. Sometimes one would fall or sail to the ground.

The next day, October 28, the roads were filled with a string of ambulances carrying wounded Americans from the hard-fought battles of the Argonne Forest, where the French had fought the enemy for about four years. The Hindenburg Line was so strongly fortified that it looked impossible to tear apart, but our navy took their sixteen-inch guns off their ships and loaded them on heavy freight cars. They moved them within easy striking range of the Hindenburg Line, and on about the 29th of October, they opened up with them and let the enemy have all they had for about seventy-two hours. That was the heaviest barrage of the war. The Americans tore those heavy fortifications to shreds.

Sixteen-Inch Navy Gun Being Transported to the Battlefield

The enemy was losing on every front—so badly that they started for the Rhine River. Their men wanted to get back home before their leaders surrendered. General Hindenburg of the German army had already told Kaiser Wilhelm (or Kaiser Bill, as we called him) that he thought they were going to lose the war.

We were about thirty miles from the main action, and we could hear the battle of the Hindenburg line. There was a continual roar from the bombardment. On October 29, our unit struck tents and got ready to move to the front. We hiked on to the Argonne Forests, where we halted for a day or so. We stopped right where the German headquarters had been. It looked like a pleasure camp. They even had underground theaters there. We felt comfortably safe, but we had to be very careful about stepping on boardwalks or anywhere that the Germans could have set explosive death traps for us.

We hiked on along the Argonne Forest and crossed the Hindenburg Line. There weren't any trees left there, only a few stumps and snags. Near the lines, the devastation was about a mile wide. They had been bombarded for three or four years. We met several detachments of German prisoners. (We had captured about five thousand.) They knew they were whipped, so they surrendered to any American soldier they could. They didn't trust surrendering to any of the other allies, who might not have any mercy on them. (We were good to our prisoners, and somehow, the German soldiers must have known that.) At the last of the war, they got so they would surrender to us at any chance they had—if they could get away from their commanders.

On the thirtieth of October, we resumed our pursuit of the Hun. At about 3:00 p.m., we stopped to rest for a few minutes. During our stop near Varens, France, close behind the front lines, some of the soldiers became rowdy. Our captain in command got their attention and told them they had better rest while they had a chance. We were liable to go into action at any time, and we could be in battle for two or three days without rest. We hiked until about 11:00 p.m. We were pretty tired, almost worn down, and the rain was falling in a cold drizzle when we stopped for the night. We didn't want to lie down on a soggy wet sod of grass, but we were glad to have the opportunity to rest. We pitched our tents and laid our raincoats on the wet ground.

Our raincoats were made of cheap material, so they didn't keep us from getting wet, but we were tired enough to sleep even if we were drenched and cold.

The skies were clear, and there was a heavy frost on the ground the next morning. Several of us had rheumatism from exposure, and some of the soldiers were so disabled that they couldn't go any further. Private Bernard, a Frenchman by descent, was about forty years old. He had to be carried to the ambulance. On November 4, we continued our daily hike. When we halted for the night at about 9:00 p.m., we pitched our tents on a hill near a meadow. The officers made us pitch our tents in formation, saddling around the hill, and we couldn't lie that way in our tents. We were very tired, and we had a lot of angry soldiers! If the officer had let us, we could have pitched our tents in better positions to rest that night. After I lay down for a few minutes, my buddy rolled down against me. That annoyed us, but we were so tired that we still managed to get some sleep.

We had just got settled when orders came to break camp and get ready to move at any minute. We struck tents, rolled our packs, and loaded them on our backs. Then we fell in line, waiting for orders to move on, but that order didn't come until six o'clock the next morning. I took a chance for court-martial. I broke ranks and tried to find a place to lie down out of the mud and water. I didn't find such a place, but I did discover a bit of high ground with a clear area large enough to lie down and rest as best I could. I lay down on my pack, which was on my back, and put my arms over my eyes to keep the cold rain out of my face. I went to sleep, and I didn't hear any complaint about it. There were others who did the same.

That day, we crossed the line where the seventy-two-hour barrage had been fired. The earth was so full of craters and ditches that it looked as if there had been an earthquake. We went on through a place named Grandpré, where there had been a little town the day before. It was torn to shambles. Later, I met a soldier who had fought in that battle after they lifted the barrage. He said, "When we bayoneted a German, he would squeal like a pig." He gushed when he talked about it. This man seemed to love his job.

We hiked on to a large field where the whole Sixth Division had halted overnight. We built fires, and I don't know to this day why the command allowed us to do that. They must have thought the war was over, but it was still going on overhead. The Hun planes began to drop their bombs on us. We threw our blankets over the fires and extinguished them within a few seconds. I jumped to a big tree and hovered close to it. A bomb hit about thirty yards from me. My friend from Wallback, Edgar Rogers, was lying in a tent when that bomb hit close to him. The shrapnel went over Edgar's tent and killed another soldier four paces away. Edgar jumped up and ran for a sector of woods. We didn't build any more fires that night.

The Hun did come back during the night. We could hear his plane motoring over us, not knowing what moment a bomb would fall on us and blow us to dust. They bombed the general's place and killed his orderly. It didn't hit our general, but shrapnel from the bomb did wound him some.

On November 5, we hiked further along the road. It was muddy and sloppy and red with animal and human blood. We halted for a few minutes when we got within a few feet of our advancing front lines. The enemy was getting away as fast as they could, but they left machine gun nests behind their retreating forces, and they would open up and kill a few of our soldiers and animals. They would rather kill our horses than our soldiers. The horses pulled our artillery and machine guns and ammunition. We would joke sometimes and say, "Our commander would rather lose a soldier than a horse." When we stopped for a minute, some of the soldiers stepped out into the brush and saw a lot of American dead lying there. I didn't want to see it.

We went through a little town that the Hun had captured four years back. They had held the old people and women and children as prisoners and used them as slaves and worse! When they left, they took the able-bodied people with them and put the old people and children in a church. From the outskirts of the town, they shelled the church where they had left the helpless people. Some of our soldiers went in and saw the dead and wounded children and old people. I could hear the mourning. To hear it was enough for me! I didn't want to look. I saw a lot of dead enemy soldiers on the roads and on the battle lines, and that was enough for me. (That was fifty years ago, but it still makes me nervous to think of all the horrible things of war that I witnessed.)

The mountain roads were mined with time bombs, but we walked over them, leaving our supplies behind. We continued on after the Hun to a little village named Stoney near the town of Artrucke. The Hun had left at about noon that day. We halted there, and we got to sleep in a barn of straw and hay. This was the first and best place we had rested since October 26. We found some money and other things that the Hun had left as they got out in a hurry. We stayed there until November 6.

Our kitchen and food were lost behind us with the other supplies. Our command sent a detail after them, but it was a few days before they caught up with us. In the meantime, we had some corned beef and a few bites of bacon for rations, but the corned beef was so salty that most of the soldiers couldn't hold it on an empty stomach. We didn't have anything else to eat except a few little potatoes that the Hun had left in the ground. They had dug their crops in a hurry before they moved out. Some of us scraped up a few little potatoes and fried them with our bacon. They were really good! That was all we had eaten within about fifty hours.

We slept in the hay barn and waited for our kitchen and our outfit to get together again so we could move on to another front. We scouted around for a mile or so, but we couldn't go too far from our outfit while on duty because we might have to suddenly move on, regardless of our supplies. There was a wrecked airplane in sight of us. We went to see it, and there were two dead Frenchmen in it, but we didn't do anything about it. I suppose the French would take care of the remains.

There wasn't any fighting to mention, and we didn't need any second line at this time. The Hun were on the run and trying to get back home before they were captured. If we had captured them, they would have been prisoners of war. They realized that if they got home before surrendering, they would be freer, but we did seize most of their army and their supplies.

Our planes blew up the bridge over the Rhine River at Coblenz, and we captured all of the men and their material—about all of a division. The planes that blew the Coblenz Bridge sailed over our heads in formation while going back to base. I counted seventy some of them. That was an exciting view. We had a good idea about what they had done to our enemy before we heard the reports about it a few hours later.

We got orders to go on to the Battle of Verdun, but we were allowed to rest for seventy hours before going any further. That was welcome news. We couldn't have stood much more of that punishment. We dug about a half bushel of those little potatoes the Hun had left in the ground when they harvested their crop hurriedly before they shipped out. There were 172 men to eat them. We also found a few sugar beets and cooked them for our breakfast.

Our kitchen finally caught up with us on November 8 at about dark. Our detail had marched back thirty miles and found them and brought them to us. That slumgullion (or beef stew) certainly tasted good! All of the company of war strength (250 men) was together again.

Our next destination was Verdun, where the hardest fought battle of the war was still being waged. The English and the French were under a continuous siege there for nine months. No Americans that I know of fought at Verdun, but if our unit had got there before the armistice was signed, we would have had a turn for our first real offensive. Our commanding officer drew a map of the battle area and explained to us how Verdun was nearly lost. If the enemy had taken Verdun, they would have gone right on to Paris. At one time, they had Verdun bottled up, but they just didn't know how to put the stopper in the bottle. If they had known it, the Hun would have had it in their hands, but this was one of God's plans, just like an Israelite miracle. It wasn't destined to be in the enemy hands.

Verdun After Extensive Bombardment

Verdun was a city of about 75,000, and it had a natural fortification. It was behind a half-moon hill from the German lines and was fortified with a line of concrete and armed with heavy artillery. On the German side—or no-man's land—was a slope of land cleared for several miles. That probably saved France from losing the war before the Americans came. We had about one million men there when we won the war, and we captured most of their army and their supplies.

We left for Verdun on November 9. On our way out, for a part of the way, we moved back over the same ground we had previously been over. We went to Buzancy and stayed overnight. We aimed to take our time on this five-day hike so we would be in a physical condition to fight and try to take any line that was still held by the enemy. We pitched our tents at Buzancy, but we didn't get much rest. It was cold and damp, and everyone who was inclined to get rheumatism was stiff. We were so sore that we could hardly walk without punishing pain. Some of our soldiers had to go to the hospital from there. I too had it pretty bad, but I didn't intend to drop out, not as long as I could keep going. I told my comrades that we might as well stay with our job and finish it. A number of us felt that we would never again be of much use to ourselves or anyone else, but I wouldn't give up. I wanted to stay with my outfit and finish the war, and we knew it was about over.

On November 10, we hiked about fifteen miles and pitched tents for the night. On November 11, we moved on toward Dead Man's Hill, and we hiked until night, then we heard that the war was over. The armistice was signed at eleven o'clock that morning—on the eleventh month, eleventh day, and eleventh hour.

We shouted and sang, shot our pistols, lit flares, and set off loose ammunition that the Germans had left behind on their retreat. We really enjoyed ourselves, even though almost all of us were almost too weak to walk and we still had a five-day hike to get to Dead Man's Hill. On November 12, we resumed our hike and continued on the move, eating only two meals until we caught up with the rest of our division. That night, we pitched tents and stayed at Fleville for a good, long rest. The weather was cold, but we could now build fires, so we were much more comfortable than we had been before the armistice.

We talked about all the narrow escapes that we had experienced, but we felt that we had hardly been in any warfare. We hadn't seen any hand-to-hand combat like some of the other units had experienced. One of our soldiers shot himself in the leg, and someone accused him of doing it just so he could go home, but I believe it was just another accident. On November 13, we continued our hike and stopped in Granville. On November 14, after another long day on the move, we camped within sight of Verdun, where we relieved the Twenty-Sixth Division. (We stayed there until November 18.) Some of my outfit went immediately to the battlefield to bury dead soldiers on Dead Man's Hill.

I wanted to go with them, but I wasn't able to go on that detail until November 17. When we found a dead soldier, we would search his pockets. We found some paper money and a few coins on a few of them. (We kept it for our next party.) The chaplain would say a prayer, and we would cover the bodies with a little dirt to protect them until the French could take them to a cemetery. They were mostly French Algerians. They were about as dark as our colored soldiers. (As I have said, the Americans didn't lose any men nor enter into any battle there.)

Stripped and Shattered Trees at Verdun

We scouted around over the battlefield and picked up cartridges, grenades, guns, and other battle souvenirs. I got a German officer's spiked helmet, which I later brought home with me. This battlefield had been turned into a mess of holes. They fought so long and had such hard battles that it looked like an earthquake had hit there.

Outline map of France showing some of the towns mentioned

I picked up a German boot, and it had a leg bone in it. I didn't want that for a souvenir! On November 18, we started on a hike at 3:00 p.m. We went a few miles, pitched our in-shelter tents, and stayed overnight. On November 19, we hiked through Verdun and on to Camp Savoryards, where we stayed in some French barracks until November 22 while we got some more needed rest. Here, we had more of the French company (cooties).

Lieutenant Harper's orderly, a little Filipino, was so short that his pack almost dragged the ground. He got completely exhausted from carrying his gear, and Lieutenant Harper asked if some soldier wouldn't carry it for him. Lieutenant Harper was from Florida, and from appearance, he had been used to ordering colored people around. He was so overbearing and bigoted that no one in our outfit liked him. We called him a shavetail. He didn't get further than a second lieutenant, and I doubt that his superiors liked him any better than the enlisted soldiers did.

On that hike from Verdun to our delousing camp, we had stopped at a little town and bought some Limburger cheese, and some of our soldiers got a little too much wine. They could hardly keep up with the rest of us. We sat down to rest, and when we were ready to continue our hike, one of our sergeants refused to get up and go with us. He was pretty drunk, but any disobedience of orders by a soldier in time of war is dangerous.

I was sitting near that sergeant when Lieutenant Harper asked him to move on with us. Lieutenant Harper pulled his .45 pistol from his belt and said, "What do you want to do? Move on as ordered or lie here?"

The sergeant said, "Well, if you are that kind of man, I'll move on."

They later court-martialed the sergeant. They could have shot him, but the war was in the armistice, and they didn't want to shoot him. They declared it a mistrial and freed him. He had always been a good soldier. That was the first time I had ever been in a court, and I was glad to see the case dismissed. I think all of us had endured enough punishment to free the devil.

We got orders to go to central France, where we would camp until we could go home. There weren't enough trucks to haul everybody. The division would always look after its own men first, and we were a unit on our own just attached to a division. (The machine gun battalion was just a small unit compared with a division.) That was a sixteen-day hike, but we would have to do the best we could. On November 23, we deloused by bathing and changing clothes (all but our shoes) and then started on our long journey.

Rheims Cathedral After Years of Shelling by the Germans

Rheims Cathedral after years of shelling by the Germans

Our officers said 75 percent of us should be in the hospital instead of starting on a long hike. I started with my company, but I wasn't able to carry my pack. I had arthritis so bad that sometimes my knees would give way. I would nearly fall, but my legs didn't both collapse at the same time. I could catch myself from falling to the ground. I kept up with my company for two days, but I wasn't able to carry my pack. There was a Greek soldier by my side who was in so much pain that balls of perspiration burst out on his forehead, but he just kept marching on. I said, "We might as well take it as best we can as we will probably never be fit for anything when we do get home."

We received an order authorizing a small percent of my company to take a furlough. Naturally, everybody wanted to stay with the company. We were going right on to Brest, where we expected to catch a boat home soon after this hike was finished. We were afraid that we might have to stay indefinitely if we were left behind. The number of soldiers who wanted to take the furlough wasn't enough to fill out the quota, but I didn't think I would be able to complete the sixteen-day hike. I was hardly able to walk, so I was glad to have the opportunity to avoid it.

We waited there until eleven o'clock that night, when we caught a train going to Southern France. We traveled until the next night before reaching our destination (Ax-les-Bains, France, in the highlands of the Alps). This was a beautiful little tourist city where the kings and other rich people went for their vacations. We got off the train and hiked about six or eight blocks to our hotel, where we ate breakfast before we were shown to our rooms. We were all very tired, but we had first-class accommodations, and we felt like millionaires. We had a good shower and bath and crawled into our beds in the expensive hotel. This was the first time we had had such comforts in the eighteen months that we had been in the army. We slept until about ten o'clock the next morning and got up and ate our breakfast at a high-class restaurant. We had civilian privileges again—with all expenses paid!

We walked to different tourist attractions, and we saw where the kings and queens had lived and where they had bathed several centuries ago in hued-stone bathtubs. We saw a stone arch that had been built in the thirteenth century still standing. It was a noted gambling resort. (This was where Harry K. Thaw and Standford White had their trouble about 1912 or earlier, when White shot and killed Thaw. This crime story attracted about as much attention as some of the murder stories that we have today.) The next night, we went to a resort where we heard some good music and saw a show.

The following day, we took an elevated train to the top of Mont Blanc, France. We climbed the hill on a cog railroad. There was a gear in the center of the track and a gear on the locomotive that lifted the train by steam or electric power. It was raining in the valley when we started up the mountain, and we climbed up and up until we went through the clouds. We got off on a twelve-thousand-foot peak that had about six inches of snow on the ground. The air was very clear, and we could look out over the clouds and see peaks of mountains sticking up like islands on the ocean. We could also see Mont Blanc, Italy, several miles from us, and we saw the battlegrounds of the Bible days, where warriors rolled stones over the mountains and demolished armies.

Trouble! The next day I wasn't well, and that spoiled the pleasures of my remaining furlough. I had influenza and had to go to the hospital. This was a new disease, and the doctors didn't understand it, which made it hard to treat, and from what my doctor said, I had an unusually bad case of it. That was the beginning of the flu epidemic, the kind of epidemic that nearly always occurs in time of war. It was pretty bad in France, but not as bad as in the States. Only a very few soldiers died of it, but that was probably because we soldiers had good hospitals and doctors to take care of us at once. We had better care than the civilians in the States.

The flu killed many people in the States. Whole families died with it. My grandmother Estep died with pneumonia (I suppose, as a complication of the flu) in February 1918 while I was in France. I never got to see her again. Other members of my family at home had it, but I didn't lose any other relatives to it.

My doctor said to some of my comrades, "You soldiers may think you've had the flu, but Boggs had a real case of flu." I hemorrhaged with it, but I got better after about two weeks in the hospital. I told my doctor I thought I could make it to my company in central France.

He said, "This is a new disease, and you think you are stronger than you are." The next day, he told me to put my clothes on and walk a few blocks. I walked without watching my route very closely, and I got lost for a few blocks. When I got back to the hospital, I was about ready to faint. I stayed another day or two and then started back to rejoin my army unit. There were about five other soldiers with me. We traveled all day and into the night, when we had to change trains.

I was almost as tired as I had been on some of those long hikes, even if we didn't have bags to carry. (We shipped our baggage by freight or express from the hospital and didn't have much to carry with us.) One soldier had to go to another hospital. He couldn't make it back to his army unit. I ventured on, and the next day we made it on through the city of Dijon, where we changed trains again. We rode that locomotive about forty miles to Poinsinet, where I rejoined my army comrades.

We saw some beautiful country. France was mostly all cleared, except in the rough mountains where they grew their timber. That was pretty too, with big towering pine forests and sometimes a little green plantation of mostly pastureland with grazing cattle. We traveled along the Marne River for several miles. That was already a wide river, and now the Marne was out of banks (it had been raining a lot), but it was still clear, even at high tide. That section was all plantations, mostly grape vineyards and some grassland, and there wasn't any mud to silt the river.

I was pretty sick and tired when I got back with my battalion and reported to my sergeant. I wasn't able to stir much the next day and was sent to our infirmary to see my doctor. After checking me over, they marked me for quarters and told me to report back to them again. A soldier was sitting in my room near the door where the doctors were talking, just after I had been examined. The soldier told me that they said my heart was in pretty bad shape and that I ought to be in the hospital, but sending me there would get the other doctor into trouble for releasing me too soon.

I was ill all winter. I had chest pains while sleeping, and I would wake up screaming. That awakened my comrades. This "flu" was, no doubt, the cause of so much heart trouble thereafter. We were there (instead of going home right away) until late in May (from December 1918 to May 1919). It rained or snowed for forty-some days without missing a day. (The elements were about like we have in West Virginia, here around Charleston.) It didn't get very cold, except on a very few days.

We kept up drill practice and worked on the French roads, gathering stone and napping it into the roads. Quite a bit of the time, we worked in cold, wet weather. Some of the soldiers were so angry that they said some pretty harsh words about the French and about Uncle Sam for making us work on their roads after coming from our peaceful country and saving them from defeat in the war. We had to pay the French for every pound of stone that we napped on their roads while we used them. We would discuss it and grumble.

One day our crew was working on the road when it started snowing. We were getting wet, and I told my corporal that I wasn't able to work and that I was going in out of this miserable weather. He said, "Well, go on home, but you report to the first sergeant." I went in and found the sergeant sitting in the office by a good fire. I told him that I wasn't well and the weather was getting bad and that I didn't think it was a good idea for me to work in that miserable weather.

He said, "It's too bad for anyone to be out." He cursed those damn French and said, "Orderly, you go tell them soldiers to be getting in here to the fire." So my coming in saved our whole detail from having to stay a few more hours in that bad weather. We bathed and changed clothes, had a good warm meal, and then got ready for our beds.

Conversing, playing cards, and telling stories provided us with about all of the amusements we had. An Irishman named Ryan and I would start a sentence that rhymed. We would continue talking rhymes back and forth until we caused some amusement among the gang. We played cards a lot. Some soldiers would gamble all their pay away if they didn't win a big stake. I never gambled, and I didn't drink the French wine or the cognac. Some would go to the French saloons and get drunk. They sometimes fought with the French or among themselves until our commanding officer would stop them from going to that joint for a month or so. That hurt the French—from losing business.

Sometimes we received cigarettes and chocolate bars from the Salvation Army or the Red Cross. I didn't smoke, but I liked candy, such as it was. It was the best we could get. It was usually Hershey bars, but only half-sweetened. I ate so much of it that I don't care for chocolate flavor today.

I wrote several letters to friends and relatives in the States and some to my uncle Garee Boggs, who was in France. I also received mail from home nearly every week, usually from Aunt Florence or from a lady friend. Uncle Garee also wrote interesting letters. When they announced mail call, the soldiers rushed out to hear their names called, and when his name was called, the soldier would throw up his hand and yell, "Here!" The letter would be passed to him through the crowd. We received a few magazines to read in addition to our army newsletters. All of that reading kept down the monotony to some extent, but that was a long lonesome winter so far away from home, hoping every day that we would get orders to go back to the States.

An engineering battalion was located about five miles from our camp. Except for some of the commanding officers, they were all colored men. They kept the coloreds in a group to themselves. They were in the fighting forces for a time, but they were poorly trained for combat. When they got into battle, they got so enthused or excited that their commanders couldn't handle them. So they put them into noncombat units. These colored soldiers organized a show and invited us to see it. We all loaded on our trucks and went to see their performance. This was the only show we saw while there—from December until June. Some dressed in women's clothes. It was astonishing to watch them. They were fantastic. I had never laughed so hard as at their antics.

We stayed in French quarters during the winter of 1918, and we built a few extensions for our kitchen and mess hall. The French sold us some timber for fuel. It looked like our beech timber. When we cut a tree, we sawed it into blocks and split them. We also cut up the branches and saved every twig for fuel. We even picked up our chips, just as the French did. (They didn't lose a twig.) The ships that transported the soldiers home would bring food on their return trip now instead of war supplies, so we were fed very well! We had three meals per day.

While we were in Poinsinet, an order came for us to pass in review before General Pershing. I thought it would be nice for us to see the general of the Allied Forces before leaving the services, and the commander said that everybody that could possibly get there would have to go. I still had rheumatism and wasn't as well as a lot of the other soldiers, and I wasn't really able to make a long hike, but I was glad for the opportunity to see him. We had about a week to get ready for the parade, and we stayed on the practice field for two or three days to get back into practice. We hadn't drilled much all winter, but it wasn't much trouble to get back into the swing of it.

The parade ground was thirty miles from our station, and we had to hike the whole distance in one day. We got lined out and started early in the morning on the day before the scheduled event. With full field packs, about sixty-eight pounds, we followed the usual routine—fifty minutes of walking followed by ten minutes' rest. We stopped for an hour or so at about noon. Then we loaded our packs and started on with the rest of the division. We got to our destination at about nine o'clock that night. That was another lot of tired soldiers! We rested for about eight hours and then got ready for a big review with the whole division. We lined out in a big field and stood at ease. A few hours passed before the officers got there. Finally, our commanding officer called us to attention, but we still had to stand rigidly for an hour or so before the general and our commanding officer passed within two paces of me. It took them a long time to walk past thirty thousand soldiers. I got to see General Pershing, commander in chief of the US Forces and the Allied Forces, and I felt that this privilege was well worth all the hardships involved in getting there.

More than 2 million troops were in Europe, but a large number arrived too late to see any action. The Americans had 264,000 casualties, including about 50,500 killed in battle and about 25,000 killed by the flu.

Ira I. Boggs 1895 - 1983
Coauthor Dallas E. Boggs

I was in the Sixth Division, an old regular division. It had been General Pershing's old division. When I was first inducted into the army, General Wood was our commander in chief of the army. General Pershing took his place a little later. I was with the Seventeenth Machine Gun Battalion, attached to the Sixth Division with the Fifty-First Infantry. At that time, a fully manned war-ready division required about thirty thousand soldiers. We didn't have as many different kinds of combat troops as they do now. During the First World War, we still used horses in the Calvary Division, but we had some trucks. They used mostly horses to pull their artillery. Machine gun outfits used mules to pull the machine guns and ammunition.

Like most organizations, my division had its nicknames, but I don't think we were entitled to all of them. Because we were held off of the front lines until the last two months of the war, we were called Pershing's Pets, but we did furnish as many, or probably more, troops for the war as any other division. (Until we got to France, we were a training division, and we sent troops to other units to replace lost troops.)

We were also called the Sightseeing Division. That was natural. The first time we were on the front, we were placed where there hadn't been any fighting since the first few days of the war. That was on the border of France, Germany, and Switzerland near Mulhouse, and Gérardmer was our headquarters. (We were there for thirty-one days.) We did raise some trouble there, but I doubt if it was appropriate. We didn't accomplish much by it, just enough to cause uneasiness for the enemy. There wasn't any advantage to taking this section of the country, but we wanted some action to get the war over as soon as we could. We lost very few soldiers there. We didn't intend to make a drive for the place, but we kept some of the enemy troops tied down there. They didn't know our plans, and they had to stay alert for us. That kept them away from the front where they could do more damage to the allies.

We got ready and started on that long hike back to Poinsinet, where we stayed all winter, but we got started too late to hike all the way back before nightfall. We stopped at about halfway, pitched our pup tents, camped overnight, and got out early the next day. Our officers lined us up that morning and complimented us, and they told us what General Pershing had to say. We took a little more time on our return trip, and that made our hike easier than when going to the general review.

We played ball after the weather opened up in the spring. They formed football teams, and they competed between the companies. They had some good games. These were the first football games I had ever seen. It was of some interest to me, but I didn't know much about it. One man in my company got his leg broken. My sergeant said, "Well, he will get to go home before we do." I played some baseball. I had practiced that game before, and I understood the rules. It was a lot of amusement to me while we waited to get on our way home, but we didn't get organized very well before we moved on.

Poinsinet was a small town in central France about seventy-five miles west of Paris. This was a beautiful country of rolling hills. There were only a few people in that little farming town, and very few of them were young. About all of the French women worked during the war to relieve the men to go to the army. The people who remained in the village did a lot of farming. They raised mostly small grain such as wheat and oats. I lived upstairs in a house where a family of French people lived downstairs. There were four members of the family at home—the father and mother and two girls. One of the girls was about grown up. They were nice people, but they didn't associate much with the American soldiers.

French farmers lived in little villages. They weren't spread out like the American farmers are. Usually, the mayor of the town owned about all the land, and the people worked for him. We had bynames for some of the people around us whom we saw daily. One old farmer, Ye Ow, was always calling to his farm animals. One young woman who wasn't capable of doing work in a factory was called Cow s—.

She was silly and dirty. We got our straw for our mattresses from a barn there in town. The old people would send that silly girl to the barn with us soldiers to help and show us where to get the straw, and about every soldier in town knew her by the byname that we had given her.

The French kept their animals right in town where they lived, especially their cows and work animals—mules, horses, and work cattle (yolk or oxen cattle). They usually kept them under their dwellings. They were careless about their backyards, where there was usually a pile of manure, but they kept their barns about as clean as they did some of their homes. In spite of such appearances, the French seemed to be healthy people.

We stayed at Poinsinet until May 1919. For a homesick army of soldiers, life there was very monotonous, but we kept things as interesting as we could. We received official orders to move on, but not to go back home. We had to join the army of occupations. If you ever saw an army of discouraged soldiers, this was it! We got ready and took our hard luck as best we could. That was a soldier's life! Our unit moved out within about a week after we got those orders. I was left behind to load our mules on a train. (I was raised on a farm, and I had taken care of animals about all my life.)

We finally got on our way a day or two after the rest of our division left. We loaded our animals on a train and started to Coblenz, Germany. At times, there was some pleasure in being a soldier, especially for a person who likes to travel and see interesting sights. That was my delight. Coblenz was near a bridgehead that we blew up in the last part of the war. (That action stopped the enemy and allowed us to capture a big portion of the German forces.)

On our way to the occupation front, we passed through some of the most beautiful parts of France through level land and low rolling hills. The scenery was beautiful in the springtime, especially in the little farming sections. We stopped at Rheims for a few hours and looked at the town. It was a big city, but it was shot up pretty badly during the war. There was a fierce battle in that city, and only a few people remained—those who could find buildings here and there that weren't shot up too much to provide shelter.

The Rheims Cathedral was one of the interesting sites that we viewed. It had been a beautiful building, but it was torn up pretty badly from the results of the big battles. This building was started in the thirteenth century, and they had still been adding onto it when the war started. It towered high in comparison to the other remaining buildings around it. Before it was shot up so badly, it must have been one of the most beautiful buildings in Europe. At that time, they said that the French didn't intend to repair it. They wanted to leave it as a reminder of their enemy, Germany, but I imagine it was repaired.

Cpl. Ira I. Boggs, 1918

This was the providence of Flanders. The poppies were in a glow of red as far as you could see in all directions. This was a beautiful sight, but the graves of the casualties of war were just the opposite—no matter how straight the crosses were row by row. It made me mourn in grief, and to think that I could have been one of those among the dead. As the poem by John McCrae, a physician in the Canadian Army, goes:

In Flanders fields the poppies blow Between the crosses,
row on row, That mark our place; and in the sky The larks,
still bravely singing, fly Scarce heard amid the guns below.

We are the Dead. Short days ago
We lived, felt dawn, saw sunset glow, Loved and were
loved, and now we lie, In Flanders fields.

Take up our quarrel with the foe:
To you from failing hands we throw The torch; be yours to
hold it high. If ye break faith with us who die
We shall not sleep, though poppies grow In Flanders fields.

We moved on toward our place in the occupation forces where
we would be guarding the French and German border. (The borders
were not entirely safe, even after the armistice was drawn up and
peace was declared.) Some of our army stayed there for a few years
before we turned it all over to the French and Germans, but about all
of the soldiers who had enlisted or were drafted for the duration of
the war were back to the States within a year. Some of our soldiers
reenlisted, and they stayed until transport ships brought enough newly
enlisted men to relieve them after they had replaced the soldiers who
were to be released from the service.

We halted in a little town not far from Luxembourg or
Belgium. There we stayed for a day or two. We didn't know why
we had stopped, then we learned that our orders had changed. We
got orders to go to Le Mans, France, and wait for a boat to sail for
the States. After all of our disappointments about it, my battalion
didn't have to join the occupation forces. On May 12, we started
back the way we had come. We went back through France,
following our previous route, and we traveled through Versailles,
where the peace conference was going on. President Wilson and
some more American dignitaries were still there. Versailles is a
beautiful city just on the outskirts of Paris. It seemed more like an
American city than any city I had seen in France. We were there

for only a few hours, but we had time to see part of the city. Then we traveled through the outskirts of Paris near the Eiffel Tower.

We stopped in a freight yard in a little town for an hour or more. There was a car sitting on another track near our car, and it was loaded with barrels and kegs. Some of our soldiers said, "If you French are going to treat us like animals, we'll act like animals. Animals help themselves to what they see." They stole a ten-gallon keg of wine and hurried it into one of our cars.

By the time we moved out, almost everybody had had a drink or two and filled their canteens. When the keg was empty, they dumped the container, and it rolled over a hill. We didn't see where it went, and we didn't care much. About everyone was pretty tipsy. The keg may have hit a dwelling, but nobody cared. We didn't get along very well with the French after the war was over. Nobody felt very good toward them. It wasn't hard to start a row, especially when the soldiers were drinking wine and feeling pretty brave.

Ground That Has Been Fought Over and Churned by Explosions

We stopped in Rennes on our way to Brest, the port where we were to take a boat. Someone yelled, "The Americans won the war!" The French didn't appreciate that boasting by the American soldiers. It started a riot! Some of our soldiers got hurt pretty badly, and I heard that a Frenchman was killed. We got out of there as soon as we could. The American officers were about as responsible as anyone for this trouble. They got their share of the wine, so no one was unaccountable for our outlawry. We went on, and I never heard what the French did about our actions. They probably couldn't do much, and they were just glad that we were going home and that they were through with us.

We landed at Brest and unloaded in a soldier's camp on the outskirts of the city. We stayed there a few days while we rested and got ready to sail for the States. We received official notice that there was a ship waiting for us at the port of Brest, a ship by the name of the *Henry R. Malery*. It was considerably smaller than the *Desney Belfast*, the ship we had sailed to France on. This one was only three hundred feet long, but we were glad to get any kind of a ship back home to God's country. We got to port early the next morning. We got to see the *George Washington* in the bay there. It was the ship that had brought President Wilson to France for the peace treaty. It was a big beautiful vessel, one of the largest on the ocean. The bay was full of ships and small sailing boats about as far as we could see.

It was about dark before we finished loading and got started across the Atlantic that day, June 2. We boarded the ship and found our quarters down in the bottom level. Our bunks were spaced one over the other. I had the middle bunk. There was one under me and one over me. Our vessel finally got underway, and we were soon out of sight of land for the next twenty-one days.

For the first day or so of our voyage, we got along very well. The water was fairly calm until we were about midway across the Atlantic Ocean, then a storm came up. It was just an ordinary storm, but it didn't have to be a bad storm to rock that small boat. The waves were high enough to splash onto the deck at the bow of the ship. Everybody who was inclined to get seasick got a touch of it. I got deathly ill. If you ever get a bad dose of seasickness, you will be in such misery that you won't care much if you die. The smell of that saltwater made me more terribly miserable. I got out of my bunk to go to the restroom, but I was so sick that I nearly emptied my stomach before I got there. I had such a bad case that I was still trying to vomit after emptying all the contents of my stomach. (I had the dry heaves.) Almost everybody was ill, and the floor was so slick and slimy that we had to hold onto the bunks as we walked along. Regardless of who was sick, the boat was rocking so swiftly that anyone could fall into that mess, and a few soldiers did faint and fall.

In a day or two, we began to get over our seasickness, and we soon got hungry. Having emptied our stomachs to the limit, we had room for a big meal. This was my second voyage on the ocean, and at the time, I hoped it would be my last. One of the officers of the ship's crew also got seasick. He said he was going to try one more trip, and if he got sick on that trip, he would have to break his life's career. It's very unusual for a seasoned sailor to get seasick after getting accustomed to the rock of the boat and the scent of saltwater.

I started a casual conversation with another soldier on the boat, and I asked him where he was from. (It is customary for soldiers to inquire about where you are from, especially in my division. It was an old regular division made up of men from half or more of the states.) He was from Clendenin, West Virginia. His name is Lone Rucker. (He later returned to the gas and oil industry and has spent his life there, just as I have. After more than fifty years, I still see him sometimes when I go to Clendenin.)

We sailed on, and after we were able to eat and refill our stomachs, we started feeling pretty good. We didn't have any more high winds, so we enjoyed the rest of our voyage. Early in the morning of June 22, someone yelled, "I see land. We are entering port soon." Everybody got out on deck as soon as they could. We sure were glad to get off of that boat, especially onto our good old United States soil, and to get started on for home again!

We unloaded at New York harbor. From there, we caught a small schooner and sailed across the Hudson River to Hoboken, New Jersey. From there, we went a few miles to Camp Mead. We rested there for a few days and got ready to be mustered out of military service so we could go home. I met an old friend (Fred Summers from Wallback whom I hadn't seen for a few years) there, and we had a good visit.

I was at Camp Mead for about two weeks, resting from our sea voyage and waiting for a chance to take my final physical examination before discharge. I didn't feel too well, but I thought I would probably be okay sooner or later after I got out of the military service. Now I think that I made a mistake by not staying in a few days longer and asking for a medical disability from active service. My health didn't prove to be good, and it was nearly a year before I went back to the veteran's hospital for a checkup on my condition. (They did give me a disability rating, and the doctors decided that it was related to active service conditions. They gave me a 24 percent disability and paid me from the time I was discharged.)

I left Camp Mead and traveled to Orlando, West Virginia, where I had to wait a few hours to change trains for the final lag of my journey. At about 10:00 a.m. the next day, I got off the train at the Camp Creek railway station. None of my family was there to meet me. They weren't expecting me so soon. It took me about forty-five minutes to walk home across the hill from Camp Creek. I carried only a valise with a few clothes and toilet kit in it. I had shipped my trunk by rail.

I got within sight of the house and still didn't see anybody, and I was within one hundred yards of my home before anyone spotted me. Mother, Dad, and my sister, Ona, met me about halfway. We hugged and wiped the tears from our eyes. It was a glorious meeting. I had been gone for about twenty months, about seventeen months longer than I had heretofore been away from home at any one time, and when I left for the war, we didn't know for sure whether or not we would ever meet again on this side of heaven.

My brothers were not at home. They were working here and there. Alvah, the oldest, was the only one that was living any distance away from home. He was staying in Clendenin. By the next day, I had met all of the family. Alvah, Guy, and Cornelius were teaching a school and doing some work on the farm. I believe Ray was working for a telephone company. Glenn, the youngest of the family, was only about seven years old. We thought of him as the baby, and we all adored him. I do remember that he slept so sound that if you had to get him up (especially at midnight), you had to lead him around or watch him for a half hour or so. Otherwise, he might get out of place and wander away.

I was very nervous, and that lasted for some time after the war. While at home and convalescing, I tried as best I could to adjust myself to civilian life again, but it was pretty hard for me. I was almost as jittery as a shell-shocked person, and that made men very restless. It was hard for me to get busy, and work was getting scarce. A very bad panic was coming on, and it lasted for several years.

I didn't have enough education to do office work, and at that time, there wasn't much I could do that wasn't manual labor. We had very little machinery to take the drudgery out of work. Employment in the oil fields required some very heavy labor, but it was better for me to keep busy—if it did hurt. If I had not had the mind to work and the bodily constitution to stand it, I don't know what might have happened to me, but after about two or three years, I began to get better and more encouraged. One thing helped—my work always seemed to please my boss. Then, too, I did get enough employment to get by until I could finally work myself into a job that didn't require so much hard labor, a job where I could make a go of it.

I began to get adjusted to civilian life again, but I did miss some good friends whom I had known and lived with for two years. I did write some of them for a while, but I soon lost contact with them.

While at home, I visited a few of my relatives and friends for a few days, but I felt restless and didn't tarry long about finding a job. I hadn't seen my granddad Estep, my aunt Florence Hill and family, or my uncle Bob Estep and family, so I went across the hill and stayed there for a day or two. I missed my grandmother Estep so much; I didn't mention her because no one else did, and I didn't want to bring any sorrow to anyone. (My grandmother Boggs also died while I was in France. She died of rheumatic fever.)

We played ball some and played games at night and had a nice time. Aunt Florence was only about four years older than I. She was Mother's youngest sister and almost like a sister to me. We had lived near them for several years. We walked through the woods where I had played from the time when I was eight years old and where I had later hunted and killed rabbits, squirrels, quails, and coons. Only a few families lived in that area—about a half dozen families within a three-mile radius (in the head of the two King Shoals and Pigeon Creek). Granddad, Uncle Talty Hill, and Uncle Robert Estep farmed and logged.

Uncle Robert sawed lumber on a large sawmill at the mouth of Upper King Shoals Creek. He walked two and one-half miles to work six days a week, and then he worked ten hours per day lifting and rolling those big logs with a cane hook. People worked hard in those days for $1.25 to $1.75 per day, but that would buy more then than fifteen dollars would in 1972. People didn't need to buy much, only a very few groceries. They raised corn, wheat, oats, beans, pork, beef, potatoes, tomatoes, fruits, chickens for eggs and to eat, turkeys, guineas, and sheep. They even knitted some of their clothes. People didn't depend much on money to live on like they do today.

I stayed around home until about the first of November 1919. During the little while I was at home, we had a few get-together parties. I visited some with friends and relatives, and I associated with the girlfriend I had written to while in service. I decided that it would be best if I kept busy, so I got the scythe and started to work on the farm. Dad said, "You had better be careful, or you will get too hot. You haven't done any hard work for a while." I took my time and worked a few hours a day until I could stand to do a little more each day. There wasn't much work to be found, except on the farm.

I did find a few days of work in the oil and gas fields, such as casing oil and gas wells. I made about two dollars a day at that. That was top wages for labor. I decided to learn a trade if I was going to work in the oil and gas business. I thought I would learn to drill wells. I had to stay on the job about one month without pay to train to be a driller and learn to heat and sharpen drill bits and pound them out with a sixteen-pound sledgehammer. You had to know just how hot to make them, or you could get them too hot and ruin them, but you had to get a drill bit hot enough to hammer it into the shape you wanted. You had to learn to build a furnace and to fix the gas lines so they would blow into the furnace at a certain pressure to heat the bit. When the bit got hot enough, it would blow white-hot sparks. If you didn't get it out of the furnace soon, it would burn and ruin. Those bits were made of the best of steel. They weighed from 300 to 2,500 pounds, according to the size—from five inches to twenty inches or more.

I went to work on a well near Clendenin. Clarence Leisure was the driller, and he was the boss. I teamed up with Grant Ross, the tool dresser. (I had known Grant from the time I was a boy, and Clarence married Grant's sister, Estel. I knew her too as they were from Wallback, where I had lived from 1906 to 1911.) I could come home on the train once or twice per month. I worked there for about six weeks.

Everything began to slow down after the war ended, and the oil and gas business wasn't so good in West Virginia. I stayed around here until about October 1919 before I decided that if I was going to follow those industries, I'd better go to where there were some big producing fields and lots of work.

4

Texas

My cousin Harry Estep and I (and about four others) decided to go to Ranger, Texas, where there was a rushing field. We got together in Clendenin and boarded a train to Charleston, where we bought tickets to St. Louis. When we got there, we decided to stay for a day or so to see a big meat-packing center on the westbound bank of St. Louis. We caught a streetcar and went to the plant, where we got permission to go in. We started our tour in the building where they were butchering cattle. It was a big shed, about a hundred yards long, and there was a platform on the side, the full length of it. They drove several cattle into the narrow lane and filled it with cattle until they could hardly turn around. They had a platform about as high as the cattle's heads along the side of the pathway. A man stood on the platform holding an eight- or ten-pound sledgehammer, and when an animal turned toward him, he would hit it in the head with the hammer. It would fall and roll down the floor to a scaffold where they could hang the animal. Two or three men attached a rope to its leader with a hook on the end of it and swung it up by its hind legs. (I didn't like the looks of that. It reminded me of what I had seen in the Meuse-Argonne battlefield.)

We went on to where they were killing sheep. They drove them into a pen and tumbled them over to cut their throats. Those sheep bleated as though they knew what was going to happen to them. We continued on to where they were butchering hogs. They drove them into a little pen by a big wooden wheel about eight feet in diameter. They put a hook in the hog's leg and rolled it over the wheel. They butchered it as it went over the wheel and into a tank of scalding water while it was dying. (The law finally put a stop to this cruel way of butchering.) We went on through and watched them dress and cut the meat in shape to pack and then on into the packinghouse. We watched them strip the entrails of the animals to make weenies. They stripped the inside lining out and filled it with meat. Then they twisted it at the right length to make a hot dog or weenie.

We caught a streetcar back to town and found a hotel, where we stayed overnight. Then we got out the next morning and caught a train bound for Texas. We went down the Mississippi River and crossed over it on a long railroad trestle. This was the largest river that I had ever seen. It must be a mile wide at the place where we crossed it. We went south through Missouri and Arkansas and crossed the state line into Texas at Texarkana, a little town on the border of Arkansas and Texas. We continued through Greenville and Dallas and got off the train at Fort Worth, where we stayed overnight.

As we continued on our journey to Ranger, Texas, the next morning, we traveled through big farming sections, mostly grazing and cotton. This was the first cotton I had seen since 1918, when I was in Georgia, but it was getting late for cotton, and it was mostly all picked. There, I saw the largest herds of cattle I had ever set eyes on. Most of them were the famous longhorn cattle, and some were black polled Angus (mule heads without horns). Those long horns are dangerous to the cattle handlers, and to the other cattle too. (They have now bred cattle that don't have such long horns.)

That scenery was in the prairies of Texas. The land was almost level, with some small rolling hills. It was green and alive with vegetation, yet this was far south. It was beautiful—the Lone Star State. (But it lost its boasting rights as the biggest state when Alaska was admitted to the union.) Most of the Texans I met were nice and sociable, like most Southerners, but some are overly boastful about their state. It is one of our best farming states, and it is as wealthy as West Virginia in natural resources, especially oil and gas.

We arrived in Ranger, Texas, at three o'clock in the afternoon. We got off of the train and hunted us a hotel. That little town—about one hundred miles southwest of Fort Worth—was lively with the oil and gas business. To save expenses, my cousin Harry got us a room together. We got out the next morning and looked around the town, and we talked to several people about different oil and gas companies and their wages and working conditions. Harry soon found a job at drilling wells. (He had quite a lot of previous experience at dressing tools, and it paid good wages.) It took me another day to find something to please me.

I went to work with a casing crew. It paid a little better than tool dressing, and there was plenty of work, but the hours were irregular. Some days they worked us several hours, and others we didn't find so much to do. We had to install two strings of casing before we could rest. The contractor was paid for each string of casing we ran into a well. In the two weeks I stayed there, I made about as much money as I would have made in a month at tool dressing, but work got a little slack. So I inquired about tool-dressing jobs, and I found an employment office that was hiring. I stayed around a few hours and found a new job that suited me.

I admitted to the driller that I hadn't had too much experience in that trade. He asked, "Where are you from?" I told him that I was from West Virginia. He said, "I'm from Blue Creek, West Virginia."

I answered, "I'm from Clay County, near Clendenin." I learned that he was glad to get employees from West Virginia. The wells in our state are more difficult to drill, and he thought that anyone who could dress tools in West Virginia would be worth a chance to see what he could do. He also realized that I was a long way from home and would probably be more dependable than the local workers. Also, he felt that West Virginia men were easy to get along with and took more interest in their work.

We drove to the site about ten miles from Ranger and got there in time start the afternoon shift. The boss told me that his regular tool dresser had gone home and that he wasn't expecting him back for a month or so. He said, "I have five strings of tools, and I think I will have work for you most of the time." I realized that if he couldn't keep me busy, there would be a lot of other contractors in that area that would hire me—once I had a chance to show my worth.

I arrived at the well at about ten o'clock the next day. I looked around and met the other members of the drilling crew. Most of them were from Ohio. My boss arrived on the job at about eleven thirty. When I met him, he asked, "Where are you from?" When I told him, he replied, "I'm from Pennsylvania, from near where the Drake well was drilled, the first oil well ever to be drilled."

I said, "Yes, I have read about that job."

"I see you are considerably better equipped to drill than Mr. Drake was."

"Yes," he answered, "it took him about a year to get that well to producing. He had a lot of hard luck and had to rebuild his rig or derrick about three times, and his hole fell in several times before he got it cased in, but that became a prosperous field in about three years. They found a way to handle the gas. The drilling business made slow progress, but after so long, it has finally become one of our principal industries. It can make one a rich man overnight."

"Yes, I knew a man in the Blue Creek field who leased his few acres of land. He was a very poor man with about ten children. They drilled about three oil wells on his lease, and he got one-eighth of the oil. It brought him several thousand dollars in just a short time. I heard later that some skinner offered him a small sum for his lease, and he sold it for about one-tenth of what it was worth. He was an ignorant poor fellow, and he never had any wealth. He was proud of a little money, and he didn't get a lawyer to do his business for him. He got cheated out of it somehow when he signed the deal."

My boss said, "Boggs, you go fire your boiler and get it up about one hundred pounds of steam. We'll pull this bit out to see if we need to dress it." My boiler was about two hundred yards from the well. We had to keep it far enough away to avoid any danger of setting fire to the well when it came in. If there was a strong producer and the well was too close to the fire of the boiler where we made steam, it might catch fire and burn us and everything else nearby.

We pulled the tools out, and I got the gauge out of the tool carrier and gave it to my boss. He put the gauge on the bit and moved it around to be sure that the bit wasn't worn too much and was still round and sharp enough to run back into the well. He said, "I believe it will be okay to run it into the well at least for one more session of drilling." I slipped the ropes in place (on the bull wheel) and got ready to run the tools into the well. I pushed the bit over the well hole as soon as he lifted it off of the floor and as it was swinging close to me. He slowly released the brake from the bull wheel and started lowering the bit back into the well. He loosened the brake a little more, letting the bit drop faster. I watched the marker string that he had tied on the rope. When the marker went past the bull wheel and over the pulley wheel on top of the eighty-four-foot derrick and back down to near the ground level, I said, "It's about at the bottom of the well. I see the marker string coming down on the rope." He slowed his engine and lightened his brakes on the bull wheel. It stopped when the string was about six feet off of the floor. Then we eased the bit on down to the bottom of the well. I put the walking beam on the crank of the drilling wheel and wedged it. I drove the wedge good and tight to hold the beam to the wheel. The driller started his engine, and the wheel rolled over slowly. As the wheel turned over, the drilling rope stretched tight from the weight of the stem and the heavy bit. The walking beam went up and down each time the wheel turned over. The bit would drop about four feet onto the bottom of the well, and with the added weight of the stem (together they weighed about two thousand pounds), the bit started churning away at the bottom of the well. The driller felt the rope to see if the bit was hitting bottom. As the bit churned away, he turned the lever on the drill screw slowly to keep it hitting bottom and drilling away. Sometimes it would advance pretty fast, and at other times, the operator wouldn't turn the screw for a half hour. It progressed according to the hardness of the stone he was drilling into. Sometimes the machine would churn and churn without showing any headway.

I worked on that well near Ranger, Texas, for about a month. It was the second well in that field. The first one, about three hundred yards from the one I worked on, was a wildcat well. (That's what they call an exploratory well, one that requires a lot of risk of hitting a dry hole and ending up with nothing.) It was eight or ten miles from any other active well. It was one of the most productive holes ever drilled. It had several hundred pounds of pressure and was so strong that it blew out around the casing at the bottom. It tore a crater in the ground about one hundred feet in diameter and forty feet deep, and it threw boulders weighing several tons out of the pit. After several days of scheming and working at it, they got the well under control by just opening the valve and letting the pressure escape through the casing. They filled in around the outside of the casing with stone and cement and let it set solid. They finally piped the gas away, and that lessened the pressure by giving more volume for the gas to expand into.

One time, there was a rupture in the gas line at that well. It blew out so strong that there was a blue smoke of mist from it. We received orders that to run for our lives if this well blew out again because it could pollute the air with enough gas to catch fire from our boiler three hundred yards away. It was just by luck that the well didn't catch fire when it did blow up.

I have seen a well come in with such force that it threw gravel against the metal rig at enough speed that it caused a fire. One well five miles from the town of Ranger ignited and made enough light that people in town could read a newspaper by it. In those days, the best way available for stopping a fire at a well was to create steam pressure strong enough to cut off the gas feeding the flame. The flame didn't ignite for several feet above the outlet of the gas because the pressure was too strong for it to mix with air.

At another location near Ranger, lightning struck an oil tank that held seventy-five thousand barrels of oil, causing another big fire. They couldn't get it out. The tank was too big to steam it out. It burned for twenty-four hours or so. There was water in the bottom of the tank, and it got hot and exploded. It sent flames so high into the air that the burning oil fell back onto the ground and spread the fire near other tanks. That could have ignited all of them. I was two hundred yards from that fire when the tank exploded. A lot of men had to run for their lives, and I got plenty hot before I got out of there. I ran to a bridge and got to safety on the other side of the river. They managed to keep the fire away from the other oil tanks, which were the same size as the one that ignited. A few days later, I was talking to a girlfriend there in town. She said her father had an interest in that well and that he was so worried about his loss that he got too close to the fire and barely missed getting burned up when the tank exploded.

The boss said, "Boggs, get the walking beam down. Uncouple it and throw the cable over the bull wheel, and we will pull the tool out of the well. By the time we get it out, the relief crew will be here, and we will go home." I was running the evening shift from noon until midnight. We washed up and were soon ready to leave. I finished eating my lunch before the next crew relieved us. The shack that we went home to (where I slept) was built of rough lumber, but I didn't worry much about how it looked. We usually felt like getting right to bed after working twelve hours, and we didn't have to look at it.

When I got out at about nine o'clock the next morning, the proprietor asked me if I had slept well. I answered, "I don't often fail to sleep good. After working twelve hours, I'm tired enough to sleep." He was a rouster in the field, and his wife helped him provide us four crewmen with board and room. In my spare time of about three hours in twenty-four, I would often get my gun and shoot jackrabbits just for sport. There were a few cottontail rabbits in the area, but except during a few months of the year, they weren't good to eat in that climate. There were also a few squirrels. They lived on pecans, acorns, and a hickory nut or some kind of nut that looked about like the nut of a hickory.

When we went back to work at noon to begin our evening shift, we ran the drill into the well and drilled for about four hours, then we pulled the drill out and exchanged the bit for a sharper one. We ran the drill back into the hole and restarted the machine. I looped the rope around the middle of the dull bit and lifted it with a block. We lined it up and balanced it, and using the crane, we rolled the pulley toward the forge. There we let it down and placed the bit just a few inches off the floor of the furnace. I lit the gas and turned it up. Then I gave it a little air to make a hotter flame. In about thirty minutes, the drill bit was beginning to turn red. I watched it for about fifteen minutes longer. My boss said, "Boggs, that bit is getting about ready to hammer out."

I hooked the crane onto the cable that I had looped around the drill bit, and we pulled it up with the block and line. I swung it around and placed it on an anvil in a position to hammer it. I picked up my sixteen-pound sledgehammer and handed my boss his. We went to work on that bit while it was red-hot. We pounded it about as long as we had enough breath to hammer. By the time we turned it over and began to hammer again, it had cooled enough that we had to put it into the furnace and reheated it good and red. We pulled it out and began to hammer it again. We stopped pounding it while I handed the drill gauge to the boss. He put it on the bit and measured it. We had to hammer it in shape to fit that gauge so it would make a round hole that fit the casing pipe. If it wasn't exactly right, it might drill a crooked hole and foul our tools. We let the bit cool just a little more. Then I picked it up with the block and line and swung it around into a tub of water to temper it for that hard stone.

That hammering limbered me up, but a little more of it might have limbered me down! Yes, but that hard work made my muscles strong, and I felt like eating those good country-style meals our cook prepared for us. Yes, they sure were delicious! That's one thing that a laboring man can enjoy better than one that doesn't work enough to have a good appetite. Yes, and we poor people don't worry over losing millions of dollars.

We came back the next day and drilled for a few hours, then we pulled our tools out of the hole and examined the bit. It was getting dull and out of proper shape. We pulled it off of the stem and screwed the other bit on. We ran it back into the hole and started to drill again. The sharp bit cut pretty fast, and we made more progress than usual. Bill said, "We must have done a good job sharpening that bit, or else we have struck a softer stone." We left the dull bit for the other crew to sharpen. It was their turn because we had dressed the one before that.

Bill said, "Boggs, I hate to tell you, but Blake will be back tomorrow, and I suppose the field boss will take you back to the office and put you to work on the yard until he has another place for you on a well. I don't like Blake. I think he's a crook. The reason he was off is that he had to go to Oklahoma to stand trial for stealing a horse. He will have to go to jail if they find him guilty. I hear the trial was postponed." Bill was an hard-boiled ole Pennsylvanian, but I got along fine with him. He realized that I was new at drilling but that I was willing to try hard to do things right.

The field foreman came out with Mr. Blake the next day and said, "Boggs, I don't have a job for you on a well right now. I can get you a job on the yard until I have something on a well for you. I can't tell you when that will be, but likely in a few days. They don't pay so much on the yard, but you will only work eight hours." It didn't hurt me to have easier work for a few days. Until I started the drilling job, I hadn't done any hard labor for some time, and I needed to taper off a bit.

When I went to the new job, Mr. Easterly, the field foreman, introduced me to the yard boss, Mr. Gray. He told Mr. Gray that he would like for him to furnish work for me until he could use me again. "Yes, I think I can use him."

"Boggs, you hunt for you a boardinghouse. I'll allow you a day for today. You can come back tomorrow at 8:00 a.m., and start work for Mr. Gray. I think you will find him to be a fine man. I always have."

I had about all day, so I decided to see if I couldn't find a private home to board at. I left my suitcase in town and started down the street. I told some people whom I met on the street that I was looking for a place to live and that I would rather stay in a private home. "Well," one of the men said, "my wife may have room for you. Get in my car, and we'll run down the street a few blocks and see." He drove about five or six blocks and stopped. He said, "Get out and come in, and I'll talk with my wife." He told me to have a seat in the living room, and he would talk to his wife about the circumstances. In a few minutes he and his wife came back.

She said, "All my rooms are occupied, but I have a large room that you can share with another nice young man. If that will please you, I'll put another bed in there."

I said, "I think I can get along fine with the young man if he doesn't care to have me in the room with him."

She replied, "I think that will just suit him fine."

I said, "I left my suitcase in town. I will go get it."

Mr. Langford, the proprietor, said, "Get back in my car. I'll go with you and bring you back."

We drove to the train station where I had left my baggage, and we picked it up. Mr. Langford asked, "Where will you be working?"

I answered, "For the Mid-Kansas Oil and Gas Company—in the yard."

He said, "That's where I work."

I told him I didn't know how long I would be there as I was a well worker or a tool dresser and would be there for only a few days until they had another assignment for me. I said, "I hope I can still stay in town when they do find me a well job."

He asked, "Where are you from, Mr. Boggs?" When I told him, he replied, "Well, you are a long ways from home. I've always lived near here in Texas. I never was in West Virginia or further east than Mississippi."

I said, "I never was out of my state until I went to the army in 1917."

He said, "I didn't get into the service. I had a family and was thirty-eight when the war broke out. Did you go across?"

"I was in France for a year."

"How did you make out? Did you see action?"

"Yes, I was in the Meuse-Argonne Offensive, but I didn't get a scratch. I guess I was lucky. I was in the service for two years, but I didn't see much action."

"I'll show you your room, and we'll have you a bed by night. Have you had dinner?"

"Yes, I ate a lunch up town just before I met you."

"Have a seat. Here're some magazines you may read—and the daily paper." I thanked him and read the morning paper. Then I walked around town for a few hours.

I walked to the yard where I would work the next day and looked it over. My boss showed me around and told me about the work. "You have a big yard here. You must do a lot of business."

"Yes, we have all sizes of pipe and casing, pipe fittings, drilling machinery, boilers, rig timber, tools, or anything that goes with the oil business." I walked back to my boarding place and slipped in as though I was already at home. That's what I like about staying at a private residence. It's more like home to you, especially where you are treated as one of the family. These were nice Southern people and much more sociable than the Northern people.

My roommate came in from work, and Mr. Langford introduced us. I found him to be as the missus had told me. He was a few years younger than I and as nice a man as I have ever met. His name was Earnest Schmidt. His father was born in Germany. We ate supper and then walked up town and went to a movie. We came back and went to bed. I asked, "Where do you work?"

"I work for the Lincoln Tank Company. I build steel and wooden tanks in the fields for oil storage."

"I work for the Mid-Kansas Oil and Gas Company. Dressing tools on a drilling well is my regular occupation, but I will be working in the supply yard for a few days until I can get onto a new project. These fields seem to be diminishing somewhat. I don't know whether it's for lack of exploring for more oil and gas or the lack of business to sell it. I rather think that it's a lack of sales. The war is over and there is a scarcity of business."

I got up the next morning, ate breakfast, and went to my new job. I worked in the supply room sorting pipefittings and placing them in the bins. There were about ten people working there, not including the office force. I continued at this work for a day or two. For some reason, the crane operator had to be off from his job for a few days. Mr. Gray, the boss, asked me if I had ever operated a crane. I said, "No."

He said, "I would like for you to unload some pipe from a railroad car."

"Well, if you can't find anyone, I might as well see if I can learn to operate it."

I said, "You had better keep everybody out of the way. I might hurt someone."

I started the gasoline engine and took hold of the throttle. I ran it for a few minutes to learn how it worked. I operated a lever and the throttle with my hands and worked the brake pedal with my foot. I said, "Hook the rope to the pipe and get out of the way—well into the clear." I swung the crane over to see what I could do with the machine. My helper fastened a hook to a steel line attached to each end of the pipe. The hook was on a cable that ran to a block and pulley at the top of the crane. I threw the lever that operated the spool and carefully started it to rolling. I raised the pipe up over the freight car and put my foot on the brake, then I reversed the lever and swung the beam out over the pipe rack. I loosened the pressure of my foot on the brake pedal and eased the load down onto the rack.

My helper released the hooks from the ends of the pipe. I worked my lever and my brake, and after a half day or so, I could operate the crane pretty well. We soon got the pipe out of that car onto the rack. I worked there for about two weeks before the field foreman came after me to work for Bill Kennedy again. (I don't know what became of Mr. Blake. I didn't ask, and I don't suppose that Bill thought enough of him to tell me. But I guess that he just returned home and wouldn't be coming back.)

We went to work on the usual shift—from noon until midnight. I worked there until the well was drilled in. It was a strong producer, but it didn't blow up or cause any trouble. Probably the neighboring seventy-two-million-foot-per-day gas well took the pressure off of the new well. The two wells were only about three hundred yards apart. We ran a string of casing into the well and screwed a six-inch valve onto the head of it. We closed the valve and turned it over to the field foreman. His crew laid a pipeline to it, and it was another productive well.

We started taking our tools down from the derrick. Bill said to me, "Boggs, you take a line up to the top of the derrick and tie about three half hitches around the stem and to the drill line. I'll pull it up just enough for you to unhook the stem from the block." I had never done anything like that before! I climbed up the eighty-four-foot rig and swung around inside of it. I locked my legs around a board on the rig and held to it until I got the tie on the drill stem. I told Bill to tighten the rope with a gentle pull. He started the engine and gave it a try. It tightened and held fast until I got the drill stem uncoupled from the blocks. Bill said, "Come on down, and we will take it down." I took the bit and swung it to the far corner of the rig as far as I could. Bill eased it down as I took a rod and kept pushing the end of the drill stem outward while he leaned the other end to the far side of the rig. We soon had it on the floor. "Well," Bill observed, "you did that as well as anyone could." I had been afraid that the knot would slip and let it drop, but it held fast.

Bill told me to turn the fire out in the boiler and to let the steam run down. He said, "Leave on just enough gas burn to keep it from freezing." (That didn't often happen this far south, but we didn't take any chances on bursting a boiler by letting it freeze.) Then he commented, "I don't know what we will do now. The boss said he didn't have another location to move to, and business is slowing down considerably. Boggs, you go back to the yard. I'll give you an extra day to make up your mind."

I replied, "I can't afford to stay there at four dollars per day, not if I can get twelve at drilling wells."

I went back to work on the yard and jimmied around at just what they had for me to do. Business was slow there also, and they too were laying men off. I worked there and looked for a drilling job in my spare time. After about week, I still hadn't found anything to suit me. That weekend, I was in town and met the superintendent.

He said, "I have a clean-out job for you and Bill. Come to my office Monday morning, and I'll take you to it. It pays the same as for drilling, and it will be day work."

I met the supervisor on Monday morning, and he took me to the well. He said, "Boggs, you had just as well stay with this company. We don't pay quite as much as some other corporations, but I think you will find us about as good as anyone to work for. We have better working conditions than some companies, and we won't lay a man off unless we have good reasons for it. There isn't any reason for skipping about just for a few more cents on the day."

Bill and I rigged up our tools, and we were ready to get something done by noon. Bill said, "Boggs, did you ever run a gas engine?"

I said, "No, I never had anything to do with one."

"I haven't either, but it's up to us to try. We will do what we can." We got rigged up and were ready to start cleaning out the hole. Charley Easterly, our main supervisor, came by at about that time. Bill said, "Charley, I never had anything to do with a gas engine."

Charley said, "I'll show you what I can about it. See that your spark plug is working right, just as you would on your automobile. This engine runs on natural gas, not gasoline, but it works on the same principle as a gasoline engine. The ole Ajax engines are powerful. That's what it takes to handle those heavy tools." We examined our spark and ignition and got ready. Charley set his foot on the flywheel spoke in a safe position, and then he took hold of the wheel. "Now you will have to just get enough of your foot on this spoke that it will slip off when the wheel rolls over. If you don't hold it right, it will throw you like a bullet." Charley started the engine just to show us how. Then he shut the gas off and had Bill start it. Then he told me to start it up. "You will have to be sure you don't get that big foot of yours in a position where it won't slip off the wheel when the engine starts. One time, we missed a pumper, and then we found him dead. He had tried to start an engine, and it threw him thirty feet. His head hit a pipe, and I don't suppose he ever knew what happened."

Charley, Bill, and I finally got rigged up and started things to rolling. "I'll see if I can hook the cable to the bailer." I looked at it, and there wasn't any link on top of it. Charley had already left for another location. "Well, the Dickens," said Bill. (He was pretty wicked and didn't care to rip out a big ugly oath.) "What's the matter, Boggs? Can't you swear some too?"

"Bill, I never swore but once in my life, and that was when I was about thirteen years old. My chum backed me out or dared me to swear. He said, 'I will if you will.' I said, 'You cut down on it. I don't take a dare.' He ripped out a big black oath, and I tried it. I have never felt so ornery in all my life. I've never cursed since."

Bill said, "We'll have to solder a link onto the bailer. I'll get the ladle and put a few pounds of lead in it." We built a fire to melt the lead, and we screwed the head up on the bailer and put a link in it. Then we poured the lead in it. The bailer wasn't as heavy as a drill and stem, so we were able to handle it without much trouble. We had to let the lead cool overnight, so we didn't get any well work done until the next day.

We came back the next morning and hooked our bailer to our bailing line. I gave that flywheel a turn or two, and it started. Bill turned the throttle a little and threw the clutch in. I released the brake on the bull wheel, swung the bailer off of the floor, and started it up the derrick. I guided it over the casing while Bill operated the clutch. We bailed water from that well for the rest of that day and all of the next day.

The engine would slow down when the bailer got near the top of the well. At times, it would stop if Bill didn't shut the throttle off on time. Bill said, "Boggs, you tell me when you think the engine is about to chug to a stop, and I'll throw the throttle out to make the engine go faster to pull the bailer on out. Then I'll throw it back in." We soon caught onto the tricks of the trade. From then on, we let our engine start fast, and we didn't have any more trouble with it.

Within a few days, we had bailed the water out of the well and found the leak. It was near the bottom of the casing. It was leaking so fast that it took us three days to get the water level down to the leak. We could hear the gushing noise when the bailer hit the water. About all we could do was to pull the casing and replace the joint that was leaking.

"Bill, do you think that ole Ajax engine will be strong enough to pull that casing?"

"Yes, since we have learned to operate it, I think we can arrange that. You see, we will have Charley bring us a heavy triple block to hang at the top of the derrick. We can use this double block to hook to the casing, and that ole Ajax will haul it right out."

Bill commented, "What's worrying me is, Will this old derrick stand the weight of the casing?"

"There is quite a strain on it. This well is twenty-five hundred feet deep. I don't know just how far down this casing goes. We'll have Charley bring the logbook. It will tell us almost everything about the well—how deep it is, what kind of sand the drill went through, how many barrels of oil it produced when it was freshly drilled, just what grade of oil it produces, and I imagine, who drilled it. The logbook contains a lot of information about the well that the company won't tell just anyone."

The chief, Mr. Easterly, came around the next morning with a triple block that weighed about three hundred pounds. Bill said, "You take the single block about forty feet further out on the walk. We will unwind enough of the rope from the bull wheel, and then we'll unlatch the blocks."

"Did you ever thread a double or triple block, Boggs?"

"I've helped to thread one or two. I know you have to be careful. If you get the ropes into any position where they will cross, they just won't work. I think we can handle this job okay. You put the single or double to the bottom of the derrick to hook to the pipe, and the double block goes to the shaft on top of the derrick. That gives you more leverage. Yes, that would be enough power to pull this derrick down. I have heard of the likes of that happening."

We got our blocks threaded, and Bill said, "Boggs, tie a half hitch, or a square knot, around the block and another half hitch about the rope. Then we will have things as ready for the casing crew as we can get them."

We couldn't find a casing crew. There wasn't enough drilling going to occupy a crew. Charley said, "I think I can find enough men in our field crew that have enough experience to help you."

"Okay." We couldn't do any more that day, so we went home at about noon.

We came out the next morning and waited until about ten o'clock, when Charley came with a new crew and tools. Bill said, "Boggs, hook that line to the block and take one of these men with you to the top of the derrick. I'll pull it up, and you two can slip the shaft through the hook in the block. In a few minutes, we will be ready to pull casing."

In addition to Bill and me, we had six men. I asked those men what duties they usually did at casing. We were soon lined out and started our different jobs. One of the men took the front truck to one end of the pipe, and the other crewman took the rear truck to the other end. Two handled the heavy calipers to latch under the collar of the casing, and the other two handled the pipe, or tongs, that unscrewed the casing. I hooked the block onto the calipers. Bill tightened the rope and gave it a pull, easy at first, to loosen the casing from the hole. We must have worked at it for four or five hours. Bill kept pulling at it and slacking off, trying to work it loose from the wall of the well. He kept pulling a little heavier each time. He pulled so hard that I thought that derrick was going to collapse, but the casing finally worked loose, and we got one joint out of the well.

Bill said, "Boys, throw that other caliper under the collar, and we will see if we can get the tongs on that joint to pull it." They threw on the calipers and latched them. Then they attached two pairs of tongs to the pipe. All six of the casing crew gave it a pull, but the pipe wouldn't turn. Bill said, "Try this heavy pair of tongs, and I'll hook this ole Ajax engine to it. That'll either break it loose or cave the pipe in." He gave it a pull, and it started to loosen up. We soon had it out and on the rack. I hooked the block to the next one, and so on. "Put that rope with the clamp on one end and a loop on the other on this joint and wrap it three or four times around the pipe. Then put that eight-foot hickory pole through the loop and draw it tight. Then I'll take this three-pound hammer and pound the top of the collar while you six men push on the pole. I believe it will break. Then we can swing the pole around and have the joint out in a couple of minutes."

We worked there until about six o'clock, and we still had only about half of the casing out. Bill said, "Men, it will take us until after midnight to get all of this pipe out. When we start a casing job, we usually finish it before we stop, but we're not in a hurry for this old well to produce. It has about served its time." We threw the calipers onto the next joint and fastened the latch. We locked it so no one could kick it loose and drop the string of casing back into the well.

The next morning, we returned to that job at seven thirty. By 3:00 p.m., we had pulled one hundred joints of casing out of the well. We found the leak in the pipe that had allowed water to fill the well and shut off the oil. Bill said, "There are about twenty-five more joints still in the well. We had better pull the rest of it and put a new shoe on the bottom joint to seal the water off. The old one was not the cause of the leak, but it probably won't last more than two more years. If we don't put a new shoe on it, the pipe might have to be pulled again by that time."

Before we went home at 7:00 p.m., we had the entire casing out of the well and on the rack. The next day, Bill and I got ready to run the casing back into the well. Charley came out and inspected it. He said, "I'll have about twenty-five joints of good casing brought out today. I imagine we will find that many that won't be in shape to run back in. That saltwater is pretty hard on casing. It soon eats holes through the metal." Bill and I didn't have much work to do that day, but we stuck around and got our tools and the blocks and all of the good casing ready to start relining the well. Charley got the pipe delivered that day, and we showed the truck drivers where to unload it. Charley said, "I'll send the casing crew out in the morning, and you can start running the casing back into the well. Run the new casing in first and sort out the best of the other to finish the job. I'll send out an extra man—one that knows how to sort the pipe. I'll have him out here by ten o'clock. The crew can stab those twenty-five new joints into the well before he gets here."

The next morning, we started work at nine o'clock, and we had those twenty-five joints in the well by eleven thirty. By then, the expert inspector had graded some of the pipes, and the good ones were ready in time for us to go ahead with the job. I said, "Bill, those men sure know how to get that casing in the well, and they are doing a fine job. Everything worth doing is worth doing well, and that's the way they are doing it."

Bill answered, "I like to encourage men. That keeps up their interest and spirit to make our job more pleasant. That sure is a jolly crew, and that's what makes the wheel go around smoothly."

"That shoe we put on the bottom of that first joint won't wear out scrubbing the wall going down, will it, Bill?"

"No, it's spongy inside that solid rubber. It will fit the hole loosely on the way down. Within a few hours after we put it in the well, it will swell and tighten against the wall of the well. It will do the job."

We had all but about thirty-five joints into the well by five o'clock. Before it got late, Charley came out to see how we were getting along with this string of casing. He said, "Men, it isn't very safe to leave a string of casing hanging above the bottom of the well. Go ahead and run this in, and I'll have that country cook fix you a good meal. We'll have it out here in about an hour and a half, and I'll see that you get extra pay for overtime. We will have this work finished by midnight."

Charley sent a man to tell the cook. She had to go to town and get some groceries, but she soon had some of that good ole solid grub ready for our hungry crew of strong laboring men. I said, "Charley, get you a plate and some of those eating tools and have some of that food."

Charley said, "I'm not hungry, but a man don't need to be hungry to eat that food."

We finished our lunch and went back to work feeling fresh and strong. We got our job done a few minutes before midnight. Charley said, "I'll have men out at about noon tomorrow. They will help you clean up here. Bill, you and Boggs can bale the well out. After you get all of the water out, you may test it the next day. If you don't find more water in it, you can rig up and drill down to its old level. Bale it out good and clean. If it doesn't produce oil soon, we will see what we can do for it." We worked on it for three days to get it in good shape, and we left it undisturbed for a while to see if was producing any oil.

We came out the next day and ran our bailer into the well. When we pulled it out, the bucket was full of oil. We got about ten bailers full of oil out of the well. Mr. Easterly said, "It ought to produce more oil than that. I'll send the shooting crew out tomorrow, and we will try a light shot of glycerin. That might help it to produce. There's a gas well right over there a half mile or so. We're right between the oil and gas fields." The next day, they gave it about two quarts of glycerin. That shook it up a little. Bill and

I cleaned it out, and it started producing, but not strong enough to flow.

Charley said, "I'll send a string of two-inch pipe tomorrow and two or three men to help you and Boggs run it. We'll run pumping rods into the well, and it may make enough oil to pay off." After a few days, we finished putting in the two-inch pipe and ran the pumping rods into it. We started up that ole walking beam, and it proved to be a very good well. It produced about thirty barrels per day.

I commented, "Bill, I don't like this cleaning out job as well as I like drilling a new well."

Bill answered, "I don't either. I'd rather make something new anytime than to repair something old."

"Yes," I said, "I like to run a good sharp bit into a well and hear it hit the bottom." When it rings like a church bell for a few licks, we can run some drilling fluid into it. Then we can hear it chug and slush. When we pull the bit out and run the bailer into the well, we can bail it out good and clean. I like to see that white sand run into the waste pond. And when you feel that you are getting near the pay sand and hit a little gas, you feel excited about the prospects. You watch for your drill to blow out of the top or for the derrick to blow off. It's a little scary and dangerous, but when you drill a well like that, you can feel that you have really done something worthwhile. It's really exciting at times. Drilling is like coal mining. Once you get it in your blood, it's hard to get away from it."

I liked to sit around the employment office and hear those older drillers tell their exciting stories about drilling and about how near they nearly met their doom. Yes! That makes me think of when I was about eighteen and was helping on clean out a well. (I had forgotten about this incident until I got into a conversation with James Williams, who was standing next to me.) The driller was trying to break a string of casing loose so he could pull it out of the well. He had the brake rod up and fastened and was throwing the throttle of his engine back and forth, churning and jerking with all the power of his engine. He had a two-inch pipe on the brake lever, and it was hung up. He gave a surge on that bull wheel and caused about a two-ton jerk. The two-inch pipe came unlatched, and it didn't miss my head more than an inch. James was standing almost as close to it as I was. If it had hit either of us, we never would have known we had been hit.

Another time, I was working on a well about five miles from the one Bill and I cleaned out. It had just come in, and it was gushing oil at a high pressure. Eight or ten of us were trying to get the well under control. It was spurting oil to the top of the derrick. One of the stockholders was standing by, and he got so excited about getting rich overnight that he pulled out a big cigar. He was reaching for a match when one of the crew members noticed him and knocked the match from his hand. If he had lit that match, that place would have exploded over an area of one hundred and fifty yards in diameter. That's one time I felt proud that I never smoked. That fellow nearly fainted, and he left there in a hurry. The gusher made so much noise that you couldn't hear anyone talk for a long distance from the well. The oil and gas oil spewed all around. We got that well clamped in, and after we laid two four-inch lines and hooked them up to the oil tank, it flowed with such strength that those two four-inch lines jumped and rocked until it looked like they would break.

Bill said to me, "We're done with this well." Charley left without saying what we would do next. We returned to the site the next day and stayed there until about 2:00 p.m. before Charley showed up. He said, "Bill, I have just started a well about three miles out from Ranger. The driller and the tool dresser want to go home to West Virginia for a vacation. They will be gone for about two weeks. I want you and Boggs to take over until they come back."

When we got to the well, we learned that they had just spudded in. The stem wasn't underground.

"Oh!" I said, "that's a twenty-inch bit. I never saw a bit that large. We never use a bit larger than ten or twelve inches in West Virginia."

All we had to do was to rev up that ole Ajax engine and start drilling. I set up the walking beam and wedged it tight to the crankshaft. Bill cranked up the engine, and we were off—*chuggety-chug-chug*. I let in a little water, and Bill opened up the throttle. That one-thousand-pound bit went down into that soft dirt and stone in a hurry. We drilled fifty feet before our relief crew came out. (Bill and I were on the morning. We worked from midnight until noon.)

We went to town, and Bill put up at a hotel. I went back to my old boarding and rooming house—Mr. Langford's. They took me in, and I learned that Earnest Schmidt was still staying in the room where we were partners before. I was tired. I crawled in bed and was soon asleep. I got up at about 6:00 p.m., and Earnest and I went uptown. We just gadded about for a little while and came back. I sat in the living room and talked with the folks until about nine thirty. There was only Mr. and Mrs. Langford and a niece they were raising or had raised. She was about eighteen. They didn't have any children. There was another young man boarding there. His name was Hue Moore. I hadn't met him on my previous stay, but we soon got acquainted. He was a nice young man. He was from Texas too. Earnest, Hue, and I pulled together most of the time. Hue lived at Fort Worth, and Ernest lived at Clyde, Texas, about twelve miles from Ranger. Miss Little, the young lady Mr. and Mrs. Langford raised, worked at the post office. She had a friend, Miss Wilson, who worked with her. Miss Wilson was from Tennessee. She had a brother who lived in Ranger, and she stayed with him most of the time. She chummed with Miss Little, and I saw her quite often at the boardinghouse and around town. We soon got acquainted.

I went to bed for a little rest. I got up at eleven o'clock, and Bill soon drove by and picked me up. We went to the well and relieved the crew. We drilled until about 6:00 a.m., when we pulled that big twenty-inch drill out to change the bit. I said, "Boy, that's a monster!" I hadn't seen a bit so large. I lit the furnace, and Bill helped me get the bit into it. It took a hot blast of fire to heat that big bit! We got it set where we wanted it, and I increased the gas pressure. It took about an hour to get it good and hot through and through. I kept my eye on it pretty well. Sparks started flying off of it, and I noticed that it was getting white hot. I said, "Bill, I believe this bit is about ready for the hammer."

Before we placed the hot bit on the anvil, I had taken the walking beam off of the crankshaft and replaced it with a rod that was about four inches thick and about eight feet long. They called it a ram. I said,

"Bill, show me how to use it." I got hold of the end of the ram and guided it to the bit. Bill started the engine slowly. Every time the crank turned over, the ram crashed onto the big bit. We soon shaped it as much as we could before it got too cold to pound anymore, then we put it back in the furnace and heated it again. We got it white hot and set it back on the anvil. We got our sixteen-pound sledgehammers and used them to finish shaping it up to fit the gauge. That was the first time I ever used a ram. (In West Virginia, we never had a bit so large as that one.) I put the walking beam back on the crank, and Bill started drilling again. I put the bit back in the fire and heated it hot enough to temper, then I pulled it out and eased it into a tub of water.

We drilled until our relief crew came out and relieved us at noon. We decided we were deep enough to run some casing, so our relief got everything ready for us to run the casing the next day. Jack, the other driller, said, "If we don't get this casing in tomorrow, we will have to work on Sunday." (We couldn't chance letting the dirt wall of the well cave in.)

"Yes," I answered, "I like to have one day off per week, especially when I have to work twelve hours in twenty-four."

It took only about three hours for the other drilling crew to get ready to run the casing. They went home early, and all of us came out the next morning. By two o'clock on Saturday afternoon, the four of us had that big twenty-inch casing into the well. Jack and George, the other drill crew, didn't have much time to rest. They had to be back on Sunday night at midnight. We were scheduled to trade shifts, and Bill and I wouldn't have to come back until midday on Monday. I went to my boardinghouse, changed clothes, took a bath, and got cleaned up. Then I walked up town and wandered around until suppertime. When I returned to the boardinghouse, Earnest and Hue were there. We ate supper and then got into Earnest's Ford Model T and drove uptown. Hue walked up the street, and Earnie and I went into a restaurant for a Coke.

I asked Earnest, "What do you have in mind?"

"Let's go up to the post office and see when the girls will get off from work." We agreed to see if we could slip in and get a chance to see one of them. Miss Wilson was at the window handing out mail. I walked up as though I was there to inquire for mail. When I had a chance to see Miss Wilson for a few seconds without her boss noticing me, I asked her about arranging a double date for Earnest and me with her and Miss Little.

She said, "We will have to work late tonight. I'll come home with Miss Little, and we will see you in the morning." I saw Earnest, and we walked about town for a while. Then we went home and sat around and played the radio until about ten o'clock.

Earnest said, "Let's call the girls and see if they are ready to quit. We will drive up to the post office and pick them up."

"Okay." I called, and Miss Wilson came to the phone.

"Yes, we will be ready to leave in about thirty minutes." We picked them up and went to a cafeteria. We got a snack and then drove around a few blocks before we took the girls home. We returned to the boardinghouse and played a few games of rook before going to bed. I sure was glad to get a full night's sleep instead of having to get out at midnight and go to work.

We were all up by nine or ten o'clock the next morning. After breakfast, we got into Earnest's car and drove a few blocks. Earnest said, "I should go home today. How about driving down to Clyde with me? It's only about twelve miles." All of us, including the ladies, were pleased to go. We started that way and drove for about forty-five minutes. It was mostly dirt road.

I asked, "How fast will this car run, Earnest?"

"It's geared for about sixty miles per hour." We got onto about a mile or two of straight road, and Earnest sped up to about forty mile miles per hour. That was too fast! (The speed limit was thirty-five miles per hour) That Ford motor was buzzing! That was the fastest any of us had ever ridden in a car.

When we reached Earnest's home, all of us got out and went in to meet Earnest's family. They were nice people. We walked around on Mr. Schmidt's farm, and we gathered a few nuts from his pecan grove. I complimented Earnest's farm and home. His father had a few longhorn cattle, but he wasn't a big farmer.

We didn't stay there long. We were on our way and back in Ranger at about six o'clock. We went to a movie show that evening and then had a game or two of rook. I talked with Miss Wilson for a while before going to bed to get ready for six days of twelve-hour shifts at that well.

I got up late the next morning. Everyone else had gone to work, but I didn't go to work until noon. I ate my dinner and got my lunch pail ready. Bill came by, and we went to relieve the other crew. They had rigged up from the casing job and were drilling again. After running that twenty-inch casing, they started using a ten-inch bit. That suited me fine. Those big twenty-inch bits were hard to handle.

Bill and I worked there that week until the regular crew came back from vacation. Bill was now out of work for me. I decided to go back to the yard and try it for a few days. It wasn't such a bad job. I got a little more money (for running the crane), and it was eight-hour days. I told Bill that I didn't think I would be there for more than a week or so, if I didn't get on another well drilling job. Bill said he hadn't been back to Pennsylvania for about three years, and he might go home to see his folks. I saw Bill in town a few days later. He said he had decided to go home and spend a month or so. I bid him good-bye and wished him a pleasant vacation. (I never saw Bill again.)

I stuck around the yard for about two weeks before I decided it was time for me to hunt for a better job. I continued to work on the yard, and in my spare time, I looked for a tool-dressing job on a well, but I didn't find one. Business was getting very slack. My friend, Earnest Schmidt, said he thought he could get me a job with him. He saw his boss, and he said I could come out on Monday morning. I went out to the yard the next day and told my boss that I wouldn't be back after the weekend. I went to work with Earnest's employer—building steel and wooden tanks. That paid me two dollars more per day than the yard paid, so I bid the Mid Kansas Company people good-bye.

I continued to board with the Langfords, and I rode to work with Earnie. I had grown to like those fine people, and they almost recognized me as one of the family. It was just like a home to me. They certainly were nice, sociable people, like most Southern people. In the army, I had associated with people from about all parts of the states, and after a few words with them, I could usually tell where people were from. The Southern people had a long draw in their speech. Northern people and people from the eastern New England states had sharper accents and different expressions.

While working for Earnest's boss for about a month, I didn't find any promise for another worthwhile job in Ranger. I wasn't very well, and I needed to see a doctor. I didn't want to put it off too long, so I decided to go to a veteran's hospital for a checkup. I had rheumatism, and my nerves had been bad since my first eight months in the army. I thought I would apply for a pension before it was too late. I quit my job and stayed around for a few more days to learn about the best place to go for a physical examination. I decided to go to Camp Logan in Houston, Texas.

The Langfords were such nice people that I hated to leave them, but I expected to be back soon. I bid them and my other friends good-bye and left at about ten o'clock the next morning. I traveled about two hundred miles by train, and I got to Houston at about 6:00 p.m. that day. I inquired about how to get to Camp Logan, and a man showed me where to catch the streetcar and told me when it would be along. He asked, "Are you a patient there?"

"No, but I'm on my way there to be a patient."

"Where are you from?"

"I'm from Ranger, Texas, but originally from West Virginia."

"Oh," he said, "an oil worker there. That has been a very productive field."

"Yes, but it's diminishing considerably now."

"Did you get across the waters?"

"Yes, I saw some action."

"There's no wonder you need hospital care then. I wasn't over there, but I have a brother who lost his health there. He is in Camp Logan Hospital now."

He told me his brother's name, and I said I'd look him up when I got there. (He had been in some of the same offensives that I had been in, but when I did meet him, he didn't have much to say about it. I imagine he had seen a plenty and wanted to forget it. When you meet a soldier that talks about his experience in battle, you may imagine that he never saw much. If he did, he didn't want to talk about it, much less think about it. (My nerves are not so strong yet that I don't get nervous, and I didn't see as much action as many of our soldiers did.) My streetcar came, and I boarded it. I was soon in Camp Logan Hospital. I gave the entering official my army discharge paper, and he looked it over. He found me a bed and told me the doctor had gone home as it was late, and the doctor would see me sometime tomorrow.

The hospital was located in some army barracks that were used during the war. At that date, the government had built only a few veterans' hospitals. I was tired, and I rested well that night. They called me at about six o'clock the next morning. I went to breakfast as though I was in the army. They had very good food. I ate a hearty meal and went back to my bunk. I walked through the barracks and saw some of the patients. It wasn't very pleasant. I wished I had gone to a civilian hospital, but it was free here, and I had to have the government doctors examine me and learn my physical condition in order to determine the extent of my disability. I was there for two days before I got anything done. I told them that I had had trouble with my legs since I was in service. I had to do too much hiking and carrying heavy loads, and I didn't think that it was all rheumatism, as my legs would give way in my knees and almost let me down. They understood that. They told me they had no way to diagnose rheumatism. They said that my legs were just overdone and that the hardships of the war (hiking, exposure to the weather, etc.) had broken my nerves to some extent. I had sinus trouble too. They examined me and made x-rays and ran other tests. I suppose they did about all they could think of. The x-rays showed that my nose had been broken in the past, I suppose sometime when I was a child. I couldn't breathe much from one nostril. They operated on it and chipped away some of the bone. It helped me to breathe more naturally.

I was there for about six weeks, waiting for another operation and taking medicine. They said they weren't allowed to operate for another six weeks. They said my tonsils were infected and needed to come out. I stuck around for three months before they agreed to release me. Although they treated me very nice, it wasn't a very pleasant place. There were so many wounded veterans there whose circumstances were depressing. Some had lost their legs and arms, and some were very badly maimed. Some were blind, and some faces were disfigured. Some of the veterans had been poisoned by mustard gas so badly that they were skin and bones. Some of them wouldn't live much longer. Also, some of them were shell-shocked and crazy.

I was in a room about sixty feet long and wide enough for an aisle about five feet wide, with beds on each side of it. There must have been about forty patients in the room. We had a regular schedule for bedtime, time to rise, and times to eat three meals per day. As long as we weren't marked to quarters, we had privileges to go to Houston two or three times per week. Members of the churches and other organizations often visited in the evenings and provided us some amusement, and we could play cards anytime that we weren't scheduled for our doctor's or nurse's visits. We had plenty of entertainment, and there were not many patients in my room who were bad enough to cause much annoyance.

When the time came for me to go to the operation room to have my tonsils out, they had two surgeons there—a husband-and-wife team. Mrs. Davis was the head doctor, and Mr. Davis was an intern. I don't think Mr. Davis was very experienced. He got ready to take my tonsils out, and I noticed that Mrs. Davis kept telling him to wait for her to help him. He froze my tonsils and started operating on them alone. He was cutting around my tonsil, and he cut the main artery to it. I felt the blood spurt onto the roof of my mouth. He finally got out one and a part of the other. (Doctors later told me that a part of one tonsil was still in there. I never had it removed.) I was taken to my bed, bleeding so badly they put a clamp on the artery, but that didn't entirely stop the bleeding.

My nurse sat by my side and asked me to go to sleep. I was still bleeding. I told her I was swallowing blood. She said, "Not very much, are you?" I was afraid she would leave me if I went to sleep, so I kept as quiet as I could. I got sick and vomited. I must have vomited nearly a quart of blood that I had swallowed. The nurse nearly fainted and called for a doctor. The head nurse and doctor came at once. The doctor gave me a shot to stop the bleeding, but it was getting late for that. I bled so much that my hands, feet, and ears turned black. I was so weak that I could hardly talk, but I finally quit bleeding. They gave me more blood, and I went to sleep. The next day I was too weak to walk, but I was okay in about a week. A few days later, the Dr. Davis that operated on me did the same on another patient, and the chief of staff discharged both Dr. Davises.

About six more weeks had gone by, and it was time to have another operation. They told me I had an inward goiter and that it was affecting my nerves. I knew my neck was a little larger on one side, so I agreed to have it done. I had to have an anesthetic. I got on the operation table and had hardly more than lay down before they had a cap over my face. I wasn't scared, but they didn't give me time to be scared. I went out immediately. They told me they never had a quieter anesthesia patient.

While I was coming to my senses, I did some moaning. I was nauseated by the ether, but I was soon feeling good with a good-looking nurse waiting on me. "Oh, I don't want to get well! I don't want to get well! There's a beautiful, lovely nurse to wait on me!" Well, that's right. She was really pretty, but I never had a lot of confidence in nurses. So many of them are wild, but there was one little nurse I had a lot of respect for, and I had an opportunity to date her. She was Ms. Davis from Florida. She gave me some of her pictures and told me that my doctor spoke well of me. I thought that was enough to be a good hint.

She was well respected by everybody that I knew. She said she was going home because that work was too hard on her. She was too duty-bound; everything had to be just right. I told her she worked too hard. I was never in a hurry about falling in love with any woman. I was writing a girl in Silver Springs, Colorado; the Wilson woman in Ranger, Texas; and also a girl back home in West Virginia. I had known the young lady in Colorado for several years. I met her at Wallback, West Virginia, and knew her people well. I planned to see her again. She was a fair-looking woman and of a nice family. Her name was Mary Barnes. (I did see her later when I went through her city on my way to Los Angeles, California.)

I stayed at the hospital and got along splendidly with the goiter operation, and I was soon ready to leave. They were going to give me a ticket and expenses back to Ranger. I thought, *This will be a good time to go home.* I told them I wouldn't be able to go to work for a week or two, and I'd have to pay board and room. They knew that my job required heavy work and that I would have to feel pretty strong to pound metal with a sledgehammer. I asked them if they could give me a ticket to Charleston, West Virginia.

They agreed with me and gave me a train ticket and meal tickets to Charleston. I got a ticket at the train depot and was ready to travel the next day. The next morning, I bid my friends at the hospital good-bye and left for home. I had been away from September until May and had been at home only once (for about three months) in about three years. I would surely be glad to see everybody at home. I would have to slip in on them because I didn't have time to send them a letter that would get to them before my arrival date.

Even if I did have a berth and comfortable place to sleep and sit, I was plenty tired before I finished my forty-eight hours of travel. I read the late papers and some magazines and met a few interesting people to talk with on the train. I was always interested in the affairs of state and the places I traveled through, and I especially enjoyed the scenery.

My travels made me more appreciative of what we have in our own backyard. With the possible exceptions of the high mountains of Europe, the scenery in West Virginia is as pretty as anywhere that I have been. A lot of it is right here in the wilds of nature on Porter Creek (Bomont, West Virginia). When you travel through the deserts for two days and never see any living vegetation, except a little grease brush and cactus, you can think of the lively vegetation in the greenest state of our nation, and that's West Virginia. In the spring, when day by day the vegetation is turning from a light yellow to a green and to a dark green; when the weeping willow, then the river elm, the maple, the dogwood, and magnolia leaves appear and the laurel comes alive; when the wild lilies, blue violets, bluebells, and hundreds of white, yellow, or red flowers begin to appear; and when the rhododendrons bloom here in the valleys and on the rugged mountains, West Virginia is magnificently beautiful! Then in the autumn, when the trees change colors into the pink, lavender, yellow, purple, orange, then to deep red, and when the weeds bloom their autumn colors (to match the timber), you won't find any place with more beauty than the old rugged hills of West Virginia.

We have to have the awareness of a poet to see the beauties of nature. In the winter, when the snow falls on the pine, laurel, white oak, and other timber, and the ice freezes in those swift-running streams, and the cliffs form sheets of ice and rows of icicles freeze beneath the pines, you can view the real beauty that artists try to capture on Christmas cards and Christmas trees. It was as pretty as some of the places I saw in France, like the fields of Flanders, where poppies the color of solid red were in bloom as far as you could see and white tombstones dotted the green smooth lawn. It was pretty, but it's sad to think that I could have been there too.

I slipped in home unexpected, and I found all of my folks well and happy. I met all of the family in a day or two. I walked around and exercised for about two weeks, and I gained some strength and began to feel very well. I didn't try to labor much for about a month, then I began to work a little about the farm at anything that didn't require too much hard labor.

I always had to visit my granddad Estep, my only living grandparent. He was interesting to talk with. (I always enjoyed talking with old people.) He lived to be eighty-four, the oldest of any of my grandparents. I liked to see him and one of his old friends get together and talk of their experiences in the Civil War.

My aunt Florence had gotten married, but she still lived with Granddad. She had two boys, the only children she ever had. My cousins, Uncle Robert's children, had grown up and left home. It wasn't like it used to be there. Times bring on great changes in very few years. Once more, I enjoyed seeing all of those who were still at home, and it is sad that I didn't get to see some of them again after that visit.

I stayed at home during the summer and now and then worked a few days in the oil fields about Porter Creek. I helped case a few wells and did just about anything there was to do in the oil and gas fields. I didn't have much desire for staying here on account of the climate. I thought it was detrimental to my health. I like the Southern climate better.

I had written Mr. Langford. I told him how sorry I was that I didn't get to come back there, and I asked him to ship me the baggage I left with him. I got my trunk from Ranger in a few days. I was planning to go to California later. I stayed until after the election in

November as Dad kept at me to stay and vote the Democrat ticket. Dad was a staunch liberal and county chairman of the Democrat Party. Dad and Mother and the family in general didn't want me to go so far away. I didn't want to go so far, but I thought that would be much better for my health, and the oil industry business was good there. Other than farming and timbering, about all I ever did was to work around the oil fields.

5

California, Here I Come

Soon after the election, I took off for California. I bought a ticket to Charleston, and while there, I got a ticket for Colorado Springs, where my lady friend, Miss Barnes, lived. I went by rail through Kentucky, Cincinnati, Ohio, Indiana, Illinois, St. Louis, Missouri, and Kansas City, Kansas. The snow was flying as I went through the plains of Kansas early in November. Kansas is a long state, and it took about all day to get through it. I got to Colorado Springs, Colorado, in about three days. Colorado is a big state and almost as long as Kansas. Colorado Springs is about halfway through Colorado. I got there at about 9:00 a.m., and Miss. Barnes and her family were at the station to meet me.

Mrs. Barnes's health was bad. She had tuberculosis, and they had moved from Wallback for her health. Mr. Barnes farmed there and worked some for an oil shale concern. They were mining a stone and shell formation that contained oil, and they were getting a good grade of petroleum by heating it to release the oil. It was just a business for survival, and I couldn't see anything there that looked very prosperous. They were glad to see me. They had lived there for a few years without seeing anyone from West Virginia. I had a nice lovely time there for three days, and they seemed to hate to see me leave for California. (That was about two-thirds of the way to California from West Virginia.)

My train went through Pueblo, Elberta, and on through Grand Junction (on the border of Colorado and Utah). We bypassed Salt Lake City and traveled on through Utah. I learned there was some oil prospecting going on in Nevada, so on my way to California, I decided to stop off at the railroad junction to see about the prospects of staying there a short while.

When I got off of the train, there wasn't anyone at the railroad junction but the railroad agent, who was batching alone. He showed me to a dwelling where there were two old couples experimenting with farming in the desert.

I learned that I would have to wait twenty-four hours to get a train out of there to California, so I decided not to go the few miles further, where I would have to go to see about work in those parts. It was too lonely for me—miles and miles from civilization—but I didn't begrudge my stay there. It was an exciting experience for me to be in the desert. I stayed overnight with those old people and had my meals with them. I walked around in the desert for a little while. When I walked to the top of a little knoll and looked down on the other side, I saw what I thought was a lake a short distance from me. When I came back, I started talking about it to those old people, and they said, "No, you saw a mirage. You saw heat waves rising from the hot desert."

They were getting their water by drilling a little ways in the sand, and they were experimenting with corn, wheat, cabbage, and other vegetables. They said there was a river or vein of water that ran under the ground through there and that they didn't have to go very far down to get it. They thought I was prospecting, and they wanted to sell me their property (or their business). I doubt if they owned it. Anyway, I didn't want to stay there in that hot desert. I was certain about that! There didn't seem to be any living thing there, but I learned that they had a few gophers, badgers, centipedes, scorpions, and tarantulas and that it was not far to go from there to see rattlesnakes. I'm sure I didn't want to live among them.

The depot agent told me that he spent quite a bit of his time trapping badgers and shooting gophers, and he seemed to enjoy his job there. He got away from his work and back out into civilization about once every three or four months. Twenty-four hours was enough time for me there, in that desolate place, but that was an experience I'll never forget. It reminded me of some of the Zane Gray novels about the desert lands that I had read.

The next day, I boarded another train that I never got off until I got to Los Angeles. We traveled through Nevada until dark. I saw a lot of sagebrush, and some of the cactus was as large as trees as we passed nearby cliffs of red rock on the hilltops. We went clear through Death Valley, where so many old explorers started through years ago and never made it. (They perished from lack of water, and the hot air finally suffocated them.) At that time, 1920, there weren't many settlements along the train route until we got close to LA. The population of Los Angeles was only about five hundred thousand, but it was growing by leaps and bounds as a tourist city. (In four more years it was one million in population, including the suburbs.)

I stayed in LA for only a day or two. Then I started south and went through Long Beach, a small town, to Huntington Beach, where the oil fields were rapidly developing. I found a hotel and rested from my travels for a couple of days. Then I inquired about drilling wells. I learned that they drilled there with rotary machines instead of the standard tools that I was accustomed to. I had never worked on this kind of a drilling rig, so I decided to take a job laying pipelines. That was hard work for me. I wasn't strong, but I had done that kind of work before, and I knew the slant of it.

I picked a job I that I knew I could do. There were about twenty men in the pipe crew. In those days they laid all pipelines by screwing the joints together, no matter how big the line was. Welding hadn't been invented, or maybe, it just was not yet used to lay oil and gas lines. This was an eight-inch line, and it was to be run about eight or ten miles, mostly through a farming section. They had about one hundred joints laid out and ready to go into the ditch. (They had to bury the pipe where it crossed over the farmland.)

After I worked for a day or two at laying the line, the boss said to me, "Come with me." We went a short distance back over the line that we had laid. He gave me a pail of tar and a four-inch brush and told me to paint the pipe. (That was something new to me—

painting a pipeline. We never did that in West Virginia or Texas.) He pointed out a big kettle and some drums full of coal tar. A six-by-ten-foot piece of canvas with a handle wrapped around each end was lying nearby, and he described the process for coating the pipe. They put the coal tar into the kettle and heated it over a gas burner until it was melted. They took a pail of it from the kettle, and with the canvas under the pipe and a man on each end of the canvas, they poured the hot tar on top of the line and let it run down onto the canvas. The men dragged the canvas back and forth and tarred the pipe that had already been painted. Another crew came behind them to wrap the canvas around the pipe while the tar was still hot. I learned that they did this to keep the pipe from rusting. The ocean that had at one time covered those plains left salt in the soil, and if the pipes weren't sealed, the corrosion would soon eat holes in them.

The lines running directly from the oil and gas wells carried the fresh crude and gas to small separator tanks that sat over oil storage tanks. At about halfway to the top of the separator tank, the oil could flow into the storage tank. The gas seeped up through this tank and into gas lines near the top of the separator tank. That way, the gas wasn't wasted. We finished laying that gas line within about a month, but there were plenty more to lay in other locations in that oil and gas field. An oil well that was strong enough to flow from gas pressure was always a profitable one.

The new lines went through some orange groves where the oranges were at about the best stage of ripeness for eating, but we didn't bother them because some women were watching us. Later, some men came by and told us to help ourselves to them as long as we didn't break the branches. They were a superior grade of sweet oranges, the best I have ever seen, and fresh from the trees, they tasted much better than any oranges you can buy from the stores. I must have eaten a half dozen of them.

I had a room in a hotel to myself, and because I wasn't feeling too well, I stayed in it quite a bit of my time after work hours. I read a lot, and I had begun to get letters from home, from friends in Texas, and from the Barnes woman in Colorado. The Wilson girl in Texas kept talking about coming to California. I wrote her for about a year, but she never came. I think she married the Moore boy we knew there. I still wrote the Barnes woman in Colorado, but she was too homely to travel so far or to stay away from her people. I heard she married her first cousin there where she lived. I thought, *I suppose I'll have to be an old bachelor!*

I met several girls at Huntington Beach, but I didn't date any of them steady during the two years I was there. There are nice people anywhere, and in California, you could meet people from all over the United States, or from mostly anywhere in the world. This was an ideal climate, and there were favorite tourist places mostly anywhere in the state. At that time, 1921, you were almost a pioneer in California. If you stayed there for a year, you were regarded as a native, and people didn't often leave there to hunt for a better climate. One family told me they were afraid of earthquakes. They moved to Florida and ran into those terrible hurricanes, so they moved back to California.

The panic after the war had begun to take hold a little later there than in the East. I worked in the oil fields at Huntington Beach until spring, when business was beginning to get slack. By that time, I had received the results of my application for a pension—the one I applied for while in the hospital in Houston, Texas. I was awarded a 35 percent disability from the time I was discharged from the army. They gave me a little money to invest in a business. I decided I had better take advantage of that and do something that would allow me to take better care of my health. I decided to go into the confectionery business on the beach. It was a profitable enterprise for about three to six months out of the year.

I had enough money to buy supplies and pay rent to get the business going. I had three containers for soft drinks, and I bought mostly grape-, orange-, and cherry-flavored powders that I mixed in by the gallon. I made about 200 percent markup on that. I sold candies, nuts, cakes, gum, oranges, and other things, such as a few gimmicks that attracted children, and I had a special flavored hamburger sandwich that sold very well. I sprinkled curry pepper over it when I mixed it. It gave it a good flavor and made it taste fresh. I also sold a fish sandwich. I sold a lot of soft drinks and ice cream. There was a good profit in them. During the school holidays, I made quite a bit of money, but there was about three months out of the year when there wasn't anybody on the beach, yet I still had to pay rent to hold my building. I improved it in order to have it for another season. I added a room in the back where I could stay. That saved me extra from having to pay rent for a room, but the hotel people lobbied the lawmakers to pass a law against people sleeping in a restaurant establishment.

Ira I. Boggs's confectionery stand, circa 1921

I fared very well there, and I made a little money. I hired some help while business was good, but I worked long hours during the summer months. Later, when business was slow, I would often get up early and take a stroll along the beach. I collected a few nice clamshells and other beautiful seashells. I sold some of them, and I kept some that I later gave to people inland who had never been to a seashore. I later brought some to West Virginia and gave them to my mother and my aunt Florence. I also brought them some dishes decorated with seashells.

I enjoyed living on the beach, in that wonderful climate, and I met lots of nice people there. Near my business, a fishing pier ran about a quarter of a mile out into the ocean. At that time, it was the nicest pier on the coast. I didn't fish much, but a few people fished there year round. They caught mostly halibut and mackerel. For saltwater fish, they were fine to eat. The mackerel swarmed about the piers in such big schools that you didn't need to use bait to catch them. You could put a half dozen hooks on your line and just pull it up and down to snag them; sometimes you could snag more than one at a time. The halibut was a big fish, and you had to use bait to catch it.

They had a bowling alley on the beach, and I bowled some, but I didn't have time to join a bowling league. Occasionally, I went to the movies. The talking movies from the first inventions had begun to play there. I had seen a talking movie in Ranger, Texas, in 1920. It was the first one ever played in Ranger. Before they had the talking movie, they would show the picture and flash the words on the screen with it.

In 1922, I was living in Hollywood, and I often visited Culver City, where they made movies. I saw Hoot Gibson, the comedian, act for some pictures, and I saw a lot of others that I can't remember at this time. Gloria Swanson, Fatty Arbuckle, Syd and Charlie Chaplin, Douglas Fairbanks, and Mary Pickford come to mind. I had a pass to the theaters for any day of the week except Saturday or Sunday. Sunny Boy sang and acted there for his first show. He was one of the most popular singers. I usually went to the Hill Street Theater. I was in one oil field scene that they made at Huntington Beach.

While I lived in Huntington Beach, I bought fifty dollars worth of stock in Huntington Central Oil Company. They had several acres of land between two good paying wells. At the time I bought the stock, they hadn't drilled on their tract. When they did drill, the well came in good at seven hundred pounds of pressure. The price of the stock tripled, but I didn't sell. They lingered along and didn't drill any more. They changed their name and sold out. They went to Texas and got by with their outlawry. They were supposed to have gone broke.

I kept my confectionery business while looking for a job in the oil fields. There was an oil company signing a group of men to go to Brazil, South America. I always wanted to go there, so I signed up to go. I had to agree to stay at least one year. It would have paid about three times as much as I could make in California, but they didn't get enough men, or it all blew over. I didn't go. Work was hard to find, but I just kept going to the Standard Oil office every morning, and they finally signed me on. I got a job setting boilers for drilling and pumping. I did pipe fitting for oil, gas, water, and steam, and I made top wages there for about a year.

My first cousin from West Virginia, Andrew Boggs, came to Huntington Beach and was there with me a few months. We associated and boarded at the same place. He worked at pipe lining. The world's auto race was going on the next Sunday at San Antonio, and we went to see it. At that time, Millon and Murphy were two of the racing heroes. Jimmy Durante, Halsts, and others I might mention, also raced there. One racer wrecked and ran clear over the wall. He was killed.

Russell Boggs, Andrew's brother, came there and stayed a month or two. We went to San Diego to see West Virginia University play the world's champion football game with Gonzaga University of Washington. West Virginia won by 21–13. This was when that little fellow Caradosa played. He was the most interesting one to watch. He was as quick as lightning. He would dart under and around the defensive players so fast that they couldn't get hold of him. Football wasn't so popular then. Fewer than a thousand people attended that event, but there weren't so many people to draw crowds like the ones you see at sports events today. The population of California and the United States has grown in leaps and bounds since then.

There was always something of interest to see in Huntington Beach or in its vicinity. The Capistrano Hill Climb was interesting. It was very steep. Very few cycles made it all the way up the two-hundred-yard climb. They would bury in sand and wreck before they got to the top of that steep hill. The Orange County Fair was another interesting place to visit. There were many vegetables and fruits that a person from the East could never have seen before. They also had a world exposition in Los Angeles while I was there. That was very exciting. The inventions of Thomas Edison were the most interesting exhibits. He was our greatest inventor. The electric light was one of his most important inventions. There weren't many electric motors then, except the Delco motor, which ran by an electric battery. Edison also invented the flashlight and the flashlight battery. Thomas Edison and Firestone, the rubber manufacturer, were great cronies. Edison said people slept too much to be smart or intelligent. He only slept about five hours in twenty-four. He lived to be very old, and he was active up to shortly before he died.

Andrew went back home to West Virginia and got married. He had been courting a certain lady for some time before he came to California, and I think he couldn't make up his mind about whether to marry her. I think, as usually happens when a person gets so far away from his best girlfriend, he got lonesome for her and decided it would be better to be with her. He wanted a home of some satisfaction, and so he went back home and married her, but he liked California too much to stay away from it, so in a month or so, he persuaded his bride to come back with him. They lived in Monrovia, California, and he continued to work around the oil fields.

I was still working for Standard Oil in Huntington Beach. I liked my job and the crew I worked with very well. I decided to stay there. In my spare time, evenings and Saturday and Sunday, I continued to work at the confectionery. When business got good in the spring, I would have that to fall back on if my Standard Oil job gave out. A photographer built at one end of my confectionery. That blocked my end door space. He said he would give me room to come through the corner of his place, and that would save me from taking room for a new door. I needed all the space I had. I thanked Mr. Collins for his kindness and accommodation. He owned some real estate in Huntington Beach, including the building occupied by the theater.

He was from Texas, and he had a farm there, where he had raised cattle. He and his wife couldn't get along, and he came to California. His daughter was studying in Texas for a doctorate degree. He was a nice fellow to talk with, and I don't understand why a woman couldn't get along with him.

A young man had a ticket to take a ride in an airplane and wanted to sell it to me. He agreed to take some sandwiches for it. I traded with him and took the ticket to the aviator; he accepted it. He had a little Curtis plane to take people up for fifteen-minute cruises. He flew from the beach where the sand was packed, and it made a good field for a small plane. He took me up, and that was the first time I had ever been in a plane. We went up to about two thousand feet and sailed along close to the ocean and then over the town. He noticed that I wasn't scared, so he made a quick turn and put his plane up on its side at about a forty-five degree angle. I got a good view of the town. An automobile looked like a four-by-four-foot box rolling along the street.

One Sunday, during the summer when I was in my confectionery, a little Curtis plane just like that one fell within a few yards of my business place. Everybody who had time to see it was running. I was among the first to get to the plane, and I met the ones who were running to get out of the way. The plane hit the corner of the bathhouse, and it fell on one man who had lain down in the sand and gone to sleep. He, no doubt, never knew what had happened. It killed him instantly. It hit eight other people and hurt some of them seriously. The pilot and his passenger were badly injured and unconscious. They were cramped between the wires that braced the wings and parts of the plane. It took several minutes to get them out. The pilot didn't have a license to fly. He had tried some maneuvering and lost control of his plane. (He was making a nosedive and didn't get out of it.) That wasn't the pilot who took me on my first flight. (I associated with the pilot I flew with. He wanted me to learn to fly, but I couldn't make up my mind and didn't try it. I thought I was too nervous to undertake such a venture.)

The confectionery business was interesting work when business was good. I got acquainted with many good people, but I met very few people from West Virginia. There was a skating rink, a dance pavilion, and a bowling alley nearby. I bowled some but didn't try to skate. I later took lessons and learned to dance some. I tried to dance a time or two, but I never cared to dance to any music except a waltz. My teacher said, "You keep good time in your maneuvers."

I said, "Yes, I like music." I had sung some in a church choir, but I didn't know too much about instrumental music. I liked to dance to good music, and you meet so many people and have a variety of people to choose your friends from. There were usually good-looking ladies at the school, and they were good talkers. Most of them were just as nice as the average, and they had all the traits of any other women whom I met.

My dancing teacher was from San Francisco. She said she had met a lot of boys from Ohio and some from New York but hadn't met many from West Virginia. She said, "I like about all of those Eastern boys."

I said, "West Virginia is inland and isn't so heavily populated as most other states. In minerals, West Virginia is one of the wealthiest states in the union. My hometown [Charleston] has been classified as the wealthiest city in the US for its population."

"Well, that sounds like you are wealthy."

"No, most of my people are poor, but I do have some pretty wealthy relatives."

"Were you in the war?"

"Yes, I was overseas in France for about a year. I was in the Gardner sector and in the Meuse-Argonne Offensive. I didn't see much action, but I saw enough to suit me. I got scared, and my nerves are bad. That's the reason I'm in California. I think it is better for my health. The climate is so regular here."

"I don't blame you for getting scared."

"It's when you are right on the minute of launching an attack that you get nervous. You forget about yourself to some extent. You are always looking out to get your enemy." I dated this lady some, but I didn't write her, and I didn't see her much after I quit the dancing school. I liked most of the people I met in California.

While Andrew and I were at Huntington Beach, we met a couple of girls from Arizona. Their mother had died, and their father moved to Huntington Beach, where the girls could get work. We caught the Interurban electric car to Long Beach and went to Disneyland and to a carnival, where we rode the roller coaster. These girls had not been around much, and I don't think they knew what they were getting into when they got on the roller coaster. There was about a seventy-five-foot drop in the mile-long track. They got so scared that they became angry with us. Andrew and I were full of fun, and we didn't care. We just considered it a joke on the ladies and a good lesson for them about what to expect in California. I imagine they hated to wait until they got home to change clothes!

I didn't try to date the girl anymore. Andrew did see his girl a few more times. Andrew was a free spender. He and Russell worked in the harvest fields. They started in the south and moved northward, following the grain harvest. Andrew later married, and he and his wife came back to West Virginia. Andrew got a job as a brakeman on the B&O Railroad, and he stayed there until he retired. He worked on the northern end of the Elk River Road from Gassaway north. His dad, Uncle Burn, was wealthy. Their family worked hard, especially in the growing season, and they usually had three or four hundred head of big well-bred cattle to sell every year. Somebody asked Andrew why he wasn't in on the dividing of his dad's wealth. He said, "I spent it having a big time when I was young."

I worked at Standard Oil for about a year. Then I had an opportunity to go to school to learn a trade. The government offered me a four-year course at anything I might qualify for, and they would pay me one hundred dollars per month. I had a very good job, but I talked it over with my boss and thought about it for a short time. My boss advised me to take advantage of that opportunity. He said things were slowing down and he couldn't promise me a continuous job. (It was the beginning of one of the worst panics that ever occurred in America.) I worked for the rest of the month before I decided to take his good advice.

I made arrangements with the government rehabilitation officials and started to school in Los Angeles on the first day of the month of April in 1922. The government didn't have their own schools at that time, so they started us at high schools that already had the proper equipment for our courses. I enrolled at the Manual Art High School in Los Angeles, located near the University of Southern California on North Forty-Second Street. I decided to take a machinery course. That was a very good trade, and I liked that kind of work.

The government furnished me books and equipment, and I started in the machine shop with the high school pupils. I also took a classroom course to review my general education and learn to read and make blueprints. To become machinists, we needed a good knowledge of mathematics. There weren't many government trainees in my class. The high school teachers didn't like to have us there, and they got a little overbearing with some of us at times. But it was the best the government had for us.

I liked the work. It was so interesting that I could forget about my dinner. I soon learned how to trace maps and to read them, and I learned about angles and directions, material classifications, etc. Although some things were rather complicated for me, I soon knew how to use my drafting set to copy maps or blueprints and then to make blueprints for what I wanted to design.

I went to class three hours in the morning and to machine shop three hours in the afternoon. In the shop, I learned to shape metal on the lathe and other shaping machines and how to drill holes with the drilling machine and to cut gears on the milling machine. I liked the work. It was very interesting. I got trained to set my dividers within a small fraction of an inch and my caliper within three thousandths of an inch. I worked on the lathe, learning to sharpen my cutting tool to cut threads on bolts. I cut some threads and tried a nut on it, and it fit just right. The next day I learned to dress angles on rods and cut inside threads on rods. I had to sharpen a tool to the right shape to cut the threads.

I found a place to board in a private home within about five blocks of the school. A widow had a big home and was keeping boarders and roomers to pay for it. It was a good place to board. I stayed home two and three nights a week to study and read. I usually went to a movie at least one night during the week and, at times, on Saturday or Sunday when I didn't study or read.

I got acquainted with a young man from Arkansas, and we associated some. We would go to a show sometimes, and occasionally, on weekends, we would just go for a drive, touring around to see sights. He had a car. (I wasn't making enough money to afford a car while going to school, but I bought one after I finished school.) One weekend, we drove about thirty miles to the coastal mountain range. We caught a railcar to near the top of Mt. Low. It went up a 60 percent grade pulled by a wire line on the steep of the hill. We got off and walked a half mile or so around narrow paths. I said to my friend, "This is like being in the hills of West Virginia."

"Yes," he said, "to me, it's like being in the Ozark Mountains of Arkansas." We walked out to the top of the mountain and went into a hotel tavern. They had a big broad fireplace, and they were burning wood in it. There was about two inches of snow on the ground, and big flakes were still falling from the sky.

This was the first snow I had seen close-up for three years. (From LA, sometimes when the temperature there was ninety degrees, we could see snow at a distance on Mt. Low, Mt. Wilson, and Mt. Baldy.) We walked a little ways further to the top of Mt. Low, where Professor Low had an observatory. He had what was supposed to be the largest telescope in the world. It was a bright clear night, and it was focused on the moon.

Everybody took a peek at the moon. With the sun shining on it, it looked like ice. He made a speech about the science of the planets. He said people were learning so much about the heavens that he had to read several magazines a week to keep up with the times. He told us that it was 200,500 miles to the moon and that it was our nearest space object, but he didn't say anything about the prospects for us ever traveling to it.

We could see snowy peaks on the coastal ranges and on the Sierra Nevada Mountains. It was an enchanting sight. When we started back off of the mountain, we could see the "stars on earth," as they called the lights of LA, Longbeach, and all the little towns for miles and miles. The air was very clear during that season. The stars, or city lights, were as pretty from the mountains as those snowy peaks were from LA when we could see them.

Well, I'd better get back to my machinist job, or my boss will fire me. I met a man in LA, whom I knew when I lived in Huntington Beach. He was a poor man, but he had married a woman from a wealthy family. He gave me some good advice: never marry a woman from a wealthy family. He said that when you were so poor you couldn't support her lusciously, she would get dissatisfied. She had left him. She worked for the photographer near my confectionery business in Huntington Beach. The photographer asked me to date her, but I told him that I didn't date married women.

On Monday afternoon, my shop teacher gave me a piece of steel large enough to make into a one-and-one-half-inch cube. I clamped it in my shaper and went to work on it. I smoothed one side until I could place it in my vise on a level bench top. I kept turning it and dressing it until I had a one-and-one-half-inch cube, as near as I could get it. He looked amazed when he measured it, and he showed it to the high school pupils. He gave it back to me and said, "You are a mechanically gifted person, and there's not much use for a person to try to be a machinist unless he has the patience and ability to do things right."

He said, "You've done a good job at this, and I want you to finish it to as close to one thousandths of an inch as you can." I kept working on it for about two days, or six hours of shop work. I machined as much as I dared. Then I hand-filed it some. I put my dividers on it again, and it wasn't quite exact. I honed it on a stone until I had it to from three to five thousandths of an inch within the exact measurements. My teacher looked at it, measured it, and handed it back to me, and he said, "That's as close as I'll ask you to do this job for the first time." He took it to his pupils and showed it to them and complimented me on my work. Anything worth doing is worth doing well, and sometimes, in machinery, it has to be made to the thousandths of an inch. I liked mathematics and loved making blueprints, so I decided to stay with this work.

I kept using my drafting set until I understood it pretty well, and I liked the work even better as I learned more. I realized it was delicate and precise skill, but it was interesting. On a real job, you would have to get your measurements to a pinpoint, and you would have to punch your marks at the exact point to start the drill for a hole, or it would throw everything out of line. If it wasn't right, you would have to do your job over, and that would be a lot of expense to your employer. You wouldn't last long working on that job. If you got one small fraction of an inch off line and it got by the inspection, it could wreck a valuable piece of machinery and ruin the company's business. The boss could soon trace the records to see who had made the mistake.

When I went back to the classroom the next day and went to work on my mathematics and my blueprints, my teacher handed me a sketch of a blueprint. She wanted me to make one like it and gave me descriptive details of it. I worked on it for some time before I decided that I needed some help on the plan. I just didn't understand all of it. I kept waiting for her to come around to help me, and I noticed that she was reading a newspaper. I kept waiting and waiting, and I got impatient. It didn't appear to me that she was properly interested in her job. She finally came around and asked me what my problem was. I told her, and then I said, "I've been waiting for half an hour while you were reading that newspaper."

She got a little miffed about it, and she replied, "You aren't running this place."

I replied, "No, and it don't look like you are either. I think I'm more interested in my work than you are."

I continued, "You have a big class of young men who have put in their time in the war, and we are behind other young men who were in school while we were risking our lives and suffering on the battlefields. We are late now, and they are getting the good jobs. We are behind on our plans for life, and we have to take what is left for us, regardless of our ability." I said, "There has been a lot of complaining about the lack of a teacher here. We don't want to get you into trouble. We want you to help yourself by helping us." I always hate to cause a commotion about anything, but my friends said that she took more interest in the teaching from then on, and they complimented me. I said, "I imagine I did her a favor. Sooner or later, her boss would have noticed her disinterest." After that incident, she seemed to want to help me more than the others in her class. She didn't seem to hold any grudge against me.

"Well, it's another weekend, and a very good week's work has been finished." I asked my chum, Bob, "What do you want to do tonight?"

He answered, "Let's go to the show tonight and see "Sonny Boy" at the Hill Street Theater. I want to hear that fellow sing."

"Yes, that suits me. Then tomorrow and Sunday, we will take a trip out to San Bernardino—or Sanberno, for short—and on to Big and Little Bear Lakes." We went to the show and saw Charlie Chaplin, Douglas Fairbanks Sr., Gloria Swanson, and others I might mention put on an act. Al Jolson sang "Sonny Boy." That was a big hit, just out. That was a good show! Yes, I liked it! I liked the action, and that Al Jolson sure could sing. That "Sonny Boy" song was my favorite.

We got home a little early, so we could get up early and take the trip to Bear Lakes. It was about fifty-five miles from Hollywood. The roads were not all paved in 1923, and cars sometimes got stuck in that dry sand. If that had happened to us, we would have been late getting back home.

We went through Pasadena and San Bernardino. San Bernardino was a small town—or just a village. We drove on to the foot of Bear

Mountain. There was a one-way road with a few places to pass up the mountain to the lakes. It followed an old Spanish trail. Our ole Ford Model T puffed and boiled and steamed until we finally made it up the mountain to the lakes. This was one of the prettiest bodies of water I had ever seen. It equaled the beauty of Lac du Bourget, France, in the Vosges Mountains. It was so pure and clear that you could see the fish for several feet under the water. There was a strong breeze over the lake and the surroundings. We went adrift in some glass-bottomed boats to explore the lake. There were very few buildings on the lakeshores, but they were clearing the brush around the handiest places, and lots were for sale at $200 to $600. I thought about buying a couple of business lots, but I hesitated. I decided that I had better wait until I got out of school to invest. I needed about all I was making to live on.

On our way back to LA, we had to take our time going down the hill as this was a one-way road with only a few passing places along the way. As we drove back through Sanberno, we noticed some stucco buildings that were cracked so badly that they looked unfit to occupy. There had been an earthquake, and it did more damage there than to any of the other towns in the vicinity. (I felt it in LA, but it did very little damage there.)

We had lots of time and took a roundabout way back to explore the scenery. We drove through the outskirts of the Millionaire City of Riverside, where there were big orange groves all around as far as you could see. They were pretty, but not so pretty as an apple orchard or a peach orchard. The bloom wasn't so large, and the trees were in full leaf. (An apple tree or peach tree blooms before it's in full leaf.) Riverside is inland, not far from Arizona, and it's one of the hottest places in the state. That makes it a good climate for growing oranges. We drove back through Monrovia and on to Long Beach. We got back to LA in time to see the late show, but we decided to go home and get a good night's rest so we could be ready for work on Monday. Besides, we had passes to the shows for any night except Sunday or Saturday.

On Monday morning, I got up early and studied my lessons and went to class on time. I had some pretty complicated math problems to solve and some blueprints to draw. In class that day, we had some literature to read, and my teacher had us to stand and read aloud. I was rather timid about reading to the class. I never could read orally like most people, but I told my teacher I would try. She said, "You get some of your letters out of place." She thought my eyes were the cause of it (that I couldn't read fast). She was always boosting me and encouraging me in my lessons, and at times, she mentioned my fast learning abilities. She was an elderly lady, and I could see that she wanted me to date a young teacher there. I talked a little with the young lady, but I didn't ask her for a date. I was always short of cash. I had just enough to get by on while in school. She was about six years younger than I and just a beginning teacher, and she wasn't too pretty. Also she was too small for my taste, and she was apparently as broke as I was.

At the end of my first year of school in LA, an order came out to allow us veterans to take on-the-job training. I thought about it for a while. I didn't think I was getting along too well in school, and it was a big temptation for me. I was twenty-eight years old, and I thought three more years in school would delay my opportunity to make some money. This job would pay us well for a year or more. The government would still pay us one hundred dollars per month, and the corporation would pay us an additional one hundred. That was pretty big money in those days. I could see that my teacher didn't want me to go, but she dared not tell me. I could have finished a four-year course in school, and I probably made a mistake by not going on to finish, but I was pretty nervous and dissatisfied with my progress. The opportunity to earn more money was a little too much of a temptation for me.

My government overseer got me a job with the Willard & Wilson Oil Tool Shop. I worked for a few days at chipping and smoothing oil tools, and they put me on a drill press for a while. Then they moved me to another area, where I learned to use a jig to hold tools while making measurements to drill holes in them. I used a punch to mark the exact locations for where the holes should be. They had to be very accurate. I would make a punch hole for the place to start my drill, and I had to be very careful to not let the drill slip to either side. That would ruin the tool.

At first, I started at chipping reaming tools for a drilling well. One old man that had worked there for four years could do just about anything, but mostly he did nothing. He told me that I had broken the records on the number of those reamers turned out in one day. He said, "You've finished more than ever has been finished in one day."

I replied, "I just kept busy. I didn't think about how many I had done." They began to get low on work for us, and I noticed that they had laid off half of their men, but they hadn't gotten to me yet. I thought it was just because I was a veteran in training.

Most of the time, I worked at the drill press about all day, but after they had lain off several men, help on other jobs got scarce, and I helped with any job where they needed me. They had a foundry, and sometimes they would call on me to help take a large tool out of the furnace. There was a big strong Mexican that worked there, and he seemed to have a grudge against me, or maybe he just wanted to be overbearing. When I helped lift a heavy tool from the furnace, he would shove my load against me. That was a little dangerous with a hot iron as it might fall on you. Because I was smaller than anyone else, I think he thought I wasn't lifting my part. I never complained or said a word. I just watched for a chance to catch him off balance. I thought, "Mister, I'll get you if you keep that up. I'll shove you, and when I do, you're going down. If I have to, I'll show you that I'm not as weak as you think." He must have been smarter than I thought because he never did it again. I guess he saw from the look I gave him that he had made me angry. But, in general, we had a pretty nice crew of men working there. I never had any other trouble with any of them.

My friend Earnest Schmidt from Texas came to LA to see his aunt, and he visited me while he was there. He had never been in California before. We took a tour through the orange groves down next to the southwestern part of the state. He liked California so well that he said he was coming back, but he never got away from his people again. He was of German descent, and he had a fine lot of relatives, as nice as most German people I have met.

We went down as far as Riverside, where the oranges were so plentiful. They were getting ripe, and the orchards were beautiful with those nice big golden oranges hanging on them. We stopped where they were picking them, and we asked if we could pick a few with the crew. They agreed, and they gave us a few good ripe ones to take home with us. We told them we had never seen oranges growing in the fields before. They had English walnuts and pecans in Texas, but I never saw oranges growing there. When I was there, pecans were important to the economy. They grew in the forest, just as hickory nuts grow wild in the north. I have picked them there and also in Mississippi. I understand that Texas is now a major orange exporting state.

Three of our biggest battleships were docked at San Pedro (LA harbor), and we went to see them. There was the *Missouri,* the *Mississippi,* and the *West Virginia.* The *Mississippi* was a little longer than the others, so we decided to visit it. We took a schooner to it, and one of the crew showed us around. There were some sixteen-inch guns on it. Those are large cannons! They were dismounted onto railroad cars and used in the battlefields of World War I. They were a lot of help in winning the war. Where one of those big shells hit with high explosives, they left their mark. They used them to shell Metz, where the French had been fighting for months. We won that battle in about two days.

Aboard the USS Mississippi, 1923; Ira Boggs, left

"Were you with those guns in the battle of Metz?" I asked one of the men on the ship.

"No, I enlisted after the war was over. Some of my buddies were there. I have heard them talk a lot about the battle. They were fifteen miles from the city when firing. My buddy said he threw one hundred and five of those GI cans (shells) at them." They get their nickname from the ten- to fifty-gallon waste cans that we used to carry food, such as rice and slumgullion, for the troops on the front lines.

"Earnest, we had better get back to shore before too late. We want to go to the Hill Street Theater and hear Al Jolson sing 'Sonny Boy.' Al is quite an actor. He's a white man, you know, but he can act like a colored person." I'll never forget the show the colored soldiers gave my outfit when we were in that lonesome town of Poinsinet, France, while we were waiting for a boat to bring us home. They sure could put on some monkeyshines. Those big rough-looking colored men dressed in women's clothes, and they had quite a party. I never laughed so hard as at them. That was the first show we had seen since eight months in France.

"Well, Ira, I'm going to Texas in the morning, but I hope to be back and see you again."

"Yes, I hope so," I replied. "I'm going to continue working at the Willard & Wilson Oil Tool Shop. I will make some more oil tools."

Earnest said, "I've been working for a cotton gin company since the oil fields went dead at Ranger, but that don't pay too much."

"If you come back, I'll try to get you on at my company. Good-bye and good luck. I'll see you in about a month." (But I never saw him again.)

I went back to work at making oil-drilling tools. I had been working there for about six months, but we were expecting another layoff. They had already laid off about half of their men. The panic was just starting in California. It was already serious in the East. (It began to affect California about a year after layoffs started in the East.)

At the end of the week, my boss said, "Boggs, I hate to tell you. We just don't have any more work for you after this week. We are not getting much to do. The supervisor has quit and left the layoffs up to me. I suppose he didn't want to be here when we had to shut down. I'm keeping just a few of my oldest men, and I don't know how long it will be before we will be completely out of orders."

My veteran's counselor came to see me on Monday, and he said he thought that he could find another job for me. He called me about the middle of the week to tell me that he had a job for me at a machine repair shop, but he didn't know how long it would last. I would still be getting one hundred dollars per month from the government but hardly that much from the new company I would be working for. I went to work on a drill press at just anything they had for me to do. My boss came around and showed me where to oil my machine at the beginning of every shift, and he gave me a blueprint of my work.

I had saved a few dollars while making double wages for training with the government and the company I formerly worked for. I saw some good opportunities to invest in some real estate. I bought three lots in Alhambra, a suburb of LA. That little town was growing fast. I had bought a dwelling lot, but the realty company had failed to live up to their contract. There was going to be some delay in getting the streets paved, so I decided to sell it. I wrote Dennis, my brother in West Virginia and explained the situation. It was good property, but I didn't know how long it would take to get things moving again. We would probably have to go to court to get the realty company to do what they had agreed to do.

That was a hilltop track of land with a beautiful view to the valley to the west and the high coastal mountain range to the east. Secretary McAdoo had bought the top of a knob just opposite the hilltop where my lot was. (McAdoo was secretary of the US Treasury.) I thought if he could invest money there, I could take a chance, too. To get my money out of it, I sold my lot to Dennis at just what I had paid for it. I invested in another three lots at Alhambra. I bought one forty-by-one-hundred-foot business lot on a corner for $1,200, one dwelling lot for $1,000, and one dwelling lot for $800. My payments were about $70 per month. My business lot was one block behind the main thoroughfare through town. I made a few months payments on those lots and tried to sell the two dwelling lots, but business was getting bad all along. I failed to sell them even at cost. I wanted to hold the business lot indefinitely. I knew it was a good investment.

I worked for the Repair Company for about three months. A new boss, a young man, was put over me. I went to him to ask him for a blueprint or a little better description of a job he had given me. He was busy talking to another employee. He looked around at me and said, "You go tell your veteran boss we are not running a hospital here." I knew I had been doing satisfactory work for my former supervisor. I thought, *If you are that kind of man, I'll never get along with you.* So I didn't come to work the next morning. I still had that nervous war fever, and I knew that if he made me angry I would let him have all I had. If I can't get along with a person, I want to get along without him.

That was in the spring of 1924. For some time, I had been thinking about going home to West Virginia. I hadn't been home for going on four years. My mother kept writing me. She said, "I'd rather see you coming home than anything I know of." I wasn't feeling very well, and I was getting a little anxious to be with my friends and relatives once more. Although I had been away from home about all the time (all told, for about seven years), during and after the war, four years was the longest I had been away from West Virginia at one stretch.

I had only a short while to finish my training job, and I decided to go back to Huntington Beach and see my old friend Mr. Collins, the photographer. I had been acquainted with him for the duration of my stay in California. I met with Mr. Collins and told him I was going home to see my folks. I mentioned that I had invested some money in real estate in L.A., and he said, "Boggs, you'll be worth something some of these days. That's a good investment." I tried to sell him two of my lots, but he wasn't interested. He owned the theater building in Huntington Beach, and he was very busy running a photo business. Mr. Collins said, "You'll be back."

"Yes," I answered, "when the cold wind begins to blow and the snow begins to fly, it will be pretty hard for me to stay there in those mountains. I suspect I'll be thinking of the sunny, warm winter days here in California. This is a wonderful climate, and California is a good place to make a living."

"I suppose you will bring a woman back with you."

"No, I don't have any intentions of that, but a lot of fine ladies live there." I visited with my best girlfriend and saw a lot of the old friends I had associated with and worked with, and I went to say good-bye to my former boss, the one I worked for while with the Standard Oil Co.

He said, "It's a good thing you decided to take that training with the government. I had to lay off most of my crew shortly after you left."

I returned to LA that night, and the next day, I went to the veteran's office and told them that I was leaving for West Virginia. "Well, you'll be back?"

"Yes, I don't intend to stay more than two or three months." I bid everyone good-bye.

An old sea captain that I was acquainted with at the veteran's bureau suggested, "Why don't you go to San Pedro harbor and get a job on a ship sailing to New York? I'll recommend you to an old friend there, and I think he will sign you on." I was a little short of spending money, and that was a good idea. That would be a nice trip through the Panama Canal. I had always wanted to see that wonderful job they did in building the canal.

I packed my trunk and expressed it to Porter's station near home. (I kept out the clothes and other necessities for my trip.) Then I sat down and wrote my mother a long letter. I told her that she was getting her wish, that I was coming home and that I had shipped my trunk and was going to sail as soon as I could get a ship that way. I went to LA Harbor in San Pedro and applied for a position. While waiting for a boat going my way, I worked at loading ships and doing odd jobs. I stayed there for about a week.

On the first day of May, I got assigned to an oil tanker named *Dixie* that was going to New York City. I sat down and wrote my mother that this was a happy birthday for me. I would start home tomorrow. It would take me about twenty days or more to make the trip down south, on the Pacific, to Panama and through the canal, across the Caribbean Sea, and north on the Atlantic Ocean to New York. From there I would come on home by train.

They had four big oil lines with hoses connected to the tanks on the ship. After we got our pipes connected and everything ready, it took us another thirty-five hours or so to fill the tanks. I looked after the oil pumps and kept them going as fast as it was safe to run them, and we got it done in a reasonable time. By about midnight the next day, it was full and heavily loaded. There wasn't more than twelve feet from the deck to the water. We had around three hundred thousand barrels on it. It was a big tanker. (During World War II, a German submarine sank it on the Atlantic Coast.) But they got it up and refurbished it. It hadn't been back in use more than a year or two. It was really a pretty boat. It was painted black, red and white—mostly white.

By noon the next day, we were ready to sail. As soon as we finished loading our supplies aboard the ship, we wasted no time in getting started for New York City. We disconnected our lines and lifted our anchors, the engineer blew his whistle good-bye, and we got underway. We were soon out to sea, but we didn't get out of sight of land until sometime during the night. With the exception of a few uninhabited islands, we didn't see any more land for about eight days. I wanted to get a job at oiling those big engines on the boat, but the captain said, "It's not worthwhile unless you are going to stay on the ship. That job takes training. You might get your arm cut off."

"Well, I want to be honest about it. I'm just making this one voyage to go east."

He says, "I'll get you a job waiting on the officers' tables. There's about six of us, and that will be a good job for you. It won't take much of your time, and you can view the sights as you go along." I thanked him for his help and kindness. I was well pleased to get that job and thankful for the privilege of having more opportunity to see the territory along the way. I don't like service work of that kind—that's a ladies job—but it suited me fine for this short run.

That was the longest voyage I ever made on the waters. It's nearly 6,500 miles from San Pedro to New York City. In comparison, it's about 4,000 miles from Brooklyn harbor to France by Halifax, Nova Scotia, Canada. Although in zigzagging from New York to France by Halifax, it took us about the same time to make that trip. In going to France, we sailed out to sea at New York about 500 miles or more in order to get away from the coast, where there was more danger of the enemy's subs attacking us. It took us twenty-three days to go to France and the trip from San Pedro to New York harbor took twenty -two days.

On the first morning of our voyage, I got up early to get lined out for my job as a waiter. I told my boss I didn't know much about that kind of work and that I was afraid I would embarrass someone. He showed me how to set the table in style and how to wait on the customers and the crew. I carried the food to the tables and placed it as near to its proper place as I knew how. Then I stayed nearby to do anything I could to wait on the table. When they got through eating their meals, I carried the dishes to the sink and washed them. Then I put them away in shape to set them on the table again. I cleaned the table and swept and mopped the dining room. I kept it shining and in good order—as best I saw how.

I got along very well in learning my job, but one of the crew made a nasty remark about something that I did in a hurry. He bawled me out, and it didn't look so polite. He was Danish, and he thought he was a man to be looked up to. He liked to boast about how he did things and how they managed things in Denmark. There's no American who likes a proud boaster. As far as his being Danish, I was just as respectable myself as an American. I had as much to say as he did. He wanted to slap me, but he held back. I didn't want to hit him either. He wasn't much heavier than me, but I realized I shouldn't hit him without him hitting me first. I could be charged with mutiny at sea, but I didn't have to keep my expressions modest. I thought, *I'm not in the army now.* I wasn't afraid of him. I was so angry that I wanted him to slap at me, then I could give him all I had. I was pretty strong for a little man, and I was as agile as a cat. That was the last trouble I had with him, and he was the only person I had any trouble with on the voyage. I always tried to be good to everybody, and I didn't have any intentions of mistreating anyone. If my boss heard about our trouble, he never mentioned it to me.

We had been on our voyage for two days, and each day, we were getting into a warmer climate. We saw a lot of porpoise in big schools at this time and throughout our journey, and we could see flying fish most any time we looked out to sea. They are about six or eight inches long or longer, and they would slip out of the water and sail like bats.

I had the same chores daily, and I had some time to spare. I spent most of my spare time on deck. I met the signalman, or radioman, on the ship. He learned that I had never sailed much, and he seemed to take an interest in telling me about the sea and the things that he had experienced.

We were about two weeks getting to the Panama Canal. We were getting nearer to it daily, and it was about the middle of May. It was getting so hot that one could hardly stay in the sunshine. You could look out over the ocean and see a shower of big drops of rain going or coming mostly anytime. The shower would pass by, and for a few minutes, the steam would fog the deck as though it was a furnace. It would dry up for a short while, and then another shower would hit us on and off all day long. The showers kept the temperature down some. Without them, a person could hardly stand the heat. Those sailors worked right ahead at their cleaning and painting, as though the heat didn't bother them. We saw very few other ships on our way. We were too far out to sea to get sight of the coastal ships.

We finally came into Panama Bay, and that was as far south as we went. That's about five or six hundred miles from the equator, and that's as close to the equator as I have ever been. As we sailed into the bay, it was hotter than ever. We were no longer getting so much of that good sea breeze. A camp of US soldiers was stationed near the entrance to the bay. I suppose they were there to protect the canal in case of war. They were living mostly in tents.

We passed through the cut in the hill that they had talked about so much when it was being excavated. It was about forty-five or fifty feet high. That's just a shadow of some of those five-hundred-foot cuts through the Appalachian Mountains near White Sulphur Springs, where Interstate 64 goes through. But it was quite an undertaking in 1904. We didn't have the machinery then that we have today. They did have a steam shovel. I suppose they used one of the first steam shovels ever made in America. They were about like one of our ordinary ditching machines, and it took a year or more to finish that small ditch through the knoll. I was surprised to see such a little cut. There was so much discussion of it in the newspapers, and they had so much to say about it that I expected it to be much more spectacular than it actually appeared to me. But that was a very big undertaking in those days. The St. Lawrence Canal is now the biggest canal we have. It was just finished a few years ago from the Great Lakes to the Hudson Bay and out to the Atlantic Ocean. There are plans to build a canal from the Great Lakes to the Mississippi and Ohio Rivers. Some of it is already built toward the Ohio in 1972.

We sailed on through another lock into an artificial lake about a mile wide and six miles long. The stumps, or snags, of the trees were still standing in the lake. Crocodiles and boa constrictor snakes were squirming all around the shorelines. It was a wild jungle through most of the canal. In places, we were near the bank, and we could see those big snakes in the trees, almost over our heads. There were monkeys in the trees too. I noticed that they kept clear of those big snakes! There were all kinds of pretty yellow, green, red, blue, and about any other color of birds. They were very pretty, and they looked better to me than those big snakes. This was a real wild jungle. There were lots of pretty ferns, trees, and vines. Some of the wildflowers were as beautiful as any I have ever seen anywhere on a voyage. That was the best trip I ever had, especially through those wild jungles.

We sailed on to our last lock on the Atlantic side of the canal, and we were soon ready to go across the Caribbean Sea through the Gulf of Mexico. Balboa was a small town in 1924. There were only about half as many people in America in those days as there are now, in 1972.

We passed through Balboa Bay into the Gulf of Mexico. That is usually a stormy body of water. I got a little seasick. The cook said, "Boggs, how would you like for me to get you a piece of fat meat on a string? You can swallow it again after it comes back up." He was trying to make me vomit, but I wasn't that sick. The sickness didn't affect me for more than a day or two. The sailors said the Caribbean Seas was as quiet as they had seen it. It's usually a rough sea.

We went through the Caribbean Sea and up between Cuba and Puerto Rico. I was standing on the deck with the radio signalman, and he said, "Look at that big man-eating shark. They follow a ship to get the garbage, and if you should fall overboard, they would ram that sharp dagger in you as soon as you hit the water."

We sailed to within sight of Puerto Rico and continued back out to sea. We didn't see much more land until we were near New York City. The weather was getting cooler as we sailed north, but the sun was bright. The air was blowing at about twenty-five miles per hour, and we began to feel a little chilly after being in those tropic climates. I had gotten pretty handy at my job by this time, and I was free most of my time to stay on deck and see all of the scenery. There were several ships sailing in our vicinity. We were near land and in one of the busiest coasts of the ocean. I saw the *George Washington* passenger ship that I had seen on the coast of Brest, France, when I embarked for New York in May 1919. (It had brought President Woodrow Wilson to the peace conference at Versailles, France.)

We were getting near the harbor. A lot of ships were coming in and out. We got to New York harbor on May 22. We had left San Pedro on May 1. Everybody seemed to be happy—at least the engineer of the boat. He kept blowing the whistle until the captain told him to stop it. We could be fined for making unnecessary noise in the city.

That was a fascinating voyage, even if the weather was a little too warm! For a nice trip, some conditions weren't too good. Our rations weren't exceptional, but that is usually the complaint on a boat. People who have never sailed much don't usually feel too hardy, and they usually get some nausea for a day or two during the voyage. No food tastes good when you are seasick. The boat was in good shape and up-to-date, as you'll usually notice about equipment operated by a big corporation like the Standard Oil. That was a jolly crew. We were pretty busy at games and recreation when off duty, and that made the time fulfilling, but I don't think more than half of the crew signed up for another voyage. We were mostly just travelers on the trip for sightseeing. The core members of a crew, who make sailing their livelihood, usually don't change much.

The boat pulled into the docks and anchored at New York City harbor at about noon. I had my belongings packed and ready to disembark, and I was one of the first to get off. This was my first trip to that city. I was in Brooklyn in 1918, and we camped on Long Island for about two weeks before sailing to France, but I didn't get into the Big Apple at that time. We weren't allowed any vacation so near the time for going to war.

Before we got off the boat, the radioman told me a lot about the city and how to get around. He showed me some of the skyscrapers. The Empire State Building, the tallest building in the world, was the one I remembered best. I caught a cab to the Pennsylvania Railroad Station and got rid of some money by buying a ticket to Charleston, West Virginia. I had some twenty-dollar gold certificate bills, and they would look too tempting to a thief if he got his eye on them. I left my baggage at the depot and walked up Broadway.

I saw some of the city's main buildings and sights that I had always read about. Then I got a hotel room and put up for the night.

The next morning, I boarded a train to Washington, DC, and I got there in the late afternoon. This was my first trip to Washington. I stayed there overnight and saw a few sights. Then I caught a train to Orlando, West Virginia. I had to wait there for about four hours for the next train. That was a small town—you might say only a village. I got restless while waiting so long. I was so tired of traveling and anxious to get home once more after nearly four years that it seemed more like a day than four hours.

I met a few hillbillies and spent my time very well. I enjoyed talking with people of my native state and learning what had taken place all those seven years I'd been away. I learned that my old home state wasn't so far behind times, at least not as much as some people thought it was. There are too many people who think of West Virginians as an ignorant lot of people, but I've met more ignorant people in mostly any of the thirty-one states that I've been in. Mountain folks usually have more vigor than the people of the plains or the coastal states. They take West Virginia to be a very poor and lackadaisical state, but it is very active in business and recreation, and it has more natural resources than mostly any other state.

6

Right Back Where I Started From

I boarded a train in Orlando at 10:00 p.m. and arrived at the Camp Creek Station the next afternoon. There wasn't anyone there to greet me. They didn't have any idea about when I'd be home. I left part of my luggage at the post office and walked across the hill. I was at the door before anyone saw me. I was certainly happy to get home and see my folks. Mother saw me first. She grabbed me and hugged me and cried for joy. She hadn't seen me for nearly four years. I was tired, but I didn't get to bed until late that night. Dad took my hand and shed tears with me too. Clyde and Glenn were the only other members of the family at home. They were out about the farm, but they came in after few minutes. Neither of them was grown up then. Glen was the youngest, and I'd been away about all of the time since he was born. He hardly knew me. He had seen me only a few times since he was old enough to remember. Waitman, Lee, and Ona came in late that day. Cornelius had married while I was away, and he lived nearby. He came in that evening. We had a merry time.

When I got up late the next morning, it seemed very quiet. (That contrasted with the previous two nights in New York City and Washington, DC, where there were so many noises.) The air was so fresh and calm. The sun was shining so bright here, away from any smog or fog, and I didn't smell the saltwater of the oceans and seas, which I had been accustomed to for the last month. The forests were fresh and green in their tender new buds and leaves. The dogwood and magnolia were bright with their pure white bloom. The redbuds were beautiful with their glowing lavender buds. The clover fields were in bloom with their pretty red flowers, almost ready for harvest.

Mother's flower garden was aglow with all colors of zinnias, marigolds, and assorted flowers. They looked prettier than Burpees Gardens in Burbank, Los Angeles, or Wrigley's Garden in Pasadena, California.

I had stayed too long in the dead plains and coastal ranges, where it was dry desert anywhere it wasn't irrigated or where it wasn't being used. (In places, the desert was white with alkaline salts and too dead to grow grass, brush, or tumbleweeds.) Now everything looked so lively with nature's beauty. West Virginia's natural beauty and its lively nature make it one of the most beautiful places on God's green earth.

Clyde and Glenn were working in the garden. They came in at noon, and after we ate dinner and they rested for about an hour, I got a hoe and went to work with them. I always liked to work in a garden, where there were so many different kinds of plants—fresh and green and growing so fast that you could see it daily. At this time (June), they were growing very heartily. The weather here was getting very warm. Onions, lettuce, radishes, and early vegetables were ready for the table. Garden produce is so much fresher and tastier when you get it right out of your garden the same day you put it on the table.

We came in and ate supper and chatted a few minutes, and then I picked up my hoe and worked some in Mother's astonishing flower garden. Some of the flowers, such as the Easter flower (daffodils), gladiolas, poppies, etc., had quit blooming, but they were still aglow with the pretty green colors. White, red, yellow, and pink roses were just beginning to bloom. They were so beautiful!

They had made several improvements to the house while I was away. They had added two more bedrooms, and they had built a cellar with a big room over it. We called that room the smoke house.

I had to revisit all the sixty-acre farm, most of which I had helped clear from the forest. I climbed to the top of the knob, the highest hill, where I always liked to see the pretty view in all directions. The best scenery was toward the northeast, where you could look out over the foothills of the Appalachian range toward the Blue Ridge Mountains as far as your eyes could see. You could view the high mountains until they faded from your eyes. On a bright sunny day, when the air was so clear of smog or fog, one could see for miles and miles. The mountains rise up in the blue until they are dimmed by the horizon. There wasn't any manufacturing in that direction. Charleston (the manufacturing center) is toward the southwest of our home farm while the Appalachian range is toward the northeast. Toward the south and southwest, the hills are lower. They look like small knolls side by side as far as you can see, but they are just as beautiful as the other mountains. At that time of the year, everything was so fresh and green—a light color to a dark green—and the daisies, clover, and other pretty flowers were bright with bloom. They were just wonderful. The dogwood and magnolia had begun to fade in their bloom, but locust trees on the hilltops were in full flower, and they sent out a sweet fragrance from their pretty white and pink blossoms. A gentle breeze stirred the air just enough to mix those scents with the cool moisture from the nearby trees and give the air a very fresh feel.

The summer and spring birds were busy building their nests. The cardinal, now our native state bird (the titmouse was our state bird then), was whistling its pretty soft chimes, and a bluebird was chattering with its pretty musical songs while cleaning out a hole for its nest in a tree trunk. The quail was saying, "Bob-bob-white." The crickets and some of the birds were singing their *teet-teet* songs. Everything was alive with beautiful chimes of nature. Flowers of the fresh blooming daisies perfumed the air, and the trees were alive with summer coming on. The sounds of wind rustling the leaves, bees gathering nectar from the flowers, and all of the other sounds that you don't notice over the noises of busy cities blended together to enrich the atmosphere.

I thought about the other beautiful seasons in West Virginia. The valley is the beauty of the winter, with snow clinging to the spruce trees. The pretty green ferns and the pretty green holly, with those dots of deep red berries, all add to the beauty of winter in the valleys. There's no prettier place of nature than those West Virginia hills.

Right here in Clay County, we have the pretty blue waters of the Elk River, two hundred and fifty miles long, with its swinging and winding turns in those deep canyons by those sharp points of rock, and high tea tables hundreds of feet up the steep bluffs of those hills and mountains, shining real arts of nature, which take millions of years to form. (I'm told that the Appalachian Mountains are about two billion years old.) Where will you find any prettier place of nature? Not in the Rockies, not in the Vosges Mountains of France, not in the high mountains and peaks of Switzerland. In all the thirty-one states I've visited, the fresh scenery and the majestic mountains of West Virginia are the prettiest of all. The mind can't think of words to express the stunning beauties of God's nature.

I stayed about home for a few days while I waited for the rest of my brothers to come in so I could see all of them. (My only sister was at home.) None of them were working far from home, and we all gathered to celebrate my homecoming. We found our songbooks and sang some old hymns. Guy sang soprano, Dad and Alvah sang tenor, Cornelius and I sang bass, and Mother and Ona sang alto. (Cecil was a good tenor, but he was away teaching school and couldn't be with us that night.) Alvah sang alto at times when there weren't any women to sing with us. When we were together long enough to practice, we made some good music. We often sang with the choir at church. Singing provided a lot of our entertainment in the days when we didn't have cars.

I had to see my granddad Estep. He was the only grandparent I had left. I had to go about five miles to his home. I walked across the hill to Apex (formerly called King Shoals), where I had to cross Elk River. A good neighbor, Levi Cook (his son, Patrick Burton Cook, was married to my aunt Lula, Mother's sister), set me ashore on the other side of the river. (That was the same spot where he had boated me over the river many times when I was a small boy.) I thanked Mr. Cook for being so obliging, and that's all he would accept, as always. He never charged anyone a penny for rowing them across the river, and he and his family did a lot of that. Sometimes a person would drop a coin in his boat for him, as I often did when I had the change. I then had to walk about two and one half miles up Upper King Shoals Creek, where I had traveled in my youth on my way to Wood Island School, and then about one mile over the hill to the head of Lower King Shoals Creek, where Granddad's property was located.

I got on my way up the creek, walking on the old tram road that was bridged along the steep hill bluff. I noticed a three-cornered crosstie with its sharp corner sticking out. That reminded me of the time my older brother Guy fell on one like it just about there while we were on our way home from school. He cut his nose off until it dropped down over his lip. As it would be, a doctor lived just a few yards from there, and we rushed Guy back to him. The doctor dressed it and fastened it back as best he could, and it healed very well. (He still has a scar, but you can hardly see it.)

I walked on past General Cook's place (he was the brother of Levy, who set me across the river) and on by the pawpaw groves, where I had gathered pawpaws to take my mother and dad and my younger brothers and my sister. Some of the trees were large enough to climb, and I would shake the trees to get the ones that I couldn't reach from the ground if I couldn't get them by climbing the tree. (Most of those that fell when we shook the tree were so big and so ripe that they would mash when they hit the ground. So it was better to pick them from the tree if we could.) I walked another mile or so past an old house where the old lady Widow Shaver had lived. She had passed away, and the old house was falling apart. She would watch us on our way to and from school, and sometimes she would invite us to stop and warm our feet and hands. Then she would hurry us on to school so we wouldn't be marked tardy or on home so our parents wouldn't be worried. She was a Black Hawk Indian. She and her children had a very dark complexion.

I walked on up the creek about two miles, and then I started up the hill toward where we had lived from 1902 to 1908. I stopped at one of the springs where Mr. Bill Arthur had chipped out a hole in a rock. I had a good cold drink of mountain water, and then I just sat there for a half hour or so. Time stood still. I was spellbound. I was mesmerized by the place where I had played until I was about ten years old. We had rambled among the rock cliffs and deep canyons until there was hardly a foot of this ground that I hadn't been over.

Some of the banks were covered with rugged laurel and rhododendron thickets (the rhododendron is our state flower, and it is very pretty), and there were some rough waterfalls there. There were rock cliffs sixty feet high, where we would build fires and where we would camp in the old bear dens. Wildcats were still plentiful, and there were still a few black bears and panthers in the area.

I walked on up the hill to where we used to live. The place had run down, and it looked like the house was ready to cave in. A family was living there (I don't like to mention names when I can't say any good about them, especially after they have passed away) that was accused of moonshining. They were no good, and they lay around drunk. It made me sad to see my old home place, where I spent some of my happiest days of my life, go to the dogs. This was where I learned to hunt rabbits, quail, pheasants, and squirrels. But because the timber had been cut pretty close, the small game had almost vanished. My grandfather cut over the timber, and another party had cut it again.

I went on over the hill to lower King Shoals Creek, where my grandfather and uncle Robert Estep lived. I sure was glad to see them again after nearly four years. Granddad was nearly blind. He had had operations on his eyes for cataracts. He wanted to hear about California and about my trip from Los Angeles, or San Pedro harbor, south on the Pacific Ocean and through the Panama Canal, through the Caribbean Sea, and around the Bahama Islands, Cuba, and Puerto Rico. Because I had been in the World War I, and he had been in the Civil War, we had some very interesting conversations. He talked about the battles of Gettysburg and Bull Run, and I told him about the Belleau Woods, Meuse-Argonne, Verdun, and the Vosges Mountains in France. Granddad was a very interesting man to talk with about mostly anything. He was only sixteen when he was called to join the rebel army. He was never too proud to admit that he was on the wrong side of the war. He said he didn't know that he shot anybody, except one of his rebel buddies. (He accidentally let his gun go off and shot his buddy in the heel.)

I saw my aunt Florence and uncle Robert and my cousins. They were the closest to me of any of my relatives outside the family. I'd lived near them for a long time. I was very glad to see them again. Everybody asked, "When are you going back to California?"

I always answered, "I want to stay about home for two or three months, but I do intend go back to California. I like the climate, and it agrees with me better than what we have here. Also, I have bought property in LA. I aim to go back in a month or two." I stayed with my grandpa for a day or two and then went back home.

After another week, I went to Wallback to see my uncle Filmore Belcher and family, whom I had lived with for nearly a year. Aunt Lida was my mother's oldest sister, next to Mother in age, and she was very dear to Mother. They always visited each other as often as they could, but that was only once or twice a year. In those days, people had to travel by foot or horseback. That was the only way you could get over most of the roads.

I had to hike so many, many miles in the army that I said, "If I ever get back home, I'll never walk another mile." I did walk pretty far to see my uncle Filmore and aunt Lida Belcher, but we had some very engaging conversations. He was a woodsman—timber cutter—for years. He supervised the woods crew, and he filed the crosscut saws for all of his crew. His saws cut into the wood the best of any I ever pulled. In those days, we were cutting the choice hardwood timber in virgin forests. I have cut big white oak trees that were as much six feet thick. Some of them didn't have a branch anywhere less than seventy-five feet up the trunk. That was the best timber in the eastern half of the United States. Uncle Filmore could file a saw so even on each tooth that it wouldn't run off the mark more than one and a quarter inch in a stave block that was six feet thick. The saw had to start right and go through a tree exactly right, or some of the staves would be turned out at the wrong length, and that would ruin the timber.

I asked, "Uncle Filmore, do you remember how near we often came to death in that dangerous work? Do you remember that heavy white oak branch that broke and caught on another tree when falling and how that tree swayed down and up? It threw that two-hundred-pound branch within an inch or two of your head. You had your hat on and your head down, and you didn't notice it until it hit the ground just barely behind you."

"Yes, I do," he answered, "and I did finally get hit by one that didn't go an inch over my head, and that's the last timber I felled." Uncle Filmore was such a good timber cutter that many logging firms kept begging him to work for them. He was so accommodating that he stayed on until he was seventy-five years old. He was a very good neighbor and a fine man, and he raised an admirable family.

When I came back to Porter's Creek after visiting my friends and relatives, I was still puzzled about what to do. I intended to go back to California, but I would be taking too much of a chance by bearing the expenses without knowing what propositions I might have to comply with by leaving home, where I presently had room and board without too much worry. I was getting enough money from my government pension to kind of keep up my meals, and I helped raise the seasonal crops and put them in storage. There were but very little expenses otherwise.

I helped Mother bring in the garden produce as it became ready to gather and make ready for storage. We picked beans and strung them for drying and for canning. There were different vegetables to take care of—tomatoes, cucumbers, carrots, turnips, corn, mustard, and other vegetables. This was like the old time way of making a living, and it took very little cash in those days.

I found a day or two's work on neighboring farms and some in the gas fields. I kept looking for work, but it appeared that there wasn't much use to look. Things were so slack in business that it looked pretty gloomy. There was a bit of drilling going on (for oil and gas), but there wasn't much need for that as long as business was so slow. However, the United Fuel Gas Company had drilled a few wells, and it looked like business would pick up some.

Finally, in November or December, there was talk of building a big gas-pumping station in a big river bottom about a mile and one-half below Porter Station. That seemed to be too good to be true. The Hope Natural Gas Company, a new business in this area, started the project. They began by building a railway switch to ship in material to build the plant. They broke the sod there on the twenty-fourth of December, but they didn't use more than a few men in the beginning. They had a big station in Doddridge County (Hastings Station), and they brought some of their men from there. It was a bad winter, and they didn't get much done.

I kept going there every Monday morning (and sometimes two or three days per week). Until spring, they hired only a few men at a time. I finally got disgusted at the supervisor for telling me to come back in a day or so. He encouraged me, but I was so anxious to get into something appealing to me that I began to get impatient. It had been the longest period that I was without a steady job since I was mustered out of military service. I went to see the supervisor again, and I asked him if there wasn't something he might start me to work at. I told him I had had a few years experience in the gas industry, and that I had done about everything there was to do in the oil and gas fields. I said that I would also like to get on at the pumping station when they finished building it.

He still talked favorably of hiring me. I finally told him off. I exclaimed, "Mr. People, I have been coming here for over a month, and right along, you have been asking me to come back."

In a hurry to complete a task, he snapped back, "When I want help, there's always someone handy to hire."

I said, "Okay, I'll be right here when you want a man."

There were, nearly always, forty or fifty men there by seven o'clock every morning. Many of them hadn't made any wages for so long that they were destitute. I kept my word, and I was there when they did need me. They hadn't hired anyone early that morning, and it was about 10:00 a.m. I saw Mr. People talking to his assistant, and then he walked away. The assistant started toward the ten or twelve men still standing on the railroad track. I stepped out to meet him. He took my name and gave me a mattock and shovel. He marked out a line up the hill for me to dig a ditch for a waterline to the place where they would set their first tank for domestic use. Out of fifty or so men that were looking for work that day, I think I was the only one they hired.

I started right away at digging the ditch. It would be about seventy-five yards long and fifteen inches deep. The width was just enough to get a shovel in handily. It was needed for a two-inch line to carry water to where they would set the tank. I dug it as straight as I could, and I dressed the sides down good and smooth. While I was digging, I noticed the boss at a distance talking to his assistant, and I thought I understood what he was saying. He wanted to know if I just wanted a job or wanted to work. He seemed to be watching me pretty close, but I hardly looked up. I didn't want him to think I noticed him.

I was a little tender to work at such hard labor, but I kept at it. I didn't let on to show anybody how much I was hurting, and when I got the ditch finished, I didn't wait for the boss to come to me. I shouldered my mattock and shovel and hunted him to let him know that I had finished it. He went back with me to inspect the ditch. He looked it over good. "Well," he said, "you got this job done pretty quick." When I stared on a new job, I always worked fast. I wanted to show my boss that I didn't mind working and that I always did the job as well as I could. Anything worth doing is worth doing well. The Hope Natural Gas Company always wanted everything to be neat— even if it did take a little more time.

The boss took me to where they were setting a steam boiler—an old Climax boiler like we used for drilling gas wells. It had a square firebox on one end, and the boiler tank ran out about twelve feet further and sat about five feet off the ground. There were three men working at it. Clarence "Pete" Judge was the boss of the crew, and he had set many boilers. I told him I had helped set up a few of them. He asked what I had done. I told him, and he said, "I did too. I've drilled a lot of wells."

"Well, I've helped drill several too. I was a tool dresser." I told him that I could climb an eighty-foot derrick about as quick as anyone.

We trued up the boiler and set it up in good shape by plumbing it and leveling it. Then we laid a gas line. The United Fuel Gas Company had a gas well near the boiler, and the South Penn Oil Co. had an eight-inch gas line near there. We ran our lines to the boiler from it. We also laid a two-inch line to the river to pump water into the boiler for steam. We installed a steam whistle on top of the boiler. This was the first whistle that blew at Cornwell Station on March 1925. They still blow that whistle at certain times during workdays, but there isn't a steam boiler there now. The plant has been converted almost entirely to gas-powered engines.

When we completed setting the boiler and laying all of the pipelines to it, Clarence Judge said, "Ira, you get you a shovel. Slip down the railroad and climb up in that freight car where they're unloading that sand for concrete, and you won't have to work in this mud." I got a shovel and went to work. Clarence said, "I'll tell the boss that I told you to do that." I was working there the next day, when a man came along and asked if I knew a place he could get board and room. He said he had a job if he could get a place to stay.

I said, "No, I don't, but if you want to go home with me, I think you can stay overnight with us or until you can find a boardinghouse." About that time, I saw the boss start toward me, almost in a run.

He said, "Get to work. What do you think we hired you for? To stand and talk?" (That gave me more time to stand and talk.)

I answered, "I was helping this man to get a place to stay while he works for you. You can't keep men here if they can't find a place to stay." You hardly dared to stop to look up, or you would lose your job. There were too many men hunting for work. They could just step over to the railroad track mostly anytime and get a man who would work hard because he had a family that was almost starving. People had been out of work for months, some for two or three years.

I brought that man, Mell Lipscomb, home with me, and he worked at Cornwell until he died, nearly at retirement age. He and his wife were the oldest people on the job. They never had any children of their own, but they raised a boy and a girl, their nephew and niece. The children called them Uncle and Aunt, and all of the children around called them Uncle Mell and Aunt Cora, so everybody got to calling them Uncle and Aunt. Aunt Cora married my uncle Charles Foreman a year or two after Aunt Julia died, and I still called her Aunt Cora.

We unloaded several cars of sand and gravel and cement, and we were finally ready to start putting up the main building for the pumping station. We had a cement mixer that could mix two sacks of cement at a time. It was powered by steam from the boiler I had helped set up. I looked after engineering of the cement mixer. I had it going when work time came, and I kept it oiled and watched over it during the day. Clarence Judge ran the crane that handled the concrete. Between the two of us, we ran the machinery that handled car after railcar loads of cement that went into the buildings. In addition to the floors and foundations for two fifty-by-one-hundred-fifty-foot buildings that included engine blocks for five one-thousand-horsepower steam engines, foundations, and blocks for five big double boilers. They also laid firebrick to line the furnace and red wall brick for the walls. There were five sets of boilers—one for each steam-powered gas-pumping engine. One boiler was set up over the other—two for each of five sets. Four-inch tubes about thirty feet long ran from the lower boiler to the upper boiler and through the furnace.

They built a coal bin above the furnace at the end of the boiler house. It would hold a carload of coal (about fifty tons). They had a trestle about fifteen feet high for the railroad cars to run on so they could put a coal crusher under the railroad cars. The crusher included two big spools about six feet long by four feet in diameter, with teeth on them. There were trapdoors on the bottoms of the railroad cars. To unload a railcar, someone took a sledgehammer and knocked a latch loose from the trapdoor. The coal dropped into a box over the crusher and fed into it. The coal was ground into small lumps and powder. It dropped into baskets on a belt that carried the coal to the top of a track. The baskets turned over on a shaft as they came back down. The crushed coal dropped into the bin. They had a crane high overhead to drop the coal into the furnace. It ran on a rail track and was powered by electricity. A large basket ran under this coal bin, and there was a lever to open up the coal bin and let about five hundred pounds of the crushed coal into the basket. The fireman would pull a chain to set an electric switch and start the basket to rolling on the overhead track. He would walk along under the basket clear through the boiler house from number one boiler to number five boiler. There was a hopper over each boiler, and each hopper had a spout latch. We could pull a lever and open the spout to fill the coal hopper. Sometimes we'd overfill the hopper, causing coal and coal dust to spill over, and we'd have to sweep it up and shovel it back into the hopper. The coal was fed into the furnace by a steam engine located in the basement of the boiler house. A rod ran up past the boilers to the hoppers. It turned three gears located in the hopper. The rod turned over very slowly, and it could be sped up or slowed down to regulate the feeding of more or less coal into the furnace. The furnace was about twenty by sixteen feet at its base and about twenty feet high where the flame touched some tubes with water running through them. That transferred heat to the water to make steam to run our steam engines.

There was one big fan in the basement for each of the five boilers to pull a draft of air and run it to the boilers. We could regulate the airflow into each furnace according to how much steam was needed to run those big one-thousand-horsepower engines. It took a lot of steam to pull those five engines. They had an eight-inch steam line that ran overhead to the engine house, which was about seventy-five yards from the furnace. The furnace was well closed in, and there was a smokestack for each set of boilers. Those stacks were about five feet in diameter and extended about two hundred feet into the air above the boilers. They had a powerful draft to them. There was a damper on each stack to help regulate the furnace according to how much steam was needed. When pumping the full load of gas, we would burn as much as 150 tons of coal in twenty-four hours.

Each of those engines had a flywheel that was twenty feet in diameter, and each weighed one ton. When they rolled over 115 times per minute at full speed, they had tremendous power. We didn't usually run them at less than one hundred revolutions per minute. I have seen them go as high as one hundred twenty times per minute. Then we would have to watch them closely, or they would burn out one or more of the bearings that cushioned a six-inch rod that was turning that fast. They were what you call twin engines—a low-pressure one and a high-pressure one. The low pressure pump would take the gas out of the field line and pump it into the high-pressure pump, which pumped it into a twenty-inch trunk line. The trunk line ran for twenty miles to Jones Station, and Jones Station pumped it on to Hasting Station in Doddridge County.

The field lines didn't usually handle over one hundred and fifty pounds of pressure, but when we were pumping a full load, the pressure would run as high as three hundred twenty-five pounds at the point of leaving the high-pressure engine that pushed it into the trunk lines. When you load a twentyinch line with three hundred or three hundred twenty-five pounds of pressure, you are pumping a lot of gas. We have pumped as high as 250,000,000 cubic feet of gas in twenty hours, but we didn't usually move more than 230,000,000 cubic feet in that time. Well, I'd better finish building the plant before I pump all of that gas. We finished running all of the concrete into the engine blocks and foundations for the buildings, and the steelworkers put up the buildings with steel frames and sheeting.

We went to work laying sixteen- and twenty-inch gas lines from the field lines to the engines. We used threaded pipe and screwed the joints into collars, which brought the ends together and sealed them. This was some of the last screw pipe ever used in the oil and gas fields. Later, they developed acetylene welding methods for joining the pipes, and now they can use electrical welds. For acetylene welding, they used long cylinders that were eight or ten inches in diameter and four and one half feet high, with a valve on top and a place to connect a hose. These tanks had two thousand pounds of pressure in them, and they lasted through several twenty-inch welds. When they emptied a tank, they would send it back to the chemical plant to get it filled. The tanks have been known to explode, and you dared not handle them roughly. Mostly electrical welders are used nowadays. The electric welding machine was hauled around on a motor cart or a truck. If it couldn't get up the hill on its own power, they could lift it up and let it down with a block and line, or they could haul it on a four-wheel-drive truck or on a bulldozer.

The threaded pipe that we first installed at the Cornwell Station was handled with sixteen- and twenty-inch tongs, and those tongs were very heavy. It took three men to carry them, and four to six men were needed to buck the tongs to screw the pipe together. I had done this kind of work in Texas and California, so I knew where the best jobs were. I was smaller than most of the men, and the boss would usually assign me to a light job. When I worked on the tongs, I got on the end next to the pipe where there was a short stroke. I was quick and knew when to jerk the tongs off and on. There was also what we called a stabbing man. He got on the outer end of the pipe and lined it straight with the joints to match the threads of the collar. At times he didn't get them lined straight, and we would get them started cross threaded. When that happened, we would have to unscrew the pipe and start over again. Sometimes, if we ruined the threads, we would have to reline a few joints and rethread them on a lathe at the machine shop.

That was hard labor, especially on the end of those eight-foot sixteen- and twenty-inch tongs, where there was more leverage and you had to buck the pipe further up and down. The boss would peck on the collar, where the pipe screwed together, with a two-pound hammer. That kept it jarred loose until the pipe screwed together. They had a squirt can of light oil, usually lard oil, to make it screw together smoother and to keep the threads from wearing. This was a very exacting job, and they didn't often have a leak. If we did have a leak in those days, we had to cut the pipe with a big cutting chisel that had a four-foot handle on it. A man would strike it with an eight-pound hammer to cut the twenty-inch line. Then it had to be rethreaded, matched, and put back together. To rejoin a pipe that had been cut in two, we used a follower. That had a collar to slip over each end of the pipe with a bevel on each end of the collar. It had bolt holes and a large rubber ring to fit in the bell end and a ring with bolt holes in it. We would run the bolts, usually six or eight, through the holes and screw them very tight with wrenches. The joint would hold four hundred pounds of pressure. That was before they learned the welding method, but about that time (1925), they were doing some light-pressure welding for joining heavy pipelines.

For four or five months, while another crew was setting the engines and boilers, we worked hard at laying the lines and fitting pipes. That was one of the hottest months of May that I have ever seen, and it was hot on through the summer. We didn't take much time in the shade, but we had to watch about getting too hot. We got the lines about laid, and they set the coolers for each discharge engine to cool the gas. The gas got very hot from pressure while it was being pumped through those engine valves or compressors. On one-half revolution of the engine, the intake valve would open and let the gas in, then it closed, and the other half revolution would push it through the high-pressure valve and out into the line at a high pressure. That would send it on for twenty miles, where a relay station pushed it further on to another relay station or to the consumers.

I asked Frank Purpel about getting a job for me in the producing department when they started to pump gas. He told me he didn't have anything to do with that, but he said that he would recommend me. At that time, I was working for Dallas Powell, and I knew he wanted me to work for him, but he was taking the job of operating the trunk lines. I asked Sye Zarbough about a job with him. He was taking over the station as chief engineer. He said, "You go with Dallas for now. Dallas and I plan on trading men later." Dallas assigned me and Charley Linler to watching a gas meter on the hill from Cornwell. We regulated it by pinching a valve until they got the right pressure and flow rate on the gas line. We worked there for three months, and we each worked twelve hours per day, rotating our shifts so that one of us was always on the job. We were paid forty-five cents per hour, as usual. They were building a plant at Cornwell to take the gasoline out of the gas before shipping it. The gasoline mixed with water hindered the flow of gas through the lines. It would clog the lines, and they would have to install drip valves on the low places along the lines to blow some of it out on the ground. That wasted it.

Sye Zarbough called Charley and me to his office. He said, "Ira, I want you to night watch at the gasoline station while they build it." I worked there at a monthly salary, eight hours per day, six days per week until they got the gasoline plant ready to run. Sye gave me a job as pumper—a helper on the gasoline plant. They had three shifts, eight hours per shift.

I worked at the gasoline station for about one year before the boss and others made a complaint against me. Sye transferred me to the gas-pumping station as an oiler. I didn't tell Sye anything, but he understood why they didn't want me around. They were bringing bootleg whiskey onto the job and drinking it there. One of the men would go somewhere a mile or more and get it in the quiet of the night while he was supposed to be working. Sye finally caught him bringing it to the station. He discharged that man and suspended the boss and others who were drinking it. They were off for two weeks before he let them come back.

The new job was a step up for me. It was inside the plant and a warm place to work in the winter, but it was hot in the heat of the summer. After I worked there for three years, I was promoted to engineer. That raised my pay to $125 per month. That was good wages during the worst panic that ever hit this nation.

Business was still slack during the summer months, and the company didn't have work for all of the men at the Cornwell Station. They couldn't sell all of their gas when people weren't using it domestically. They found work elsewhere for us tower men. This was before they started pumping gas into old lines and wells during the summer, storing it for winter sales as they do now. The Hope Gas Company was growing fast. They only had one station in 1925, but that was a very large one. It was easily worth $12,000,000 or $15,000,000. Now they have merged with the Consolidated Gas and Supply Corporation and are worth several hundred million. They have holdings in several states and nations. At first, they were a part of the Standard Oil of New Jersey. (Glenn Corrin, who is still president of the Hope Gas Company, said that the men who built and operated Cornwell Station were the making of the Hope Gas Company.)

They were setting a fifteen-thousand-horsepower engine at Jones Station, Cornwell's relay plant. I went there in 1926 to help in the installation of that engine. I got there at about 10:00 p.m. The boss asked me if I wanted to go to work on the midnight shift in two hours. I told him I was pretty tired. He didn't say anything more. The next morning I went to work with the pile driving crew. The piles were made from pipe that they had on hand. The welders cut out part of the end of the pipe and heated it. They drew it together into a sharp point, and then they drove it about twenty feet into the ground. They had a pile driver that they themselves had manufactured. It was made of eight-by-twenty timbers, two of them framed together with a pulley wheel on top of it. It was about twenty feet high. They had a track inside of the frame. A line hooked to a block of steel weighing about five hundred pounds, and the line ran over the pulley wheel on top of the derrick. It ran down onto a spool on a shaft turned by a gas engine. This engine would pull the heavy block to the top of the derrick and drop it about ten feet onto the ten-inch pipe, twenty feet long, and drive it into the ground until it hit a solid base. We drove several of those pilings to support the base for that big Snow engine. The engine, with the compressor and rod, was about forty feet long and weighed several tons. It could pump twenty-five million cubic feet of gas per twenty-four hours. That pile driver hit about three licks per minute. (Now, in 1972, they have a pile driver that operates by compressed air. It can hit as fast as you can drive a nail with a two-pound hammer.)

Those pipes were cut off at the top of the ground and filled with concrete. It made a solid foundation. The cement would still be there after the pipe had decayed. We finished that job in about a month. The Hope Company had their headquarters at Pittsburgh, Pennsylvania, but they were moving to Clarksburg, West Virginia. We moved our rig to Clarksburg and worked there, driving pile for a four-story office building. We worked there for about two months or longer. They didn't furnish us material to go ahead with the work, and our boss had to lay us off for about a week, telling us they would have the material mostly any day. There were six men in the crew. We were stuck there, away from home, and we were a sore crew of men. Some of the men looked for another job. They did pay our expenses, but they should have paid our wages too. They only had three of the five engines running at Cornwell that summer. They finally started the other two engines and called me back there after we finished the Clarksburg job.

I got back to Cornwell on Monday morning and went back to my job in the pump house. I liked this job better. There was very little hard labor to it, and it was a nice clean place to work, and I could live at home. I liked to work at Cornwell. It was a good job, with the exception of tower work. We had three shifts per day—day, evening, and morning. I liked the day shift better. It was an hour's less time on the job. The other workers took an hour for rest at noon. We had to watch our machines, but we could sit down by our engine at noon and eat our dinner, and our time on the clock still counted, so we could leave an hour sooner when we were running shift work. I also liked the day shift better as we had the evenings to go out for a little recreation.

When on the evening shift, I came off from work at twelve midnight and slept until about 8:00 a.m. I had to guard against being too busy at day work, or I would be very tired by midnight. I'd get up at about eight o'clock, eat my breakfast, read the daily news, and work an hour or so (especially in the garden during the summer). Sometimes, I'd go to town for pleasure or shopping, but I would try to get back home in time to rest an hour or more before work time. The morning shift was the most disagreeable shift, but it appeared to be shorter than the day or evening shift. For some reason, time seemed to go by faster on the job, but I never could sleep more than two or three hours after coming off that shift in daytime. I'd usually go to bed at about nine thirty and sleep until about twelve or one o'clock. Then I'd get up and eat my dinner (lunch) and read the news, then I'd mill about the farm at anything there was to do. Sometimes I'd get my gun and go out and target practice, or hunt some (in hunting season), or get in my car with some friends and take a short drive. There were not any paved roads nearer than Clendenin, so I wouldn't go farther than Clendenin. I'd get back home in time to sleep another hour or two before work time.

I had to walk two and one half miles to get to my job. It was a mile and a half to the river, and then I walked a mile on the railroad track. By road, the distance was ten miles. We had to take a roundabout way to drive to Cornwell Station or across Elk River from the station, where we could park our car and then walk over a swinging bridge to the station. The roads weren't kept up very well, and it was hard to drive over them a lot of the year. In the winter, the roads were very rough and slick. I could walk on it about as quick as I could drive, and at times, anyone would have trouble getting over those muddy dirt roads in a car. In the summertime, they would scrape the roads once or twice, and then I would usually drive. When the roads were in bad condition, I would rather walk than drive, even if snakes and wildcats did threaten me.

One time, I was walking along the road in the forest after dark. I could hear something walking in the leaves about shoulder high. I had a flashlight, but my batteries were so weak that it didn't give enough light for me to see a stone. I felt one by my feet and threw it that direction. I repeated throwing stones, but the animal still took only a step or two. I said, "Mr. Wildcat, if you won't run, I will." After I settled down and as I neared our house, I was swinging my hands as I walked. My dog walked up by my side, and my fingers gripped the hair on his back. I almost jumped out of my boots. My hair stood up like a scared cat's.

I got so used to the wildcats following me. I didn't mind them so much, except when they were so close to me that they could leap on me, but I never heard of a wildcat attacking anyone. I was more afraid of being attacked by a mad dog or a mad fox. Several of those animals have been killed here and proven to be rabid.

I had one more long hike through the woods while working for the Hope Gas Company, and it brought back some memories of my teenage years when I worked at cutting virgin timber. I had gone to Nicholas County to help build a small pump station on Muddlety Creek at the foot of Sewell Mountain (the Hamilton Gas Co. had a few wells there, and the Hope Gas had bought their gas.) I didn't take my car. I rode with one of the other three men from Cornwell. We drove up to Birch River and over the Suel Mountain. I worked there for about six weeks before they called me back to Cornwell. I had to return alone, so I had to find my own way to get back, and the company gave me only one-half day for the return trip. I learned it was only about six or seven miles across the hill to Buffalo Creek. I walked through a forest that was part of a track that included ninety thousand acres of virgin timber. There were trees in that forest that would saw two or three thousand feet of lumber. They were still using a big hand mill for cutting lumber from this big track of timber. (They didn't finish it until about 1966. The mill that they used to finish that track of timber was a double-band mill. It would cut a log each time the carriage ran back and forth each way. It cut forty-thousand board feet per day.) I came to Widen and caught the Buffalo Creek and Gauley train to Dundon. From there, I caught the train to Procious. (It's now the B&O Railroad.)

I decided to make a little extra money by raising poultry. I constructed a twenty-by-twenty house with a row of nests through it. I installed a dropping board over the nesting stations and put a screen over it. Then I built roosts over the dropping board. I bought a gas-burning brooder and ordered five hundred white leghorn baby chicks. I would sell the cockerels and keep the pullets. I could depend on two hundred pullets to keep for laying hens. By September, they would be laying. There were thirteen families there at Cornwell, and I would deliver them good fresh eggs from twenty-five to thirty-five cents per dozen. Then I built two more twenty-by-twenty-foot houses and could have five hundred pullets at a time. I made a little extra money at this business.

I bought fifty acres of level and sloping hilltop land from my brother. I cleared some of it and grew corn for my chickens, so I was pretty busy, working five days per week at Cornwell while clearing ground and tending it in corn or small grain, wheat, or oats.

In a few years, there were so many people in the poultry business that I quit it. I couldn't compete with them. I cleared more of my land and decided to plant an apple orchard. I sold some trees for Stark Bro's nursery, and I got my trees cheap. I ordered one hundred golden delicious trees and some winter-apple varieties. I already had about twenty-five trees on my farm, and I planted two hundred more. In two or three years, those golden delicious trees began to bear. I made a little money at this business, but the orchard soon grew until I couldn't take care of it by myself. I couldn't hire anyone at fair wages, and I had to work too hard to run two jobs. I didn't do much at that business. In 1927, I bought forty-six acres of land on Porter Creek. It was within a mile of the railroad and a little closer to my job, and there was no hill to walk up on my way to work and back. Left Hand, where I stayed with my parents, was up a fairly steep hill for a mile or so. I got the land very cheap. It cost me $347. There were two and one-half acres of bottomland, with two nice places to build. I was still single, but I intended to build a house on it and rent it out or batch. I had batched some before while in California. I wasn't the kind of person who saw many women I liked, and I wasn't in any hurry about falling in love. I had met a few ladies in Texas and California whom I thought quite a bit of, but I never got engaged to any of them. If I could have gotten married, I wouldn't have been settled, and that's a bad time to marry. I had dated some few ladies for a few times, but I hadn't yet met a woman here that I wanted to marry.

7

Marriage and the Family

I became interested in a young lady that I saw a time or two when I was delivering eggs at the coal mining town of Barren Creek. I noticed that she was nice-looking and a big hardy girl. She was visiting some people that I delivered eggs to, and she brought me a basket to put the eggs in. I didn't talk to her. I saw that she seemed to be a little shy (maybe because she wasn't dressed to suit herself). Anyway, I inquired about her and learned that I knew her people. I had known her father, Mr. Grant McCune, since I was a child. He carried the mail by my home. I also knew his brothers and his father and mother, Mr. and Mrs. Bill McCune of Procious, where Grant lived when I was growing up.

They were all nice people. I also knew her mother's people. I wasn't well acquainted with them, but I used to attend church at Barren Creek, where her grandmother went to church. They were pretty intelligent people. Her uncles were a little rough, but they didn't matter to me. It was the woman that I wanted to get acquainted with. She was quiet, and I didn't mind that. I suppose that, in a way, she was like me. (People have told me that I was pretty slow to get to know.) The next time I saw her, she was nicely dressed, and she looked very pretty. She was quite a bit younger than I was, but at twenty, she was old enough to know people and to know what she wanted to do.

I finally had a chance to get a date with her. I had a nice little car, and I took her home from where she was staying at the time I met her. She lived near the head of Leatherwood, about five miles from Clendenin. I met her family. Her dad was there. He was an intelligent man to talk with, and he was a good Christian. They were

Methodist, and I was a Missionary Baptist. That didn't matter to me, either. I never gave too much consideration to the differences in those churches. I stayed and visited with her for a while. Then we got in the car and drove to Clendenin, where we went to the movies. We held hands and watched the show. When it was over, we got some ice cream.

We drove around for an hour or so, then I took her back home. There was a little too much difference in our ages, but we kept meeting once or twice per week and driving about from place to place. She had to make her own living, so she didn't stay at home much. She worked as a maid, and sometimes she stayed with her older sister at Smith Bottom, just a mile or so above Cornwell. That was pretty handy for me to see her often. Her brother-in-law Albert Smith and I had known each other since we were children.

I first met Miss McCune in September or October. We kept dating and getting better acquainted. I had begun to like her pretty well when some boys tried to take her away from me. I was a little jealous, but I thought that was a good test to see if she thought more of me than any other man. She had a close lady friend working in a restaurant at Marietta, Ohio, and she had some plans for going there to work with her friend. I didn't like the idea, but still, it wasn't a very long drive from here. Later, she told me that she didn't go because she didn't want to be so far away from me—where she couldn't see me often. That suited me too. We kept seeing one another once or twice a week, and sometimes, more often than that. We seemed to be in love. We just weren't satisfied when we were apart. We drove here and there, and we often just sat in the car, getting better acquainted and making love. She was twenty-one, and I was thirty-four. Well, we were old enough to make up our minds as to what we thought best. I thought that if I was ever going to marry, it was about time, and at her age, a woman usually worries about letting the years go by, and they don't want to let a good chance slip away.

This next spring, I had to leave Cornwell again for about three months. The Hope Gas had another plant. It was of the same type as

Cornwell but not quite as big. They were setting an engine there like we had at Cornwell—a one-thousand-horsepower Hamilton steam engine. It took quite a bit of work to build the forms and run concrete blocks for the engine foundation. They usually used twenty-five or thirty men to build the forms and run the blocks (or foundations) and set up the engine. This was the third summer with the Hope Natural Gas Company that I had to go elsewhere for work.

Jackson Station was about forty miles from home. Homer Cook, Clemit Taylor, and I rented us a house and batched that summer. We came home on weekends. I was with Miss McCune most of the time while at home from Chelyan. I seldom got started back to Chelyan before midnight. One Sunday, I stayed a little late with Miss McCune. That night, I drove back to Chelyan unusually late. I had never been so sleepy while trying to drive as I was that night, and I haven't been so foolish about it since then. I went to sleep while I was driving my rumble-seat Star car through Marmet, but I was startled when I went off of the pavement onto the berm. That woke me. I was headed toward a house. I jerked my wheel just in time to miss running right onto the porch of the dwelling. In one or two seconds more, I would have driven into that man's home. I was so shocked that I had to stop for a few minutes. That was the only time I ever went to sleep while driving an automobile.

Nellie and I made up our minds to get married within a month. I worked three weeks longer at Jackson Station, and I asked my boss if I couldn't take the week's vacation that I had coming before I was called back to Cornwell. He hesitated before he answered. I told him I was going to get married. He said, "Congratulations. Of course I'll let you off."

That Saturday, I came home after work and went to see Nellie. We made arrangements to go to Charleston on Tuesday. I came back home on Monday night, and on Tuesday morning, before I left to meet Nellie, I told Dad and Mother that Nellie and I intended to get married on that day. "Well," one of them said, "just as we expected. We talked about it while you were on vacation."

We didn't have any doubt about it. Before we left Mr. McCune's at about noon, Nellie told her people that the next time they saw her she would be a married woman. We went to Charleston and to J. O. Morrison's store, where we bought some clothes. Nellie picked out a nice wedding dress, and I paid for it. We got to the courthouse just in time to get our license before they closed. We asked the clerk where we could find a minister. A man standing nearby told us to go to Woodrum's Home Outfitting Company on Virginia Street. We went there and found Reverend Woodrum. He called on two of his clerks to serve as witnesses and took us into a little room that he reserved for that purpose. We were married on August 14, 1929. We took our vows at about six o'clock, then we had our supper and went to a show. We came out at about nine thirty and found a room at the Holly Hotel, where we stayed overnight. We left our hotel room at about nine o'clock the next morning and went to a restaurant for our breakfast. Then we walked around town for an hour or two. We shopped some and then drove back by my home. We stayed there until early evening, when we drove to Leatherwood and stayed at her home on Wednesday night.

We enjoyed being together alone, but we did visit some with our friends and families. We went to see my grandfather nearby. He was the only one of my grandparents still living, and he was getting very old. (He was in poor health, and he lived only a few weeks longer.)

Nellie and I drove around the country a lot that week. On one excursion, we followed the highway about thirty miles to Spencer. The counties had finished paving that road, and I suppose it was the longest piece of paved road in the state at that time. (In those days, the counties paved the roads.) They finally paved a ten-foot one-way road to Charleston. In about ten years, they paved another ten-foot, making a two-lane highway to Parkersburg.

When the one-way road was paved, everybody who had a car had to try it out. Shortly after the road opened, I was driving a Buick car below Clendenin, near Falling Rock. There was about a six-inch drop on each side of the pavement. They hadn't made the berm and smoothed it yet. Another car started around us. It hit my car and knocked it off of the pavement into a rock road bank. We all got a pretty hard jolt, but none of us was hurt bad. My brother and I and Marjorie and Blanche Foreman were in my car. Blanche was the worse hurt. She had to use crutches for a few days. The rest of us had a few bruises. This was the first wreck I had had while driving. It was the other driver's fault, and he knew it, but he drove on while the excitement was on. Some people told us the name of the person that they thought was driving the car that bumped us, but we couldn't get any proof, and we had to drop it. I had a wrecker pull my car back to Clendenin to a garage, and I had to leave it there.

I had to go back to Chelyan to work that weekend. Nellie stayed at her home while I worked there for about another month. I came back every weekend until late September, when I returned to work at the Cornwell Station. This was the last time I left Cornwell to work elsewhere. Business was getting a little better. The Hope Gas Company was drilling a few wells, and they were selling more gas. I had received two promotions in the five years I had worked for the company. I was doing very well with them. I couldn't have found a better job anywhere in the country.

I wanted to build a dwelling on my property on Porter Creek, but I decided to wait until spring. After work, I kept coming to look at my land and think about where I should build. I had a little more room in another bottom from where I decided to build, but it was windier there in the wintertime. I noticed that on a clear day that the sun set at the head of Ad Hollow, and during the winter, it shined here until within a half hour of sundown. In the summertime, it didn't hit here so much. It raised over one point and set over another point, and the wind came up the creek and down Ad Hollow. The two breezes met here, and it didn't make so much draft as it did in the other bottom. I had about decided to build between the road and the creek and to keep one-half acre of bottomland on the other side of the creek for an extra garden. The road ran a little close to my door, so I had it moved some. That made a better place for the road too.

My parents had a fourteen-by-twenty house over the cellar. Nellie and I bought what furniture we could get along with and moved into it. We planned to stay there until spring or until I could build on my property on Porter Creek.

When I had spare time, I worked some on my lot to get the brush cleared. By February, I had it in shape to start building. I went to the Farmers & Citizens Bank at Clendenin and made arrangements for money to build. The cashier seemed to be anxious to loan me the money. He didn't hesitate. He asked me if I had a clear deed to the land. I told him yes, and he deposited the money into my account for me to use for the project.

We picked our house pattern from a catalog that I had received from a firm in Chicago. It gave the room layout for the house and all the details we needed to know, but it didn't include blueprints. Everybody advised me not to build a big house. Nellie and I decided to choose between two designs. One was a story and a half. The other was a one-story bungalow. We didn't want to put too much money into a home so far out in the country, so we decided on the five-room bungalow with a bathroom and two bedrooms with closets, a full basement, a hallway and backdoor, and an eight-by-eighteen-foot porch. The building was twenty-four by thirty-four. It had a dining room and living room, with a six-foot French door between them and a ten-by-twelve kitchen. For 1930, it was a nice little modern home.

Business was dull, so I had no trouble getting help to build. I knew a city building contractor who was the best of carpenters. He took my map, or blueprint, and figured every piece for the house. We went to the Charleston Lumber Company for the building supplies. They wanted to know how I wanted to pay for it. I told them I would pay cash, and they were glad to get that. Business was almost at a standstill during one of the worse panics ever to hit this country.

I contacted Elmer Samples, a neighbor who did odd jobs and had a truck, and he had my house pattern on the ground within a week. I had my house insured before it was built. The lumber was insured as soon as it was on the ground. My brother-in-law furnished a horse, and I got a scraper and a man to help excavate for the basement, four and one-half feet deep and twenty-five by twenty-six. We had that ready by the first of March. Dick Duffel was my contractor, and Enos Matheny and Bob Estep were the carpenters.

They shaped up the basement and built the foundation and form for it. I got sand (for concrete) from the creek near the basement. I could have used the sand we graded out of the basement site, but it was a little fine, and it would have taken a little too much cement. I got about all of my sand within fifty feet of my house. I piled it near the basement site, and we made a box to hold about a yard of concrete. I borrowed some shovels from the Hope Gas Company and got fully ready to run the foundation and basement wall. I set some bolts in the basement wall to anchor the foundation. In a day and a half, we had the basement and foundation ready for starting the rest of the building. We bored holes in the two-by-eight foundation and bolted them to the basement wall, tight and level. That would keep the house from shifting in case of a wind or flood. Before it would shift, the force would have to be strong enough to tear the building apart. I used twenty- and thirty-penny nails to anchor the sleepers good and solid.

Dick plumbed the corners and set the two by fours around the walls and rooms, and he soon had them in good shape. I told him that I was going to quite an expense to build my home, and that the reason I got him to do it was that I could trust him to do it right. A home is a permanent abode, and I wanted it to be sturdy, even if it did cost a little extra. I ordered number one grade lumber for all but the storm sheeting. It would be covered with siding material. I shellacked all of my framewood and doors before I put them up. That protected them from the weather and kept them from warping or cracking. I don't think the house is one-fourth of an inch off in either frame or room. Someone asked me why I was so particular about my house here in the country. I said a home is something permanent, and I wanted it put up that way. Also, if I ever sold it, I could have something to sell. I hired a man to paper the walls, and he said he had never papered walls in a house that was as plumb as ours. I used clear oak for all the framing except for the doors and windows. We framed them with pine. After forty-one years, it's as good as it ever was. In about twenty years, I had asphalt shingles put on over the siding. That made it more airtight, and it would save fuel to keep it warm. In hot weather, it would stay cool longer through the mornings.

We put dressed sheeting on the roof and covered it with asphalt shingles. We have oak floors all around. I doubt if there's a home on Porter Creek as plumb as this house. Enos Matheny had built about all of the houses in our area up until I built mine, and he said that Dick Duffel was the best carpenter he ever worked with. One day, Mr. Matheny got in a hurry with some of the framework, and he didn't get it just right. Dick was gone, but he himself did it over when he got back. We graded about one hundred square feet of level space for our lawn. We pulled the dirt from above to below the house, leaving an elevation of about four feet on each side of the lawn. The dirt from the basement helped to build it up considerably.

In May, 1930, the house was about finished. I had quite a bit of work to do to it yet, but we could be more comfortable here than in the fourteen-by-twenty smokehouse room on my parents' property. Also, I had about three-fourths of a mile less to walk to work, and none of it was uphill. (I had been walking to work for five years, and the last part of the walk, coming home tired, was uphill.) We bought more furniture and moved in.

Nellie and I have never paid any rent, and in forty-one years, rent expenses would have paid for two homes like this one. My total cost was $2,100 by the time it was ready to live in. I painted the outside (with two coats) right away, and I finished trimming the Sheetrock inside. I kept at it whenever I had time, and I soon had the walls painted and the floors varnished. It was a nice little modern home, and it was very comfortable.

We had lived here only two months when, on July 11, 1930, our first child was born—an eight-pound boy. I never saw a child look so much like his dad as he did. He was skinny, and he looked like me for that. When he got a little flesh, my picture diminished. We parleyed for a name. Nellie said, "Let's call him Norris. I've never heard of a Boggs by that name." I agreed to call him Norris Wayne. He was a healthy child. We were a happy couple with such a fine baby. He came before the doctor got here. (In those days, women didn't go to the hospital to have babies like they do today. The doctor came to your home to see patients then.)

We had discussed the size of our family. I thought I was too old to raise a big family, as I was old enough to be his granddaddy. Nellie thought it was wrong to prevent having children. I rather agreed with her; anyway, I didn't feel it was right to have her do something she thought wrong. We wanted another child to grow up with him, but not too soon. On April 20, 1932, Dallas was born. We thought we would lose him, but he was soon okay. He wasn't born naturally. His was a breech birth. I guess we need not have worried after he was born, but the doctor was rather nervous about him too. His middle name, Ervin, was after my second name, although I spell my name Irvin. Now Nellie and I were happy; we had two boys so near the same age to raise together.

From our new home, I didn't have quite so far to walk to get to work as when we lived up Left Hand. I was still working in the pump house in the compressor department. I liked my job, but it would have been much better, in a sense, if I could have worked days instead of doing tower work. In a way, night work was convenient. I had some days to be at home during daylight to look after things I couldn't do well when working on the day shift. One trouble, I would work too much at home, and if I was tired before I started my shift, that made my job more miserable. We would get too tired imposing on ourselves, which most tower men did.

For a year or two longer, I worked the day shift through the summer because they didn't sell much gas and they didn't need to run all of the pump engines. On the day shift, I worked at mostly anything there was to do, and when the men started taking vacations, I took their places on the tower shifts. Until we had worked for five years, we got only one week of vacation. In 1932, most of us had five years or more, but a few of the men had less time on the job. I had six years. Because I didn't like the day work so well, I managed to take my vacation while on the day shift. On day work, we never knew what we might be called on to do, and some jobs weren't so good.

When business was good, I went back to the pump house to work at my regular job. I liked it better as I knew just what I had to do and how to do it. I was promoted to engineer. That paid me $130 per month. That was fairly good wages in those days. Lawrence Dolen was my tower foreman. He was a little overbearing, and that attitude was encouraged by one of the men that I worked with, a man who wanted my job. He was next in line for an engineer's position. We didn't have any particular problem, but it seemed that he wanted to make trouble for me. (I didn't know until later that the foreman intended to can me, but if he had tried, I doubt that he could have gotten by with it. I could have transferred to day work, where he didn't have any authority over me. I think the chief liked my work.)

As it turned out, the chief engineer moved to Jackson Station, and we got a new chief, Burl Neusom. He was as fine a man as I ever worked for. Instead of me losing my job, Dolen lost his. Burl called me out and told me that Dolen had intended to get rid of me. He said that he was glad Dolen had left, and then he let me know why Dolen left the Hope Gas Company. Burl and Dolen had worked together elsewhere, and they couldn't get along. Burl said, "I'll give you a chance." He and I never had a cross word. Later, when the new tower foreman took his vacation, Burl gave me that job for three weeks while the foreman was off.

I worked in the pump house for two more years. At that time, we had to do some maintenance work in addition to the engineering work. For example, we painted the walls (up to the windows) and the window frames. The oilers painted and the engineer looked after the engines. At intervals, the oiler would break from his painting work to go over his bearings and see that they didn't get too hot. He would paint near his engine, where he could see and hear a rod knock out of place, or anything that was out of order.

Before we quit, we would oil our parts of the engine where the oil pumps didn't reach, and we'd fill the oil cups to keep them dripping properly onto the bearings. Then we'd go over the engines with towels and wipe up any oil that dropped from the bearings. On the morning shift, we mopped and swept the floors. Since we burned coal, we usually had to sweep cinders from the floors. About every two or three months, we painted the floors. We kept things as clean as we would in our living quarters. We painted those big engines and compressors too. They also required us to paint the outside of the building and the outside pipe and valves, but we weren't required to get off of the ground or onto a ladder.

I was hunting the tower foreman to report something. There were several men there building a water plant. The area was very muddy, and I was trying to avoid the mud. I was jumping from curb to curb. The four-by-five curbs were built around valves. I thought I was jumping over a four-by-five curb, but I landed on a curb that was built around the wall of the plant that they were putting up, before I saw what it was. When I landed, I looked down and saw a thirty-foot drop below me. If I had stumbled, I would have fallen thirty feet down onto a concrete floor or onto a man who was directly below me. I was so frightened that I nearly fainted. I walked off through the mud and sat down. It took me a few minutes to get over the shock before I could go back to my job. I went back to the pump house, and my boss noticed me. He asked, "What's wrong, Ira?" I told him how close I had come to getting killed. That's the last I heard of it. The boss should have had a barrier around that wall at least four feet from the curb. They weren't long about getting one up. I was pretty nimble at that time. I was used to running along the railroad and jumping those ties when I was late for work. That probably saved my life. That's the nearest that I ever came to getting killed on the job at the Cornwell station.

Sometime after I started work at the Cornwell station, there was an explosion on a sixteen-inch gas line loaded with over three hundred pounds of pressure. I was at work when that explosion happened. It was about quitting time. We noticed the gas pressure going down, but we hadn't heard what the trouble was that caused the pressure loss. I got in a car with Ray Stats and started for Clendenin. We got to the road that goes up Broad Run Creek. There, at the cab station by the road, we noticed a woman in distress. She was crying and waving at us to stop. When we stopped, she said that the gas line had blown up and killed some men. Ray and I jumped out of the car and started running up the creek. (The road wasn't fit to drive on, and it was a half mile to the site of the explosion.)

We saw where it split the line and blew it apart, throwing parts of it several feet out of the ditch. It blew one man (Mr. Rollions) two hundred yards away up over some tall trees, and he lived to tell about it. Fred Harper and I found him. He couldn't see, and he was feeling his way along. He was so badly scarred that he was hard to recognize. His eyes looked like they were about blown out. He said, "I didn't know where I was until I bumped into the tool house." Fred and I led him to the ambulance. He asked if there was anyone else hurt or killed. I said that Clarence Brown and an Estep man were killed and several more men got hurt. (I shouldn't have told him because that shocked him more.) We figured that the only way that this man's life had been saved was that he fell through the branches of a bushy tree and down onto some a brush heap. We got him to the ambulance and hunted for the rest of the crew that had been working close to the line.

The explosion had blown the Estep man about a hundred yards. He was broken and torn so much that he was unrecognizable. We carried him to the ambulance and hunted for more people. We found part of the upper torso of a man laying in a dreen, and we took it to the ambulance. I said to Fred, "This looks worse than the battlefields that I saw in the war." We saw parts of flesh from these men lying all around the area where the pipeline exploded, and we could see pieces of them and their clothing hanging in the treetops. We gathered them up as best we could and put them on the ambulance. There were three dwellings near the explosion, but it didn't hurt anyone who lived in the homes. Their cats and dogs were eating the scattered flesh. We ran them off.

In thirty-five years, I had only one lost time accident on the job. A sixteen-inch well casing turned over on my leg, and I was off for two days. I had two lost time accidents that happened off the job. Once, I was standing beside my horse, and he kicked forward with his hind foot and hit me on the leg. I don't know whether or not the horse intended to hit me. Maybe he was fighting flies. He wasn't a bad horse. I was on crutches for a few days. Another time, I was walking to work, and there was a little ice on the ground. There had been a little sleet storm that night, and the ground was coated with just enough ice to notice it. I stepped on a clod of frozen dirt between two car tracks on the level road. I fell on the clod so hard that I broke two ribs and fractured my pelvis bone in two places clear across it. Because I had plenty of time to get to work, I had been walking slowly. If I had been walking fast, I probably would not have fallen. I hobbled about a hundred yards to the post office. I didn't think I was hurt so bad.

The mail carrier was going to the railroad with the mail. I asked him to call my boss and tell him what had happened and that I wouldn't be out to work today. I sat there until the mail carrier came back—about an hour. When I made an effort to get onto my feet to go home, my leg hurt so badly that I couldn't touch my foot to the ground. Two men helped me to the car. I stopped at home and told Nellie I would go on to the hospital and have some x-rays made. The doctor read the x-ray and showed me the pictures of my broken ribs and the cracks in some others, as well as the broken pelvis bone. They put me to bed, and I lay there on my left side for eleven days.

I encouraged the doctor to let me go home, and I was back on my job within thirty days. My doctor said that was the quickest he ever heard of a person getting back to work after a broken pelvis. I drove to work and was off my feet most of the time.

We had a good safety record at the Cornwell Station. Our group won a trophy for a million hours without a lost time accident. I played my part in that. In thirty-five years, I lost only two days because of on-the-job accidents. Since the first day of work, December 24, 1924, only two men have lost their lives there. The first accident happened just through poor judgment and management in emptying a coal car. There's a shutter that fastens on a rod underneath the car in the center. It has hinges on it. The shutter fastens with latches on each side of the car. To empty the car into the coal crusher, you knock the latch loose with a sledgehammer. That drops the shutter. One young man knocked a shutter down, and it fell on him with the weight of tons of coal. He lived for only two days.

Another man burned to death from a careless accident. Two men were welding inside a gas tank that was about ten feet in diameter and twenty feet high. They closed a six-inch valve and took a plug out of a "T" on the pipe. That let all the gas that might come into the line escape into the air. When the men quit work Friday, they left the shutter open on top of the tank, but the chief engineer thought it didn't look just right to leave this plug laying there over the weekend. He had it put back in. On Monday morning, when those two welders came back to work, they got into the tank. Using a flint spark, they tried to light their welding torch. There wasn't enough oxygen in the bottom of the tank to light it. The welder handed his welding torch up through the manhole for their helper at the top of the tank to light it. It exploded. The explosion was heard and felt for five miles around the plant.

A flame of fire trapped the two men in the tank. The gases didn't burn in the bottom of the tank, but they flamed up through the manhole. One man lay down in the bottom of the tank until the flame died some. The other man, Noah Lusader, tried to get out until he became unconscious and fell back on the floor. One man at a time went into the tank to lift them out, but nobody could stand the heat for more than a minute or so. The flame died down enough for the conscious man to escape, with some help from a man inside the tank and another one outside of the manhole. I was about three or four hundred yards away when the explosion occurred. The fire had died down before I got there, but the manhole was still red hot. I helped Mr. Brake out, and there were two men in the tank to lift Mr. Lusader out to where we could reach him from outside the manhole. Mr. Lusader wasn't breathing when we took him out of the tank. Nat Prit started giving artificial respiration, but he was so excited that he was working too fast. I said, "Let me have him, Nat." I started giving him artificial respiration by the count, the way I was trained in the military service.

In about three minutes, he was groaning, and he soon started talking. He was so badly burned that he was almost paralyzed, but he wasn't suffering as much as Mr. Brake was. We had the ambulance there in a few more minutes, and the medics got them to the hospital within a half hour or so. Mr. Brake's ears were half burned off, and his face was badly scarred. He came very close to dying, but soon began to recover. Mr. Lusader lived only twenty-four hours. The nurses said his blood was cooked until he was about paralyzed, and that is the reason he didn't suffer.

Mr. Lusader's father-in-law tried to question the men about the accident, to bring a lawsuit against the company, but the men who really knew the details wouldn't talk. No doubt, it's better that he didn't bring suit. The Hope Gas Company probably did more for Mr. Lusader's family than they would have done if they had been awarded several thousand dollars from a lawsuit. They helped his widow take care of the family of three children. The oldest one appeared to be about eight years old. Several years later, I saw a picture of one of his children in the Hope magazine. The company had helped her get a college education and then given her a job. Mr. Brake recovered, but his ears and face were badly disfigured.

We had another man burned about the face pretty badly just through carelessness or unawareness of danger. We had been using gasoline to wash machinery or oil on the floor and mopping with it considerably. He got too close to some hot cinders, which were dumped from the furnace, and the three gallons of gas caught aflame and burned his face pretty badly. He didn't lose any time on the job, but the company had a system of keeping the men on the job when he was able to be out of bed so as to win the million hours without a lost time accident. They would take him to the doctor daily, if necessary, and keep him sitting in the office or give him light duty. After all, the company was careful and far ahead of the United Fuel Gas Company in respect for their employees. They kept Safety First signs where there was danger, and they put warning and caution signs on their tools. They got a cleaning liquid that wasn't flammable, and we used it to mop oily places. We were responsible for good housekeeping. We had a place for everything, and everything had to be in its place.

The chief who caused that accident by putting the plug back on the line didn't stay there more than two or three months longer. They cut his salary considerably and transferred him to a small pumping station. Everybody was glad to get rid of him. He was constantly having trouble with his men. He got so bad that some of the men would just laugh and scorn him. I had trouble with him only once. He kept following me around, complaining and bickering at me. He bawled me out for almost nothing. I was sweeping dirt off of some brick and whitewashing it. I really had about all his mouth I could stand. I was using a heavy broom. I pulled the broom up into my hand to see how hard it was. Then I braced myself. I intended to let him have it right in the face. He caught on and walked away. He went back to the office, and from what I heard, he told his clerks what had happened. They came by me laughing. I heard that he told them, "I believe that Ira Boggs would fight." Once, he met one of his employees off of the job and started quarreling about something he had done on the job. This fellow realized he wasn't on the job, and he grabbed the boss and threatened him. Later on, the chief had more trouble with that fellow. He was a good man, and the company transferred him to another job. When that chief left, we got Burl Neusom back again. Burl was a fine man, and he didn't have any trouble with his men.

On July 4, 1932, two years after I built our dwelling house, we had one of the biggest floods I've ever seen. Porter Creek was way out of banks. To this day, I've never seen so much rainfall in so short a time. It poured down for twelve hours. The water was all around my house and splashing into my backdoor next to the creek. It was one foot deep in front of my dwelling next to the road. I went down into my basement. The six-inch thick concrete basement floor wasn't thoroughly set, and it broke from one end of the building to the other. The water gushed up so powerfully that I thought the house was caving in. I got out in a hurry, and Nellie waded out to the road with our two children. We tried to shelter under a rock cliff, but the water was falling so freely there wasn't any shelter. Norris was two years old on July 11 that year, and Dallas was born on April 20. He was only two and a half months old. We carried them across the hill and across the Left Hand of Porter Creek to my dad's house, where we stayed overnight. I came back the next morning. The creek bank had washed within six or eight feet of my backdoor, and the earth had cracked clear to the basement wall. The water lacked just a few inches coming through a railroad cut through a bank at the edge of the county road.

The road agent was one of my neighbors nearby. I convinced him to let me move the road about one hundred yards against the hill, and I filled the grade between my house and the creek with rock and dirt, making it safe from floods. I built a slag rock wall along the creek, taking the rock out of the creek for about two-thirds of the wall. I built the wall eight feet high on the upper end to five feet high below the house. I put two wings on it to turn the creek away from my house, one above the house and one between the creek and backdoor of my house. I put twenty-nine bags of cement in it, some between each layer of rock. I had six men working with bars to push the biggest stones to the wall at the bottom, and we slid the heavy rocks upon the wall on skids. I built the wall twenty feet from the house and threw rock into the gulch between it and my house. This opened the creek channel from two to four feet deeper than it was before the flood. Since then, the swift stream has carved it even deeper.

Porter Creek drops one hundred feet per mile, and it runs very swift when there is a high tide. When there is high water, it runs at a speed of about thirty-five miles per hour. Big stones weighing several tons appear and disappear. They come rolling and grinding down the creek, making my house rattle from their crushing along. In the forty-one years since I built the wall, the creek bed has grown deeper. It has cut thirty feet into the hill and bank below the house and fifteen to twenty feet into the hill above the house. In the previous hundred years, this creek drifted from one side of the hill to the other, moving the main stream as much as fifty yards or more. It leaves its mark with sand and gravel deep in the earth under the sand bottoms.

On my job, throughout about three months of the summer, when we didn't sell so much gas, I had work mostly outside of the plant. That was much better than working inside. It was very hot in that big engine room. I painted most of the time. The biggest job we had was painting the boiler house outside and inside. It was seventy-five feet high from the floor to the top of the eaves. We made us a soft rope swing. We fastened a block and line in the eaves of the building and ran the rope through the block so we could pull ourselves and our paint in our rope swing to the top of the building. We would start by painting a swath as far as we could reach each way. We could tie our rope onto the swing and fasten it. When finished a section, we would loosen our rope and hold fast to it so we wouldn't fall. Then we'd let ourselves down to as far as we could reach and paint another section until we got on the ground. It took three men about three weeks to paint the boiler house. The engine room was broader and longer, but only about half as high. We learned a better way.

The next time we painted those two big buildings, we got a swing board twenty feet long, about four feet wide. We put guardrails around it and a block on each end. We pulled it up to the top of the building, and two men on the ground let us down as we painted. Two men worked on the platform. We also painted a big machine shop and several other buildings inside and out. The company also owned fourteen dwelling houses and a twelve-room hotel and restaurant. We painted those buildings every two to three years. The worst such job we had was painting the inside of the boiler house, especially over the boilers. We had to wash it down before painting it, and the heat over those boilers was 1,300. It was so hot that we had to work in short shifts. The company had us do that job during the summer. They were afraid to let us do it during the winter. They thought we might cool off too quickly and take cold or pneumonia.

We also had to paint our wooden bridge that swung on wire cables for about one hundred yards across Elk River. It was built of four-inch rough boards. The sides were fenced in about four feet high, and the boards were crossed from bottom to top. It had a four-inch strip floor, with cracks between the boards. Often, the women would step into those cracks and loosen their shoe heels. Sometimes, that would cause them to fall. The company later refloored it and made it solid, without those cracks. There were usually three or four men painting the bridge, but, for some reason, the boss had me paint it by myself. When I finally finished, he asked, "Do you know how long it took you to paint this bridge?" He said, "Eleven and a half days."

"That's a good record." I answered, "I just kept busy. I didn't know how long it would take me." While painting the outside of the bridge, I had to be careful not to fall into the river. I stood on a narrow board and held onto the bridge with one hand. Some of the high officials saw me painting in that manner, and they said that was too dangerous. They got me a wide belt with a fastener to hold me to the bridge if I did fall. There was a four-inch wire mesh outside the bridge to keep children from falling. That was difficult to paint over. It dragged the paint from our brush. The swinging bridge was suspended from one-and-a-half-inch wire cables that were attached to ten-inch gas pipes that were framed with four-inch welding pipe and anchored in concrete piers on each end of the bridge. The wire cables were attached to spindles on top of those tall piers and fastened to heavy concrete blocks buried in the ground on each end. We kept this cable greased with a heavy or thick grease so it would never rust and break.

The Hope Gas Company was a young corporation at that time, and without experience, they made mistakes—as most men do. For those concrete piers, they dug to a solid base on each end of the river, but they didn't drive piling in and around them. In a few years, while the ground was loaded with water or soaked, one of those piers tipped, and the bridge fell into the river. No one was hurt. There wasn't anyone on the bridge when the pier fell. There was one person on the opposite end from the pier who fell; he was just ready to start across the river. He was a little shaken up, but he got back to safety in a hurry. They set another pier and drove piling under and around it and around the pier that didn't fall. That happened in 1938. The bridge is still standing in 1972. We live by hopes and learn by our own experience and other people's stories.

I went back to work in the pump house, where I was promoted to engineer. After my promotion, they didn't require me to leave tower work again. I no longer had to do day work during the summer. I continued as compressor and steam engineer, and I stayed there for two or three years before being promoted again.

I worked with two oilers who helped me take care of five engines and ten compressors. (Each engine had two compressors.) Lawrence Cooper, one of he Hope Gas Company officials, designed them. The Hamilton Steam Engine manufacturers at Hamilton, Ohio, made the steam engines. They were powerful one-thousand-horsepower engines. The flywheel was twenty feet in circumference. It weighed a ton. When it rolled over at a rate of one hundred twenty to one hundred twenty-five times per minute, it had a tremendous power. We didn't—or weren't supposed to—run them any faster than that.

I have checked them when they were running at one hundred thirty revolutions per minute, and I wasn't long about getting my hands on the throttle and getting it to one hundred twenty-five revolutions per minute.

With a sudden pressure drop, as in a case where the gas load was lost through a line blowing up nearby or when a gate closed through a mistake, the engines could run away. They could reach a very high speed in just a few seconds. We were usually notified of any expected change of pressure, but in case of a line blowing up nearby, we had no warning. I have caught them when it was dangerous to be near them, but we never did let one run away to tear apart. Number one and number two engines were low-pressure machines. They picked up the gas from the gas field lines. One compressor each on numbers one and two engines picked up the gas from the field and sent it to the higher stage compressor, and the high-stage compressor would transfer it to numbers four and five engines. They sent it on through the trunk lines to a relay station or to the place of consumption. Number three engine worked independently. It had a low stage that pumped the gas from the trunk lines and a high stage that pumped it into the feed lines. That equaled the high and low stage for the five engines.

This was an interesting job, and we also felt that it was important. I imagine that during those zero temperature days in Cleveland, Ohio, and New York State, those domestic consumers thanked us for this gas. My job was to keep an eye on number three engine and to keep a log on all of the engines. I'd watch the suction and discharge pressures registered on gauges mounted on a board at each engine and check the temperature on each of the ten compressors. I recorded the readings in a book every hour. I also reported the gas pressure to headquarters in Clarksburg. They would tell me if they wanted more or less gas, and I would speed up or slow down those big engines. On very cold days, we ran those engines at top speed. Sometimes the commercial users would have to shut down in order for the residential users to have enough gas to keep warm. We had a low-pressure system in those days. We couldn't carry more than about three hundred fifty pounds of pressure because the trunk lines wouldn't stand more pressure than that.

On September 6, 1934, Nellie and I had an increase in our family. I called our doctor. He came and brought us not one but two babies, out-and-out identical twin girls. The doctor seemed to be almost as proud of them as Nellie and I were. He had four girls, and he said that if those girls were boys and were his, he wouldn't take one million dollars for them. They were so much alike that for some time, we would get confused as to which was which. We finally found names that suited us—Dorothy May and Dorcas Fay. Nellie said, "I've found a mark I can use to tell them apart. Dorothy has a freckle on her left cheek." She looked at Dorcas and found a freckle just like it. They both weighed about the same. They weighed seven and a fraction pounds, totaling two ounces over fifteen pounds. Until they were a year old, we would get confused in trying to tell which was which. When they were in high school, they looked so much alike that people couldn't tell which was which. They still do. We thought that four children would be a nice-sized family, but in those days that wasn't considered a large family. We would dress them as near alike as we could, and we couldn't get out on the streets without people stopping us and looking at them amazed.

By 1934, business had picked up quite a bit. The Hope Gas Company put in another one-thousand-horsepower engine. In the wintertime, we kept all of the engines going at a high speed, but we would have to shut some of them down during the summer.

Finally, business began to look lively. New factories were under construction, and the gas companies drilled more wells. We didn't have enough gas to supply all of our customers. The Tennessee Gas Company laid a big trunk line from Texas, and the Hope Gas Company and United Fuel Gas Company bought gas from them. To measure the gas, we had a meter with a round dial and an ordinary clock on it. We put a paper chart on the dial. It was round, with circular marks around it beginning at the pivot and extending to the outer edge. There were straight marks, also beginning at the pivot, extending to the outer edge of the dial. Those marks indicated fifteen-minute intervals on the chart. There was a hand on the clock with red ink and one with blue ink. One represented the gas pressure, and the other represented the water pressure that might be going through the line. The gas hand would rise up and drop according to the gas pressure. This hand worked up and down on the circular chart. We used a mathematical formula based on the square root of our readings to figure how much gas had passed through the meter in twenty-four hours. We would average the fifteen-minute readings to get a number for our calculations, and that would give us a fairly accurate estimate of how many million cubic feet of gas that we had pumped. The chart turned one revolution in twenty-four hours, recording the readings on the chart. That's the same way the meter in your home figures how much gas you burn monthly. But the pressure on your line is usually six ounces instead of the one, ten, or fifteen hundred pounds of pressure on those big trunk lines.

On June 23, 1936, we had another birth in the family—another girl. She broke the tie of two girls and two boys. We called her Wilda Jean. She weighed ten pounds, the largest of them at birth. That made five children. Our family was getting large too fast. It's pretty binding to have so many in school at once. (I was raised in a family of fourteen, and compared to that, five wasn't so many.) They made an interesting family, three girls and two boys. The oldest being two boys. They were healthy and vigorous children.

In eighteen months and eighteen days, on January 5, 1938, another girl was born. She was the smallest of all at birth. She was so little I was afraid to pick her up. She weighed only six pounds, but she was healthy and grew faster than any of the others. Now she's the largest of the girls, she's five feet ten inches tall and weighs one hundred sixty pounds. That's the same as her mother weighed when we were married. Now Nellie weighs about two hundred pounds and has, at times, weighed two hundred twenty pounds, but she's five feet eight inches tall. That was a tall woman then. People now average about two inches taller.

Including Wilda and the twin girls, Dorothy and Dorcas, we had four children in three years and ten months or, altogether, six in eight years. Including the twin girls, they were all hardy and vigorous, and I had to keep busy, working on my job and on my farm to keep them going strong. We called this one Norma Lea. She grew fast and was the size of a woman at twelve years, just like her mother was at twelve.

I was still working in the compressor department as an engineer, running those big steam engines. I liked my job, with the exception that it kept us close inside all day. In the summertime, on the warmest days, it got pretty hot, but we could step outside some, just so we didn't go so far that we couldn't hear the engines rolling along. We would go over the engines every hour and feel the bearings and see that the oil was circulating properly. We had a pump that drew oil from a tank that held about thirty gallons or more and circulated it through the bearings and back and forth through the pump, and vice versa. We kept the oil tank in the basement, where the intake and the outlet gas steam and water lines were. They came up and connected to the engines and compressors and back into the basement and outside, underground.

We had our gas valves on the outside. It took four men to close or open those big sixteen- and twenty-inch valves. To open or close the valves, we turned them with our hands. (Nowadays, they just press a button and the valves operate by compressed air or electricity.)

One day, the chief called me into his office. He said, "I. I.," (they noticed my initials on the work order board and got to calling me I. I.) "I have another job for you if you want it." He described the job to me. "It's inside and outside work. It's the strictest job we have. When it goes down, about every wheel stops rolling. It's the auxiliary engineer's job."

I said, "I'll look it over with you and consider it." He took me into the electric turbine room, where they had two five hundred-horsepower steam engines, and he showed me the gauge boards and how they operated. They usually ran just one turbine engine. The other one was a spare. It served as a backup source of electricity for when something went wrong, but sometimes, when things were going at full blast, they would use both. When those engines were going full speed, I could hear those generators humming on top of the hill on my farm two and a half miles from there. They had to be set so solid and true that you could hardly see those turbines moving or rolling over. The chief took me on through the water plant and reservoir and down into the basement, where the water pumps were. They had a two-hundred-fifty-horsepower water pump that pushed the water from the condensers to two seventy-thousand-gallon tanks for the steam boilers. It took an hour to fill one of those tanks. I would open the valves to the tank that I wanted to empty into the reservoir and close the valve on the tank that had already emptied. Then I had to start the electric pump to fill the empty tank and open and close the valves to the reservoir, which had steam lines in it to warm the water for the boilers. There were two one-hundred-horsepower pumps in the basement (one for a spare pump) to move the water from the reservoir to the boilers. When the plant was in full production, it took all of the capacity of a six-inch water line to supply those five or six boilers.

This water was picked up from the big condenser pit next to steam pump house about two hundred yards from the boilers. This pump didn't deliver the water direct to the boilers but to a big tank by the end of the boilers. It was heated there to almost boiling temperature before going into the boilers. This helped to keep fuel expenses down to fire those five big boilers.

The big condenser that those big steam engines connected into caught the steam from those engines and used it to heat the water in a big tank that overflowed into the condenser pit. Exhausting the steam into the condenser tank, sealed by back pressure of water at the condenser pit, also kept the noise down. You didn't hear those big engines chugging along like those at the United Fuel Station at Cobb Station, a few miles down Elk River.

I said to my boss, "I'll take the job, and we will soon see if I can do it." This was a better job, in a way. I had it all to myself. I didn't have a foreman or anyone to bother me. I just went about doing what I knew was to be done and did it the best I could do. I got along without any complaints. It paid me ten dollars more than the steam-engineering job in the compressor plant station.

I stayed near those electric turbines when I didn't have other work to do. Once an hour, I went to the water plant at the river. To reach it, I went down a flight of forty-nine steps to a platform level with the riverbed, where there were three two-hundred-fifty-horsepower electric-powered pumps run from those turbines in my turbine room. I looked at the oil in the bearings on those water pumps to see that there was enough oil in them, and I felt the bearings to see if they were overheating. Then I looked at the water gauges to see that they were pumping enough water through the sixteen-inch and the twenty-inch line. The sixteen-inch line ran to the condenser of my turbines, and the twenty-inch line ran to the condenser for those big steam engines. Those pumps also supplied water for cooling those big compressors that pumped the gas.

Allis Chalmer manufactured the turbine engines. They operated by steam and rated five hundred horsepower. When in full speed, they ran at five thousand revolutions per minute. They made a keen humming sound, but I soon got used to the noise. They would automatically speed up or slow down as the pressure hit them for more or less power. Sometimes, I would have to regulate the voltage by turning a wheel an inch or so. I soon got well acquainted with this job, and I got so I could listen to the changes in the tune of those turbines, and as the noise went lower or louder, I could tell their speed, and I could tell if something had gotten out of order about as well as if I was looking at the gauge. I had to notice the voltage and amperage and keep it going right to run all of those water pumps and other motors. There were several of them. I might also mention our coal crusher and other small motors that run on the electricity generated by our turbines. Those turbines also furnished lights on the job and for fifteen dwellings and for the bridge across Elk River.

This was the auxiliary power plant. It was the heart of power to keep things adjusted and running. We could get power for our lights from the Appalachian Power lines when we shut down a few days every year for maintenance repairs, or in case we had to shut those turbines down because of a noisy bearing or other emergencies.

When the plant first started operating, there wasn't much to do at this job, but it got to be a pretty busy job. When a new job came up, it was easy for the boss to say, "Let the auxiliary engineer take it, he doesn't have anything to do."

One of the major responsibilities assigned to the auxiliary engineer was testing and treating the boiler water and the domestic water to keep it pure. When the river was muddy, we had to use chemicals to clear and soften the water that went to the boilers. We used copper sulfate and aluminates to clear it and soda ash to soften it. I have used as much as fifty pounds of copper sulfate to clear it, as much as thirty pounds of soda ash to soften it, and as much as twenty pounds of aluminates. When the river was in tide from sandy or loam soil, we didn't use so much of the chemicals. When it was muddy from red clay soil, it took more chemicals to clear it. When there was a big tide in Buffalo Creek from coal mining, we also had a black water to contend with. We just couldn't get that water cleared up properly. We usually used from three to thirty pounds of soda ash, but a few times, I have seen Elk River so pure we didn't need any chemicals at all to clarify it.

We always used some chlorine in the domestic water to make it safe from bacterial contamination, but we used very little at times. We had a small tank of chlorine gas, and we regulated the flow of it by the number of air bubbles per minute. We would reduce or increase the bubbles as needed. We tested it with a little seeing-eye instrument. We looked through a glass to tell the color of the water to test it for purity. The tank of chlorine held up to two thousand pounds of pressure. I have seen it spring a leak, and I have breathed enough chlorine to make my throat raw at times.

They found another task for the auxiliary man or engineer when he didn't have anything to do. We put a soapy chemical called burman in a small tank in the boiler basement. It came in flakes that looked like broken glass. It was supposed to keep the boilers from scaling and to keep them clean. We had to regulate a jet of liquid from this chemical as it flowed into the boilers. There was a one-half-inch pipe from each boiler where we got our test water. We would boil a half pint of this water in a container and put chemicals in it to bring a sludge. Then we would pour it into a small tube with small scale marks on it. We would increase or diminish the flow of the burman according to the level of sludge that showed in the tube. Then we could increase or diminish the flow of water in those one-half-inch pipe drains from the boilers and increase or decrease the burman accordingly. Most of this extra work was for the day shift and the evening shift. The morning shift had the least amount of extra work to do.

When we had to change turbine engines, usually on day shift, we couldn't always get all of the make-busy work done up properly, no matter how fast we worked. Changing those turbines was a particular job, especially when they were loaded to full capacity. We had to be sure our water drain valve was open when we opened the steam throttle. Otherwise, water would collect in the engine and fill it up, and it would blow to pieces. We would keep the steam flowing through the engine until all water was drained while the engine was hot from steam. Then we closed the water drain valve and turned on the steam by opening the steam throttle a little at a time. Before kicking it entirely off, we closed down the throttle on the other engine a little until we had about the same amperage on that dial as on the engine we had started to shut down. If we made a little mistake, we would lose our electric load, and our water pumps would all shut down. The chief and another helper, the tower foreman or the machinist, was usually there to help change turbines. It was a demanding job. If we kicked the turbine off and lost our load of water, the steam engines would go noncondensing, and the fireman would have to make more steam. Then we could hear those big steam engines exhaust into the air or into the empty condenser tank. They didn't make quite so much noise by exhausting into the tank as they would if they were exhausting into the air like the United Fuel Gas station at Cob Station does. (At that time, Cobb Station pumped more gas than we did. Later, we put in three more of those big thousand-horsepower engines, and then we pumped more gas than the United Fuel.)

Another increase in our family! It was a fine, big, hardy eight-and-one-half pound boy. He was born July 17, 1939, the year before the Second World War broke out (he was the only child born in an uneven year number). We named him Granvel Cornelius. He was the seventh one. They all kept us going strong.

I worked daily on my job and continued to farm quite a bit. I had some timber to cut. I had a sawmill moved onto my place to cut it, and I had bought a ton and a half truck. Business got slack, and I didn't do much good at it. I couldn't sell anything but crossties for the railroad, and they finally quit buying them. I had my truck about half paid for. I got an order for mine posts, but I couldn't meet expenses, and I had to quit that. I made about three trips to Virginia. I hauled about five hundred bushels of apples and sold them, but I had to hire a man to help do this, and I couldn't make it pay out. On the weekend, I would quit work at midnight and go with my truck driver. I'd get back just in time to go to work. My driver would sell the apples during the week while I worked, and I would make another trip. I made two or three trips to Ohio. On each trip, I took a load of coal and sold it. Then I brought back hay or corn and sold it. I made a little money at this until winter. I had paid sixteen hundred dollars for the Diamond tee truck, with monthly installments of seventy-five dollars. It was a good truck, but there was nothing to do with it. I made a few payments and borrowed five hundred dollars from the bank. I paid off the lean on the truck and paid the bank thirty-two dollars per month until that note was cleared. After business picked up a little, I sold my truck and the balance of my timber to Uncle Charlie Foreman.

After I worked at my auxiliary engineer job at the Hope Gas Company for a few more years, the district engineer wanted me to take a different job. When they started buying gas from Hamilton Gas Company, they installed a new one-thousand-horsepower gas engine to pump it, and I would be running that engine. In a way, it was a better job, but it would be quite different from what I was used to. It was too monotonous for me. I had so much to look after here and there on the auxiliary job that anytime I got tired of staying in one place, I could get up and move around, whether I needed to or not. No one but me knew I was just tending to my business, and I could meet people and talk for a few minutes. The gas engineer job was an inactive job, and I wouldn't be close enough to speak to anyone except when the tower foreman came around. I didn't take it.

Later on, the district engineer fell into a scheme to make me take it. I thought I understood him. I knew that he and the tower foreman had a mutual friend who wanted my job, but I had too much time on the job, and it was against our organizational rules to go over seniority. He went to a lot of expense (for the company) trying to take the position. They sent for the chief electrical engineer at Clarksburg. Then they had me meet with the other three electric plant engineers, and all of us took turns changing those turbines, shutting one down and putting the other one on. We had to know our system, or we would fumble the job. If one of us made a mistake and kicked off the electric power, that would cause a lot of trouble and expense.

We all spent a half day changing those turbines, each at his turn. When we got through, I noticed that the district chief called the electric chief out for a private talking. I decided I could talk to the electric chief too. I called him into another room and told him what the plan was and what the district engineer wanted. "Yes," he said.

"I understand too. I told the district engineer you did a better job changing those turbines than any of the others." That settled it for me, and the district chief didn't get his plan to work out. I got an extra day's work, with overtime, and I kept my job.

A few years later, as I grew older, they offered me the job again. My auxiliary job was getting to be a little rough for me, but I learned that the new job wouldn't last more than two years or so, but I thought I could get my old job back if I had to change. I was a little worried that if I took the job and it went out, my seniority wouldn't count. But I learned that if the job was canceled, I would probably have enough seniority to get back to the old job. I had so much running to do on the auxiliary job (and I had to walk to work and back; that was four and a half more miles per day) that I finally decided to take the offer.

The new job was the nearest no-work of any job I ever had. I was in a twenty-by-thirty building all alone, and there was a lot of noise from the V-type engine, which operated from natural gas. It was built just like a Ford engine, but it was much bigger. I just had to pour a little oil once a day and check the pressure on my books every hour. I had about a half hour's work to do each day, and I could just sit or walk the other seven and one-half hours. It was the most monotonous job I ever had.

On the day shift, I did have an extra chore that got me out of that noisy engine room for about a half hour. I had to run a test on the gravity of the gas. One day the chief sent the tower foreman to help me run it. (I suppose that the test results didn't look right to him.) In a few days, the assistant chief came by, and I said to him, "You tell the chief I'm ready to run that test again now. If he wants to send a man to help me, I'll take all the help I can get." He smiled, and I think he told the chief what I said. (I could have used the help on the morning shift—someone to relieve me while I slept!)

We didn't have any extra work to do on the morning shift, and we didn't do any work that didn't have to be done at that time. We sat a lot of the time, and occasionally, when we had lost sleep at home, we would get very sleepy. I read some because if I had anything in my hand when I started to nod, I'd drop it. When it slipped out of my hand, I'd awaken. If anyone came through the door next to those howling turbines, it would cut off the sound enough that I would notice it and awaken from my snoozing. I had a boss to wake me only once, and he just rubbed by me and went on. He didn't say a word. He came in from the opposite door from the turbine engine, or he would have awakened me. Some of the men just couldn't sit down without going sound asleep.

If I got too sleepy, I would brace myself against something, and my legs would give way when I nodded off. I told my friends I wasn't like a horse; I couldn't sleep while standing. One of the firemen just couldn't seem to stay awake. The boss caught him sound asleep a few times, and they laid him off for two or three weeks. They finally had to discharge him. To go to sleep while firing all of those big boilers endangered everything. Finally, as a last resort, the company would discharge a man, but very few men were discharged at Cornwell Station.

One of our men kept coming on the job too drunk to work. He was their electrician, and he associated a lot with one of the bosses. I had some trouble with the hot plate, where I heated my boiler water, and he rewired it. When I came on the job, before I went out to the river pump house, I would turn on the switch to heat my boiler water. He had connected the wiring to a two-forty-volt instead of a one-twenty-volt wire. When I got back from the river, the place was on fire. The hot plate set on a wooden table. There was enough voltage on it to kill a person if he was wet or had wet feet. They laid the man off a few times and finally had to discharge him. His wife taught school, or his family would have starved. Once, he was away from home for a day or two. When he came back, there wasn't anyone there, and all of the furniture was gone. When he found his family, his wife told him that when he quit drinking, he could come home. That weaned him from his bottle for a while, but I have seen him drinking since then. Other than being an alcoholic, he's a pretty well-respected man. (I had worked on public works since I was fifteen years old. The Hope Gas Company had the finest, most respectable crew I ever worked with. They were very particular about whom they hired permanently.)

One day, the chief said to me, "I. I., I want you to fire those big boilers for two weeks. My fireman is going on vacation."

I had fired a boiler with gas on a well-drilling job, but I said to the boss, "Chief, I never fired those boilers."

"Well, you've done everything else here. It will be on the day shift, and the tower foreman can help you out if you need help." This was during the summer, at a time when they weren't selling much gas. They fired those boilers with gas when they couldn't sell it all. There were only three boilers to fire at that time. About all I had to do was watch my water level on each boiler and watch my steam gauge and regulate the gas as needed to keep up the steam pressure. They would let me know ahead of time when they were going to start or stop one of those big steam engines. I managed my turn at that job and didn't blow up any of those boilers or lose enough steam to cause those engines to stop.

I worked some in the machine shop. There's where I ought to have been all the time. All of it was day work, but I didn't try to talk myself into the job. If I had always worked on the day shift, I couldn't have done much farming, and I couldn't have worked on my house. I worked at the relief shift for about five years. That gave me more time to work at home. I'd work two morning shifts, two evening shifts, and one day shift. The worst of it was that when I worked my last evening shift, I would come off at midnight and have to go back on the day shift that morning at eight o'clock, but that gave me eight more hours off on my weekends.

I grew a little corn, wheat or oats, and all the vegetables we needed in the summer, and Nellie canned a few hundred quarts. We kept a horse to do the farming, one or two cows, chickens, and hogs. I killed an OIC hog that dressed out at nearly seven hundred pounds. Its middling was six inches thick. We just couldn't have made it if we had not raised a lot of our food.

On August 1, 1942, another child was born, a seven-pound boy. We called him James Douglas after James Doolittle and Douglas MacArthur. This was about the time that Jimmy Doolittle led the air raid over Tokyo, and his name was very popular; also, my dad's name was James Curtis Boggs. The doctor didn't get the baby straightened out properly before he was born. He broke the baby's arm and didn't tell us it was broken. We noticed that it was swollen. If there was anything wrong with a child, Nellie would notice it about as well as a doctor would. She was a good nurse. Douglas didn't get along good, and we didn't think we would raise him at all. Once, he turned so blue that Nellie thought he was dying. We took him to the hospital, and two doctors took him into a room away from me. I heard him scream for life. They set his arm without taking time to give him any relief by freezing his arm or giving him an anesthetic. I could have fought those doctors. I knew what they had done without mercy. A lot of the time, doctors are just too busy to take proper care of patients, and those men may have been like the doctor who brought Douglas into this cruel world. They may have thought he wouldn't live anyway, but he had a good careful mother who saved him. He soon became as healthy as any of his seven siblings. This gave us four boys and four girls—tied for the second time. That made eight in all.

One day, I had just eaten my dinner, and the children were at the table. Nellie said to them, "Don't eat all of that chicken. I want some left to put in your daddy's lunch pail."

The boys were three and four years old. They went to the chicken house and caught one of Nellie's best-laying pullets. They took a six-pound ax, and one held its head, and the other chopped its head off. They brought it in to their mother and said, "Now Daddy will have some chicken for his pail." It's just by chance that they didn't cut their fingers off. They had cleaned up all of the chicken on the table. I suppose they thought to get another chicken would be a polite way to make amends and that it would save them from a scolding.

On March 1, 1944, another boy was born. (Douglas and Earl were born during World War II.) We called him Earl Edsil. He weighed seven and one-half pounds. He was another fine child. We had a lot of trouble getting proper food for children or anyone during the war. We were given food stamps for all varieties of food, but we couldn't find it. The wealthiest people would pay a high price for more than they would really need for themselves. They could get it, even if it was against the law. (They ran the black market, as they called it.) I got so angry at my merchant that I could have sued him, but there was very little we could do about it. I did quit dealing with him, but that didn't make it any better. About all of the merchants did this black market outlawry. Meat and lard or anything you seasoned with was the hardest to find.

Earl was an especially hardy child, and he made a big strong man, as strong as any of my family. He was the most playful one of the children. He was always playing tricks and making jokes on the other children. Earl called light bread easy bread, and he called corn bread and biscuits heavy bread. Once, when he was only three years old, he watched Nellie until she got busy in the kitchen, and then he slipped out the front door and, with the other children, started to the farm where I was making sorghum molasses. It was a half mile through the woods, and there were three roads to lead him off, but he took the right one and was just getting to us when Nellie caught him. He had been up on the hilltop only a very few times, but he must have remembered the roads because he got on the right one.

In the spring of 1945, I planted four acres of corn. After it was partly hoed the first time, I got sick with stomach trouble. I thought I had an ulcer. I went to the Veterans Hospital in Huntington for treatment. They found that I had a bad acid stomach but no ulcer. After about three weeks of treatment, I came home. I soon got sick again, and I went back to the hospital. They were so crowded that they sent me to the army hospital at Fort Lee, Virginia. The doctor said I had a badly ulcerated stomach. He treated me for about a month, and I got to feeling much better. After about thirty days, my boss at Cornwell Station called to see when I would get back to work. I told my doctor that I had a job to take care of and that although I got full pay while off, I thought I should go back to work soon. I didn't have any hard labor to do, and I felt that I was now well enough to handle my job. The doctor agreed to let me go home, but he told me to rest for a few days before going back to work.

A few days after I came home from my thirty days in the hospital, I went to see how my four acres of corn was doing. I never was so surprised to see such a fine field of corn. Norris and Dallas had finished hoeing the four acres of new ground corn the first and second time, and there was hardly a weed to be seen. I had never kept the weeds so clean myself as Norris and Dallas did. Norris was fifteen, and Dallas was only thirteen. New ground gets very foul with weeds and sprouts, but they kept it clean. I never had a better field of corn.

Norris and Dallas worked so hard that Nellie said she had never felt so sorry for anyone. Norris said, "Mother, I'm just too young to take care of a big family." Nellie felt so much sympathy for him that she shed tears. Norris seemed to think that I'd never be able to work again. They were the most attentive children I ever saw. Dallas was very interested in farming. He was a 4-H member, and he later belonged to the Future Farmers of America. He had several projects to improve the farm, and he made good at it. He got some good awards for his work, and he made As in almost all of his courses.

On April 7, 1946, another girl was born into the family. We named her Connie Kay. She was a fine, strong, seven-pound baby. This was another tie in the family—five boys and five girls. We never had more than a very little trouble with her obedience. She seemed to just naturally listen to what she was told to do, and she did it whether she liked it or not. If Nellie had to leave the house for a few minutes, she would sit Connie on a chair and tell her to sit there until she got back. She would be sitting there when Nellie got back. She was one of the prettiest children of the family, and she is still pretty at twenty-five years. This is the last girl to be born in the family.

Another boy was born on April 22, 1948, making six boys and five girls, a total of eleven children in our family. We named him Arthur Curtis Boggs. He is now twenty-three years old. We named him after the doctor who brought him into this world (Dr. Arthur Smith) and his granddad Boggs (James Curtis Boggs). We already had one named James Douglas. We gave him Dad's first name, and Arthur got his middle name.

I can hardly realize how Nellie and I ever took care of such a large family or ever got by on a normal income, but we managed to get all of them through high school—all that would finish school. Some of the girls quit early and got married. I tried to get them to finish after marriage, but they didn't. All but one of the boys finished high school, and all of the other five have had some college work. Three of them are in college now. One or two have had at least three years of college work. My second boy, Dallas, liked schoolwork and was very good in his ability to learn. He earned a scholarship for part of his college expenses and worked his way through four years at West Virginia University. I couldn't afford to do much more to help him, only to encourage him and help him to get a loan of a few dollars. He completed eight years of college and repaid the loan. He has a doctorate degree from Cornell University, and at age thirty-eight, he is a laboratory director. Norris is a manager for McJunkin Corporation, a tool repair and supply business. Douglas is a store manager for a Woolworth retail corporation store. Earl and Arthur are still in college while working and making about average salary and wages. They all are industrious workers and doing well. The youngest one, Arthur, is the only one who hasn't married so far. He's twenty-two years old, still in college and working for FMC.

The girls have married very well and are quite successful. The two twins, Dorothy and Dorcas, both married soldiers who will retire in the next two years and six months on twenty-year retirement—at thirty-eight and thirty-nine years old. Both husbands have learned good trades that will keep them in good jobs after they retire from the military. The other girls' husbands are doing well and making above-average wages. They also have very good trades. One is a mechanic and welder, and the other is a mechanic and crane and heavy equipment operator. Connie is a legal secretary, and she also makes good wages.

I don't think I have any reason to complain about any of my family. These days, there are not many families that don't have at least one black sheep, but there aren't any in my family of eleven children. They are all diligent workers. They all have interests that keep them going, and they're always learning to do better.

I continued to work as auxiliary engineer at Cornwell Station until I retired in 1960 after thirty-five years. At that time, the station had changed from steam power to gas and electric power. I had worked at about every chore that there was to do there, even if no more than long enough to fill in for someone on vacation for some of the jobs. I had worked at jobs that ranked from pick-and-shovel labor to tower foreman, and I had worked some as a machinist. Although I liked the auxiliary job (where I mostly stayed for twenty-seven years) best, I could have had a machinist job if I had applied for it, but it didn't pay any more money. It would have been day work, but I would have been working away from home quite a bit.

Last spring, I was in the hospital with a heart attack, and the Lord inspired me to write a short poem. There was a picture, about twenty-four by sixteen inches, on the wall at the foot of my bed. It was as natural a picture of nature as I have ever seen. It was a picture of the mountains going up, up into the horizon into the sky and clouds in the fall of the year. There was a camp or lodge built in the style of homes of a century ago. The roof extended down over a long front porch. There was one small square window in its broad end and a door at the corner of the house. It stood near an eddy of water—a stream running in from the mountains. The timber was different colors, yellow and gold as autumn, with green hemlocks on each side of the water, and the grass was as natural a green color as could be. It looked like grass appears when there has just been a shower of rain that washed all the dust off of it. It looked so natural, as if you were walking on it or sitting on the grass on the bank of that beautiful, clear stream.

> I sat on the green,
> Looking down into a beautiful clear stream.
> I sat on the green and looked up into the beautiful clear sky in the heavens so high.
> I wondered what the Lord would have me do. Whatever it is, I'll do it with a smile.
> I'll look down on this earth, but it's hardly worthwhile.

And the Lord blessed me with his heavenly spirit. So I didn't care much to die, but I hate to leave my family behind. I don't think people should want to die, not as long as they can be of some interest to this world. I just prayed and left it to the Lord, and I'm still here at age seventy-six. I've prayed that the Lord would take me away before any of my eleven children are called home forever. I'm much older than anyone else in my family. Nellie is thirteen years younger than I am, and I was thirty-five at the time our first child was born.

I didn't finish the story about the picture. There's more still that turned out good for me. I had just thought about buying this picture, but I didn't intend to buy it unless they placed another picture in its place for the next patient that entered my bed. I had read a book of literature and poems Connie brought me while I was in my bed. Until I read that little book of about one hundred sixty-five pages, I never took much interest in poetry. I never had the education to understand literature, but the book was so full of nature and godly poems that I did take an interest in it. Poems express beautiful thoughts of reality and nature. The little book that Connie brought me dwelled on godliness so well that I could understand it.

The picture? About two days before I left the hospital, my nurse came in and said, "Mr. Boggs, I'm going to take your picture." I was too late. Somebody had beaten me to it.

I said to my nurse, "I'll look at my friend's picture in the bed next to me." (There were only two beds in my room.)

After twenty-three days in the hospital, two days after the picture disappeared, I got released. I came home on the Saturday before Father's Day. I was still mostly confined to my bed for another six weeks. On Father's Day, while I was in bed, Connie brought that picture to me. She turned it around in front of me and said. "This is your Father's Day present."

I was so happy that I almost went into shock. I said, "You couldn't have given me a present that pleased me better." I'm writing this poem on the back of the picture. I want it to stay in the family until a home burns, and sometimes that's a long time. It's worth a lot to me. When I finished writing this poem, the Lord blessed me with His unspeakable heavenly blessings. I wrote it on a blank page of the poetry book that Connie gave me, and I signed my name under it. There was another blank space on the opposite page. I signed Nellie's name at the bottom of that page—for her to write a poem and send it to the hospital for me. She obliged with the following verses:

> Love does not cease when pleasures cease their thrill. When passion has grown still, blood that raced madly is thin and cold. Yet time has never our love grown old. Each other's frailty has tried us both with poor pretense and clever art to hide. He tells me of the things I failed to see when he forgets that I am his memory.

> Friends have gone on that loved us in the past; we ask with frightened glance, "Which will be last?" Oh, let us go together, if we may. I have more courage, dear God. Let me stay—if one must stay, for who would know his ways, and how could he endure the lonely days?

> But if he went to rest, I would not weep. Contented, I would wait for eternal sleep. Young love the dawning, old love the light, shining the livelong day, sending its scarlet into the darkness, into the night!

I have another paragraph or two to write about while I was in the hospital in May and June. I had a dream, but it was so plain that you might call it a vision. "Young men shall see visions, and old men shall dream dreams" (Acts 2:17). I was feeling pretty poorly one night before I went to sleep. I dreamed of seeing Dad and my deceased brothers, Alvah and Cecil. I thought they were working in a field side by side and stooped over while picking up something and laying it to their sides, and they were talking to one another and to me. I don't remember what the conversation was about, but all were talking and working continuously.

I also dreamed that there was a little child standing by the side of my bed, a little boy with curly brown locks of hair. He appeared to be about four years old, but he was looking at me with a cheerful smile. He appeared to have the intelligence of an adult. It came to me that it was my little brother Scott, who died when I was about nine years old. When I think about it, Scott did have dark blond hair, curly and in locks. It was customary to save a lock of hair from a relative who died. Mother did save a lock of his hair; I remember seeing it at times years afterward. I woke up about this time, and I wasn't breathing. I was about ready to leave this world of suffering and trouble. I didn't care to die, but I thought it wouldn't be fair for me to want to leave my family. I prayed for God to spare me a while longer if it was His will. I wasn't suffering at all, but I was about as bad off as I had been during that heart attack. I didn't call my nurse, nor did I think to call her. I wasn't suffering either, but I started breathing normally again. I've never told this dream to anyone except Arthur and Nellie.

I've often dreamed of talking to Mother too, but somehow, I didn't think of her in that dream. I have dreamed of talking to Aunt Julia and Uncle Robert at times. We know not when we will be called to give up this life. It may come as a thief in the night. The idea is never to lie down and go to sleep without asking God to make us safe for His kingdom and thanking Him for sparing our life through another day.

Now there is not so much to write about. I have lived around here since I returned from California, and I worked at Cornwell Station for thirty-five years. My job didn't change much while I was there, but it started changed drastically shortly after I retired. They put in gas engines and went on automation, which cut the crew by about 80 percent. In sheer numbers, there are now about as many people out of work as there was in the Hoover panic, but we now have unemployment compensation, social security, food stamps, and training programs, and we have better means for keeping things on the level by regulating the money supply to control overproduction and to keep prices down and wages up.

I have lived in the most progressive times of history, but the twentieth century has been a time of great turmoil. I survived the Great Depression of the twenties, and I have lived through the Spanish-American War, World War I, World War II, the Korean War, and the Vietnam War. (Two of my sons served in the Vietnam War. Douglas was a radio operator in the combat zones of Vietnam, and Earl was a payroll clerk in Hawaii.) I grew up in the horse-and-buggy days. We had only a few roads that we could get a horse and buggy over, and most of them went only from town to town. Now we have been on the moon and are trying to get to the planet Mars.

With all of those narrow escapes, I know that I have had been blessed with a charmed life, but I pray that my grandchildren and great-grandchildren will not have to go through as many hard times as I did. Scholars have predicted that the world is due for a century of peace. They say that throughout history the world has alternated between a hundred years of war and a hundred years of peace, and I hope that they are right. I cannot imagine what an all-out war would be like in the age of megaton bombs. But in the end, our descendants may have to start over again and relearn the way of living that we experienced at the turn of the century—without running water, electricity, rapid transportation, and all of the other modern conveniences. Many families of the younger generations might starve to death before they get into the swing of it.

Ira I. and Nellie J. (McCune) Boggs & Progeny at their Fiftieth Wedding Anniversary

1. Ira 2. Nellie 3. Douglas 4. Dorcas 5. Dorothy 6. Dallas 7. Granvel 8. Wilda 9. Norris 10. Norma 11. Earl 12. Connie 13. Arthur

*Specialist E-4 James Douglas Boggs
Bien Hoa, S. Vietnam, 1965*